2002 BLACKBOOK PRICE GUIDE TO UNITED STATES PAPER MONEY

THIRTY-FOURTH EDITION

BY MARC HUDGEONS, N.L.G. & TOM HUDGEONS

H C

HOUSE OF COLLECTIBLES

The Crown Publishing Group • New York

© 2001 by Random House, Inc.

House of Collectibles and the HC colophon are trademarks of Random House, Inc.

Published by: House of Collectibles
The Crown Publishing Group
New York, New York

Distributed by The Crown Publishing Group, a division of Random House, Inc., New York, and simultaneously in Canada by Random House of Canada Limited, Toronto.

www.randomhouse.com.

Printed in the United States of America

Buy It • Use It • Become an Expert is a trademark of Random House, Inc.

ISSN: 0195-3540

ISBN: 0-676-60167-7

Thirty-fourth Edition: June 2001

10 9 8 7 6 5 4 3 2 1

CONTENTS

OFFICIAL BOARD OF CONTRIBUTORS

The author would like to express a special thank you to:

W.R. "Bill" Rindoné, Bank Notes North West, PO Box 406, Wilsonville, OR 97070, for his collaboration and Market Review,

Hugh Schull, Confederate Currency Expert, for his pricing collaboration,

and **Regina Banks and Larry Felix at the Department of the Treasury,** Bureau of Engraving and Printing, Washington, D.C., for the articles on the BEP.

PUBLISHER'S NOTE

The Official ® Blackbook Price Guide to United States Paper Money is designed as a reference aid for collectors, dealers, and the general public. Its purpose is to provide historical and collecting data, as well as current values. Prices are as accurate as possible at the time of going to press, but no guarantee is made. We are not dealers; persons wishing to buy or sell paper money, or have it appraised, are advised to consult collector magazines or the telephone directory for addresses of dealers. We are not responsible for typographical errors.

NOTE TO READERS

All advertisements appearing in this book have been accepted in good faith, but the publisher assumes no responsibility in any transactions that occur between readers and advertisers.

THE OFFICIAL®

2002
BLACKBOOK
PRICE GUIDE TO
UNITED STATES
PAPER
MONEY

MARKET REVIEW

We have had another amazing year! Collectors and dealers of fifty years ago would never, in their wildest imaginations, have dreamed of today's marketplace. They would undoubtedly be pleased to see the widespread interest in their hobby. Paper money has become a premier collectible, and prices continue to spiral upward. Paper money shows and Internet sales have been well attended. Collector interest is spreading into areas that in the past have remained relatively quiet. In essence, we have had another banner year!

Internet sales are brisk, and the number of notes sold online last year probably exceeded one million! E-bay handled over a quarter million by itself. Translated into dollars, that's probably about 80 million dollars in on-line transactions. Paper money auctions held in conjunction with major shows have been well attended and have produced stellar results. At the January CAA (Currency Auctions of America), a new all-time record was set when an 1882 $1,000 (Fr#1218d) bill in About New Condition brought $935,000. Len Glaser of California verified that sales in their three auctions exceeded $10 million during the past year. When asked for his opinion regarding the future, he stated "We see another banner year ahead with continued growth in the collecting fraternity and increasing activity, as well as prices, in the entire field of collectible currency." I agree.

The advent of Internet auctions has created a greater exposure to the paper money field than any other single event in the history of our nation. As a collector, the opportunity to find specialized material has radically increased, but so has the competition for that material. Where one could previously find a "sleeper," now often results in intense competition for the same note. An example of that was an obsolete note we offered on Sabine Parish, LA. The note had fallen apart, and the pieces were glued on to heavy paper backing. We opened the note at $1 and although rare, we were amazed when the bidding reached $41. You can imagine our surprise when it closed at $481. In years past we would have gladly sold the note locally for $5 due to lack of interest.

We found the following activity during the year:

Large-Size Type Notes (1861–1923): Large-size notes are, without doubt, the most beautiful and historical remnants of a time in our history that has been long forgotten. Notes such as the 1901 $10 Bison depicting Lewis & Clark, and the 1899 $5 that bears the portrait of Chief Running Antelope, depict 1800s life on the western plains. The Rainbow series of 1869 or the Educational series of 1896 showcase the engraver's art. This has been and continues to be the premier area of paper money collecting. With the two major census's available today, we know with relative security what is and isn't available. The rarer notes (above $3,000) are much sought after regardless of grade. The middle-priced notes (ranging from $600 up) are also heavily sought after, but due to availability, the buyer knows that if the price sounds high, he will soon see another priced closer to his wallet. The lesser notes (below $600) are readily available unless they are of such superb quality that another similar note may not appear for several months. With the current prices on rare-type notes, it requires deep pockets to put together an extensive collection. It is, however, worthy of a rewarding lifetime pursuit.

Small-Size Type Notes (1928–present): Major growth continues in this area of collecting. Many of the notes previously thought to be relatively common have been found to be quite scarce. Notes such as $1 1928 and $2 1928B Red Seals are seldom encountered at auction. Although Hawaii overprint notes are always available, this is not true of the $5, $10, or $20 in really nice Gem CU condition. As such, they command a staggering premium when auctioned. Other areas of high interest are low serial numbers and star notes. Both of these areas have strong collector backing. With the release of the "new" currency the demand for older small-size issues has radically increased, and from all appearances will continue to do so. There are still many bargains to be found, and this is one of the areas that new collectors continue to embrace. Look for dwindling availability and increasing prices and pressure.

Fractional Notes (1861–1923): In a single word: *hot.* Interest has been increasing by leaps and bounds with corresponding prices. Of all the paper money fields, fractionals have shown the greatest rise in interest. This is still an area where relatively rare notes can still be purchased at bargain prices. Notes with a known census of fewer than twenty may still be found in the $200–$1,000 range. During the past year, I have seen sales of all but perhaps three or four of the rarer Friedberg numbers. Proofs and specimens of these early notes have come under strong collector pressure, and prices on both have recently more than doubled. Understandably, the availability of these notes is decidedly limited. In general, the future of the fractional field appears to be quite positive. A fractional denomination set requires six (3c, 5c, 10c, 15c, 25c, 50c) and a type set contains twenty-three. Both collections are easily obtainable.

National Notes (1865–1928): Major changes have occurred in this field. In the past, notes were collected with a theme in mind. Themes included county, state, or geographic area, and state capitols. Now there is a new breed of collector. He is best described as a "trophy hunter." If the note is rare enough, than state, etc., is of little importance. Aside from the changes, this area of collecting is hot and should remain so.

Error Notes (All): This field has stablized, and current levels should remain static for a while. The exception to this is the more exotic errors that are seldom seen and that can bring phenomenal prices from the "right" buyer. Bank tellers routinely find a variety of errors due to the poor quality control in the Fed. Notes that would not escape detection twenty years ago are now routinely passed into the public sector.

Obsolete Notes (Private issues 1800–1877): Also referred to as "broken bank" notes, as most of the issuing banks went under many years ago. These notes issued by private banks give us some of the prettiest notes ever engraved. Various themes are used by collectors, and one of the more popular is Denominational (a multitude of interesting notes such as 12½c, 70c, 90c, $1.25, $3, $6, $7, $300, etc., are available). Other popular themes include a 50-state collection, local towns, or specializing in particular engravers or printers. Prices have risen radically, and items that went begging at $8 just three years ago are now commanding $30–$35. The basis for collecting is usually geographic, and when a rare note appears from one of the more popular areas, it often results in a bidding war. A resurgence in Nebraska notes is no exception. Other hot areas are Florida, Minnesota, and Texas.

Depression Scrip (1907 and 1933): After being in the doldrums for a few years, interest has been on the rise. Some states have virtually no obsolete issues aside from those put out in the Panic of '07 or the Depression of the mid 1930s. When the banks closed in 1933, several firms issued scrip that was honored by the local bank as currency of the realm. Some western states such as Oregon, Washington, Idaho, Arizona, and New Mexico are collectible only because of these issues. Bargains are definitely available for under $20. Expect this area to radically expand over the next ten years.

Colonial Notes (1690–1799): This area continues "slow, but steady." Although relatively unattractive when compared to other notes, they are nonetheless historical in content. They were first issued by individual colonies and then after 1776 by states with the approval of the Federal government. Various printers include Benjamin Franklin and Paul Revere. The notes are hand-signed, and several famous dignitaries are represented, including signers of the Declaration of Independence.

MPCs (1947–1973): Military Payment Certificates are avidly collected by a relatively smaller number of enthusiasts. These are very colorful examples of our country's military scrip. Notes are found in 5c, 10c, 25c, 50c, $1, $5, $10, and $20 denominations. They were issued and used by our armed services as currency in localized areas during times of conflict, often to transcend the sale of U.S. dollars on the black market, as MPCs were only redeemable on military bases. Rare notes or those in top condition find eager homes, while circulated or common notes often go begging.

Related Areas: Early or western checks or drafts are quite collectible and have matured into a field of their own. Pretty vignettes and historical pieces are more commonly seen then one might expect. We recently purchased a piece issued in 1870 by the Sutler (authorized store) at Fort Bridger, Wyoming Territory, signed by the company commander and issued to a 2nd Cavalry trooper for a reasonable price. Checks signed by famous persons are also of interest.

Whether it's history, the thrill of discovery, a positive investment, or collecting gorgeous engravings of the distant past, the hobby of collectible currency truly has something for everyone. We've been at it for thirty-four years and have yet to tire of the surprise of something new and different. What better way to stay involved with the history of a nation than through its money?

INTRODUCTION OF THE 1996 SERIES CURRENCY

The Series 1996 U.S. currency series incorporates new features designed to improve the security of our currency. The Series 1996 $20 note was introduced in the fall of 1998. The new $50 note was introduced in October 1997, and the $100 note was introduced in March 1996. Lower denominations will follow. There will be no recall or devaluation of U.S. currency already in circulation; the United States always honors its currency at full face value, no matter how old.

The issuance of the Series 1996 $20 note has special importance because it is the first redesigned note that is widely used in the United States. It is the most often used of the larger denomination notes and is commonly distributed through Automated Teller Machines (ATMs). All users of U.S. currency should be familiar with the appearance and new security features of the new notes. People who use U.S. currency are the first line of defense against counterfeiting; cash handlers and consumers should examine all notes carefully to guard against counterfeits.

The new Federal Reserve $20 notes are being phased into circulation, replacing older notes as they reach the banking system. This multi-year introduction of the new series is necessary because of the time-intensive printing process and because a sufficient inventory of new notes must be available when the new note is issued to ensure its worldwide availability.

In 1996, the Federal Reserve System and the U.S. Treasury Department began a worldwide public education campaign with two primary objectives: (1) to communicate to the general public that there will be no recall or devaluation;

and (2) to provide information that will enable the public, law enforcement personnel, central banks, depository financial institutions, and other cash handlers to authenticate the new series notes.

HISTORY OF THE NEW SERIES

Until the late 1920s, U.S. currency was redesigned frequently. There also were several types of notes in circulation: United States Notes, National Bank Notes, and Silver Certificates. Since the introduction of the Series 1928 Federal Reserve Notes, changes in the design have not affected the overall architecture of U.S. currency. This includes the use of microprinting and a security thread in Series 1990 and later notes.

The counterfeit-deterrent features added in Series 1990 were the first step in responding to advances in reprographic technologies. Although these features have proved effective and will be retained, additional measures are necessary to protect U.S. currency against future threats posed by continued improvements in copy machines, scanners, and printers. The new design, beginning with Series 1996, is the culmination of a five-year study aimed at staying ahead of the counterfeiting threat and is part of a continuing process to protect U.S. currency. At the same time, the redesign process has provided an opportunity to incorporate features that will make U.S. currency more readily identifiable, especially by the low-vision community.

The process began with the New Currency Design Task Force, which comprised representatives of the U.S. Treasury Department, Federal Reserve System, U.S. Secret Service, and the Bureau of Engraving and Printing (BEP). The Task Force made its recommendations to the Advanced Counterfeit Deterrence Steering Committee, also composed of representatives of the Treasury Department, Federal Reserve, Secret Service, and BEP. Based on a comprehensive study by the National Research Council (NRC) issued in 1993, the Steering Committee then made recommendations for the new design and security features to the Secretary of the Treasury, who has statutory authority to approve such changes.

More than 120 security features were examined and tested,

including those submitted in response to a BEP solicitation, those used in other currencies, and those suggested by the NAS. Evaluation criteria included impact on security, proven reliability, ability to be manufactured in large quantities, and durability over time. Among the features evaluated were holograms, color shifting films, thread variations, color patterns, and machine-readable enhancements. The strategy of the Design Task Force was to incorporate as many features as are justifiable. The security features ultimately selected have proved successful in other countries as well as in test environments at BEP and the Federal Reserve, and since their incorporation into U.S. currency have been an effective deterrent to counterfeiters.

In its second report, the NAS evaluated features to help those with low vision differentiate between currency denominations. These included variations in size and shape, holes, and other tactile features that the Task Force deemed were not sufficiently durable to be practicable for U.S. currency at this time. The Task Force agreed that a high-contrast feature, such as a large numeral on a light background, would be useful to the approximately 3.5 million Americans with low vision, and could be easily incorporated into the new series design without compromising the improved security of the new notes or adding cost. In addition, a new machine-readable feature was incorporated on the $20 note for the blind. It will facilitate development of convenient scanning devices that could identify the note's denomination.

The Design Task Force will continue to seek and test new features to make U.S. currency even more secure and more readily usable as technology further evolves.

THE NEW DESIGN

The new currency has the same size, color, and feel as the old notes, with the same historical figures and national symbols. "In God We Trust" and the legal tender wording also remain on the new bills. This continuity facilitates public education and universal recognition of the design as genuine U.S. currency—an important consideration since there will be dual circulation of the old and new currencies around the world.

The $20 bill includes several important security features.

These features also appear in the $100 and the $50, with some variations:

- A larger, slightly off-center portrait is the most noticeable visual change. The large portrait incorporates more detail, making it easier to recognize and more difficult to counterfeit. Moving the portrait away from the center, the area of highest wear, will reduce wear on the portrait. The $20 bill features a portrait of President Andrew Jackson.

- Shifting the portrait off center provides room for a watermark, which is created during the papermaking process and is difficult for counterfeiters to reproduce. The watermark depicts the same historical figure as the engraved portrait.

- The background of the portrait incorporates the technique of fine-line printing, as does the background of the picture on the reverse side. This type of fine-line printing is difficult to replicate accurately on scanning equipment or by other means of printing.

- Color shifting ink changes from green to black when viewed from different angles. This feature is used in the numeral in the lower right-hand corner of the bill front.

- The use of a unique thread position for each denomination guards against counterfeiting. In the $20 bill, the thread is to the far left of the portrait and glows green when held under ultraviolet light; in the $50 bill, it is found to the right of the portrait and glows yellow; in the $100 bill, it is found to the left of the portrait and glows red. The denomination of the note is also printed on each thread; for example, "USA TWENTY" and a flag are repeated along the thread in the $20 note. The number "20" appears within the star field of the flag.

- The numeral in the lower left-hand corner of the $20 and the $100 and the side border design of the $50 incorporates microprinting, a printing technique using lettering that can be read with a low-powered magnifier. Extremely small print appears as a thin line to the naked eye and yields a blurred image when copied. On the new $20 bill, microprinting can also be found on the lower edge ornamentation of the portrait's oval frame. On the $50, similar microprinting is used in President Grant's collar, and on the $100 bill it is found on the lapel of Benjamin Franklin's coat.

- Serial numbers on the new currency differ slightly from old currency. The new serial numbers consist of two prefix letters, eight numerals, and a one-letter suffix. The first letter of the prefix designates the series (for example, Series 1996 will be designated by the letter A). The second letter of the prefix designates the Federal Reserve Bank to which the note was issued. In addition, a universal Federal Reserve seal replaces individual seals for each Reserve Bank.

Although all denominations of currency will have security features, the number of features will vary according to denomination. While the $20, $50, and $100 notes have a full package of features, lower denominations may have fewer and less sophisticated features.

Federal Reserve Indicators A new seal represents the entire Federal Reserve System. The letter and number under the left serial number identify the issuing Federal Reserve Bank.

Portrait A larger, off-center portrait allows room for a watermark.

Microprinting "The United States of America" is on the lower edge ornamentation of the oval framing the portrait. On the front of the note, "USA 20" is repeated within the number in the lower left corner.

Fine Line Printing Patterns The fine lines printed behind the portrait and building are difficult to replicate.

Low-Vision Featur The large numeral on th back of the $20 note is easy to read.

$100 note, issued in March, 1996.

Security Thread A vertically embedded thread to the far left of the portrait indicates the $20 denomination. The words "USA TWENTY" and a flag can be seen from both sides against a light. The number "20" appears in the star field of the flag. The thread glows green under an ultraviolet light.

Watermark
A watermark identical to the portrait is visible from both sides against a light.

Color-Shifting Ink The number in the lower right corner on the front of the note looks green when viewed straight on, but black at an angle.

Serial Numbers
An additional letter is added to the serial number.

$50 note, issued in October, 1997.

COLLECTING PAPER MONEY

Paper money can be a fascinating hobby. Though of more recent origin than coinage, U.S. paper money exists in enormous varieties and can be collected in many ways.

Potential specialties are numerous. The following is not by any means a complete list.

1. Series collecting. Here the collector focuses upon a certain series of notes, such as the $5 1863–75 National Bank Notes, and attempts to collect specimens showing each of the different signature combinations, points of issue, seal colors, or whatever varieties happen to exist in the series. This may sound restrictive but, as an examination of the listings in this book will show, most series are comprised of many varieties. Generally, the older the series, the more difficult or expensive will be its completion, while certain series include great rarities beyond the budget range of most collectors. The cost can be brought down somewhat if one does not demand the finest condition but is content to own an example of the note in whatever condition he can reasonably afford. It should be pointed out, though, that in reselling paper money there is generally a greater loss—or smaller profit—on notes whose condition is less than Very Fine.

2. Set collecting. Sets are groups of notes of different denominations, issued at the same time (or approximately the same time), which were in current circulation together.

3. Place or origin collecting. Collecting notes by the city whose Federal Reserve Bank issued them.

4. Signature collecting. Collecting one specimen of every note bearing the signature of a certain Secretary of the Treasury.

5. Confederate currency collecting. The notes issued for use within the Confederate States of America during the Civil War.

6. Portrait collecting. By the individual or individuals depicted on the note. This is sometimes known as topical collecting.

7. Freak and oddity collecting.

8. Fractional currency collecting.

Imagination, especially if placed into use in a coin shop well stocked with paper money, will suggest further possibilities. All is fair; there are no strict rules on what makes a worthwhile collection, so long as the material included is not seriously defective or of questionable authenticity.

Don't expect to build a large collection rapidly. Paper money is not comparable to stamps, where a beginner can buy a packet of 1,000 different stamps and instantly have a sizable collection. Nor should the size of a collection be regarded as a mark of its desirability or worth. Many prizewinning collections contain fewer than a hundred pieces; some consist of only two or three dozen. Direction and quality count much more in this hobby than weight of numbers. Collectors seeking to own a large collection generally end up with one whose only recommendation is its size. It may impress beginners but is not likely to be regarded highly by more experienced collectors.

PUBLICATIONS

Get a global perspective on paper money collecting from *The Bank Note Reporter*. This monthly tabloid is devoted entirely to U.S. and world paper money, notes, checks, and all related fiscal paper. Find current prices for national and international bank notes, plus an active buy/sell marketplace. *12 monthly issues are $29.98.*

The *Numismatic News* delivers weekly news and information on coin and paper money collecting with exclusive reports from the hobby's only full-time Washington Bureau. Accurate retail/wholesale value guide, current events, and up-to-date calendar make this the most comprehensive numismatic forum available. *52 weekly issues are $29.98.*

For more information, please contact:

Krause Publications
700 East State Street
Iola, WI 54990
Phone 715-445-2214, Subscription Services 1-800-258-0929

COIN AND PAPER MONEY COMPUTER SOFTWARE

By Tom Bilotta,
Carlisle Development Corporation

Over the past year, there has been widespread growth in the use of the Internet by collectors. This has occurred as many information sites have been created and collectible auction sites have proliferated and become more sophisticated. This trend increases the value that a collector will receive from computer software to work with their collection. By maintaining information about your collection in your computer, it may be easily and selectively shared with other parties. You may also download information from the Internet and incorporate it into your inventory. This could be in the form of a download of current values, a picture, or a listing of available items.

Collectors have a need to keep track of their collections and communicate information about them to other parties. Coin and paper money collections tend to contain many items with a significant variation in value. There are many reasons to maintain an accurate inventory of your collectibles. There are security concerns, such as assuring adequate insurance coverage and your ability to document a loss. You will want to be able to easily identify and list currency that is on your want list. You may wish to monitor the value of your collection or find where a particular item is stored.

Inventory software is designed to minimize the effort needed to create and maintain a coin and paper money inventory and also to add to your enjoyment of the collection process by allowing you to work with your collection in a productive manner.

Interactive Books on CD/ROM provide access to a wealth of coin and paper money information in an easy-to-use format. This format also provides higher quality photographs than can usually be printed in books. This information can also be coordinated with currency inventory programs and/or other electronic sources of information such as the Internet.

RECENT TECHNOLOGY ADVANCEMENTS AND THEIR IMPACT ON COLLECTION SOFTWARE

The continued growth of the Internet is the most significant technology trend affecting the use of computers by collectors. With the increases in speed supported by higher bandwidth connections, it is now practical to electronically transmit high-quality images of collectibles. This has fueled the growth of the on-line collectibles auction and also makes it possible for collectors to share a wide array of information with others. Collectors can have a variety of choices as to where to obtain sought-after items, no longer limited by geography or impacted by the delays and risks inherent in blind mail-order transactions. As the use of higher speed connections grows, it will be commonplace for dealers and collectors to transmit pictures rather than paper money, avoiding insurance and shipping charges and mailing delays.

The continued enhancement of digital cameras has resulted in very low-cost scanners that are capable of producing high-quality electronic images of currency. These new-generation scanners may be operated without any special knowledge or skill.

COIN AND PAPER MONEY INVENTORY SOFTWARE

One of the most important parts of a currency inventory program is the database. The database contains standard information about coins and paper money and saves the user from having to type this information manually. The greater the amount of information in the standard database, the easier the task of data entry. Another important aspect of the database is how the items are organized into groups. Proper grouping allows the user to easily locate an item and also provides guidance as to how to organize a collection.

The ability to extend the database is also of significant value, allowing the user to add new items immediately or to add more specialized items that are not considered part of a standard listing. This is especially true for world coins and paper money, which are so numerous that it is very likely that a user will wish to add items to the database. In addition to the basic information about the coin or paper money item, it is very valuable to provide pictures and values from reliable sources. Pictures are useful to the collector in identifying items that are unfamiliar. Electronic values ease the process of tracking movements in valuation of your collections.

With the growth of the Internet, the ability to download electronic updates to the database is now feasible and enables the collector to be current with recent mint issues.

Carlisle Development's inventory software, Collector's Assistant 2000, provides a comprehensive database of all coins ever minted by the U.S. Mint. This includes all types of coins by date and mint mark, bullion coins, sets, old, and new commemoratives. Recent additions to the database are the fifty states circulating quarters and the new Sacagawea Dollar. Coin values are licensed from Coin World, Inc., an industry leader in providing coin valuations. Quarterly updates are available by subscription, allowing collectors to maintain trends of their values. Carlisle Development's Currency Collector's Assistant has a complete database based on *Friedberg's Paper Money of the United States*, 15th edition. This database includes all U.S. paper money, including Confederate notes and encased postage stamps. A relationship with CDN, publisher of the Greensheet, makes value information available to the paper money collector in electronic format.

FLEXIBILITY OF GROUPING YOUR COINS AND PAPER MONEY

There are as many ways of collecting coins and paper money as there are collectors. A very important feature of collection inventory software is its ability to organize items the way the user prefers to do so. Some collection inventory programs require that the user group items exactly as the database is organized. These programs typically have great difficulty handling duplicates and cause the collector to work in an uncomfortable manner.

More advanced programs allow you to group items from the standard database with complete flexibility. The following are some common examples of how collectors group items:

Item type: (Morgan dollars, Indian Head cents, silver certificates)

Metal: (gold pounds, silver dollars, old copper coins)

Period: (year of birth set, 18th-century silver coins)

Feature: (signer, seal color, doubled die, errors)

Often collectors have several types of groupings, treating items in their primary collecting interest differently than duplicates, miscellaneous pieces, or accumulations that they might wish to trade or sell. An advanced program, such as the Collector's Assistant 2000, enables you to use all of these different kinds of groupings and freely move items between them as your collection interests change and as you buy and sell items.

VIEWING INFORMATION ABOUT YOUR COLLECTION

Your ability to find and display information about your collection can significantly contribute to your enjoyment of the hobby, as well as your effectiveness as a collector. It will also assist you in exploiting the information and opportunities on the Internet. Collection inventory software allows you to view your collection in many different ways. At one session, for example, you may be connected to some on-line auctions and need to display a list of items that you are interested in obtaining along with your target grades and price objectives. At another session, you might be analyzing the change in value of your collection over time. One of the new features in the Collector's Assistant 2000 is an extensive facility for tracking the history of value changes in a collection and presenting this information graphically. You may also need to print the detailed contents stored at a specific location such as a safety deposit box for insurance purposes.

You will sometimes want to see listings on the screen and sometimes require printed reports. More frequently, you will want electronic listings that can be transmitted over the

Internet. Most likely you will want to view both detailed listings and/or summaries of all or a selected portion of your collection. Here, again, an advanced collection program, such as the Collector's Assistant 2000, can allow you to change your view with a few "clicks" of a button. In addition to the ability to determine which items are to be included in a report, you will also want to control the information fields that are included. You might want to produce two versions of a want list: one with values and one without. An insurance listing might include inventory number codes. You will also want to be able to sort your listings based on any information fields.

Finally, due to the number of items, you will want facilities to easily locate an item meeting criteria that you specify.

INFORMATION FIELDS

It is very important that the collection inventory software contains an adequate set of information fields enabling you to store the information you want in an efficient manner. The Coin and Currency Collector's Assistant 2000 divides information fields into a set of tabbed folders, organized in a convenient manner. A Purchase and Sales folder provides a set of fields to record information such as purchase date and amount, buyer and seller information, sales date and amount, target price or cost, and grade sought for coins on want lists. It also provides a transaction mode for investors. A condition folder maintains grade information, detailed condition descriptions, and certification information.

Detailed note and Picture folders allow the user to view and scroll a set of pictures or general information that they wish to record.

Most important is the Item Detail folder, which is separately customized for coins and paper money. This contains all of the information specific to the coin or paper money item. For example, the coin folder would contain metal content, mintage, date, mint mark, numismatic codes, weight, size, edge, and other fields specific to coinage. The paper money folder would contain serial number, seal, signers, bank names, and other fields specific to paper money collecting.

Also important for data entry is the availability of choice

lists to minimize the need for typing. Carlisle Development's inventory software provides many prepopulated choice lists for such information as country, type, metal content, and color, all of which are user customizable.

PICTURES AND SPECIALIZED REPORTS

Availability of picture support provides significant value to the collector. In some instances you will want to identify items that you have not seen before. You might wish to maintain a picture catalog of your collection, either to increase your own enjoyment or to share your collection with others.

Other specialized reports can generate labels to attach to your items, index cards, or picture reports you can mail or e-mail to other collectors or dealers. An advanced program should offer a full range of specialized reports. The Collector's Assistant 2000 provides a wide range of specialized formats and also a user customization facility that can support almost any printable size.

STORAGE AND INSURANCE

Keeping track of where a coin is located requires a two-level approach for most collectors. There are locations and containers. There may be several containers for a particular location.

Examples of locations would be a bank, office, or desk. Examples of containers would include safety deposit box, file cabinet, shelf, or safe. The Collector's Assistant 2000 supports a two-level storage system where each item or group may be stored in a particular container and easily moved from one to another. It allows as many locations and containers as you need for your collection.

EASE OF USE

As with any computer software, ease of user will determine not only your enjoyment of your collection but also your ability to accomplish the task for which you purchased the software. Advanced programs, such as the Collector's Assistant 2000, approach this in a combined manner suitable to a wide range of personal preferences. These include interactive step-by-step instructions, intuitive behavior, and context-sensitive help. Equally important is accessible, competent technical support. The Internet is proving to be a very effective means of providing technical support by leveling time differences and allowing detailed communications to occur at all times.

ELECTRONIC BOOKS—SPECIALIZED KNOWLEDGE AT YOUR FINGERTIPS

Adding significantly to your enjoyment of collections are electronic information sources that exploit the power of the computer to present you with high-quality information in an easily accessible format. Carlisle Development currently offers three electronic books for coin collectors.

Grading Assistant CD: The Grading Assistant CD, based on the *Official ANA Grading Guide for United States Coins*, contains the entire contents of this standard grading reference in an interactive format. This work contains pictures of every U.S. coin type at each of the ANA base grades (AG, G, VG, F, VF, EF, AU, UNC). It also contains the full text grading descriptions for all ANA grades, including intermediate grades such as MS-63, MS-65, MS-67, and AU-58. The pictures are presented in several formats. An initial presentation provides three pictures side-by-side of adjacent grades. You click on magnifying glasses to increase the size of a selected picture.

Tabbed folders allow you to browse the grading descriptions for the coin you are currently viewing. General grading information is provided in a browsable section of the CD organized in the same manner as the book.

TOP 100 Morgan Dollars—The VAM Keys: This CD is an interactive version of the book written by Michael Fey and Jeff Oxman. This work provides pictures, identification information, and values for the most sought-after and valuable Morgan dollar varieties. It provides a spectacular set of high-quality pictures to assist you in identifying these coins and also the full text and information provided in this work.

The Coin Collector's Survival Manual (CD Edition) by Scott Travers: This CD is a landmark work, providing a set of information that every collector of coins should have. The entire contents of this book are provided in a searchable, interactive format. This allows the user to easily locate information based on word searching, topics, illustrations, bookmarks, a table of contents, or index. In addition to the contents of the book, a set of high-quality NGC PhotoProof images have been included for such topics as identifying MS-63 vs MS-65 vs MS-67 coins and toning. An interactive grading calculator brings to life the grading methods described in the book.

Well-designed coin and paper money software can add to your enjoyment of the hobby as well as improve your ability to achieve your collection objectives. Carlisle Development Corporation publishes the most comprehensive line of collector software available, especially regarding coins and paper money.

Central to Carlisle's product line is the Collector's Assistant 2000, the most advanced and comprehensive collection software available. It is sold in a variety of configurations to serve collectors of over thirty collectible types from autographs to toys. Most extensive is support for coins and paper money. The Collector's Assistant 2000 family includes:

- **United States Coin Database**—complete listings of all U.S. coinage from 1973 to the present. Fifty State Quarter program and Sacagawea dollars are recent additions. This also includes Colonial and Hawaiian coinage.
- **World Coin Database**—a listing of over 5,000 coin types from over forty-five countries, which may be extended by the user.
- **United States Currency Database**—a complete listing of all U.S. currency based on *Friedberg's Paper Money of the United States*, 15th ed.

To learn more about Carlisle Development's product line, visit our website at HYPERLINK http://www.carlisledevelopment.com. You will find current product information and may also place orders. You can reach us by e-mail at HYPERLINK mailto:carlislesoftware@aol.com or by phone at 800-219-0257.

COLLECTING ORGANIZATIONS

PROFESSIONAL CURRENCY DEALERS ASSOCIATION (PCDA)

Looking for a reliable paper money dealer? . . . Collecting rare paper money can be an enjoyable hobby. Imagine being able to own an example of fractional currency printed during the Civil War era, or a National Bank Note issued by a financial institution in your own state.

Whatever your collecting interests, the members of the Professional Currency Dealers Association (PCDA) will be pleased to assist and guide you. The members of this prestigious trade association specialize in virtually all the areas of paper money collecting.

Once you've started to collect, it can sometimes be a challenge to locate a dealer with a significant inventory. Members of the PCDA are the market makers for currency collectors. Whatever your interest, a PCDA member is certain to be able to supply you. Whether you are a beginner on a limited budget or an advanced collector of many years' experience, you can be certain that you'll find fair, courteous, and reliable treatment with a member of the Professional Currency Dealers Association.

For a free copy of the PCDA membership directory, write to:

Professional Currency Dealers Association
PO Box 573
Milwaukee, WI 53201

Your personal copy of the PCDA directory, listing members by their specialty areas, will be sent to you promptly via first class mail.

THE SOCIETY OF PAPER MONEY COLLECTORS (SPMC)

The Society of Paper Money Collectors (SPMC) invites you to become a member of our organization. SPMC was founded in 1961 with the following objectives: (1) Encourage the collecting and study of all paper money and financial documents; (2) Provide collectors the opportunity to meet and enjoy fraternal relations with their fellow collectors; (3) Furnish information and knowledge about paper money; (4) Encourage research about paper money and financial documents and publish the resulting information; (5) Promote legislation favorable to collectors; (6) Advance the prestige of the hobby of numismatics; (7) Promote rational and consistent classification of exhibits, and ENCOURAGE participation by our members; (8) Encourage realistic and consistent market valuations.

Paper Money, SPMC's bimonthly journal now in its 36th year, has repeatedly been selected by the ANA as the Best Specialty Publication in numismatics; the Numismatic Literary Guild has also selected *Paper Money* for first-place recognition. Virtually every article in every issue is written by an SPMC member, who receives no monetary compensation. SPMC coordinates and judges the exhibits at the largest all-paper show every year. SPMC co-sponsors many large all-paper shows held in the U.S. each year.

Information about membership may be obtained by writing to:

Frank Clark
P.O. Box 117060
Carrollton, TX 75011

RECOGNIZING THE
VALUABLE NOTES

Every note ever issued by the U.S. government is worth, at minimum, its face value. This applies even to notes of which one-third is missing. Whether a note is worth *more* than its face value—to collectors and dealers in paper currency—depends chiefly upon its age, condition, scarcity, and popularity among hobbyists.

All obsolete notes (such as Silver Certificates) are worth more than face value when the condition is Crisp Uncirculated (or CU as it is called by collectors). Many notes, hundreds in fact, have premium value even in lower grades of condition due to their scarcity. The premium on a collectible note may be double or triple face value or more. There are early $1 Notes worth more than one thousand times face value. While 19th-century notes tend to be more valuable, as fewer were printed and saved, notes of considerable value did occur among those of the 20th century.

A note may be valuable as the result of belonging to a series in which all had limited printings, such as the historic 1862 United States Note. This type of valuable note is, of course, the easiest for a beginner to recognize, as the notes look very different compared to those of the present day.

Conveniently, notes have dates on them, and an early date is yet another indicator of possible value. But even without dates and size differences there would be little difficulty in distinguishing an early note. The earlier the note, the more it will differ in design, color, and other details from later currency. It may picture an individual no longer shown on notes, such as Robert Fulton, Samuel Morse, or James Garfield. It may have the portrait on the back instead of the front. The portrait may be to one side rather than centered. The serial numbers may not be where they are normally found. Such notes are instantly recognizable as being very old. They, in fact, look so unlike modern currency that some noncollectors take them for stock or bonds or something other than legal tender.

A noncollector often believes that the value of old paper money is linked to its serial numbers. While a serial number can contribute to value, it is well down the list of ingredients for valuable notes. Among specimens of very high value, the serial number is hardly ever of consequence.

What is? Quite often the signatures. The signatures on a note play a very considerable role in the collector's world. If notes did not carry signatures, or if the signatures were never changed, the paper money hobby would be a mere shadow of what it is today. To cite just one example, the 1902 series of $10 National Bank Notes without dates yielded fifteen different varieties for the hobbyist to collect. Every one of them is a signature variety! Take away the signatures and all would be identical. Nothing changed but the signatures, yet they changed fifteen times. A rarity was created, too: the Jones-Woods combination is worth about three times as much as any of the other fourteen. If you did not look at the signatures and were unaware of the rarity of this particular combination, you would surely fail to pick this note out of a batch of 1902 $10 National Bank Notes. There is absolutely nothing remarkable by which to notice it.

There are many other notes on which the signatures are vitally important. The 1875 Bruce-Jordan combination on the $5 National Bank Note is so rare that pricing it is difficult. The other eight signature combinations from this series, while definitely of value, are not in that class.

The color of the seal, which has varied on notes in the 19th and 20th centuries, is seldom a major factor in value. In most cases where it appears to be a factor, some other element is, in fact, responsible for the note's value. An example of this is the $2 United States Note of 1878 with red seal and signatures of Scofield and Gilfillan. It is quite a bit more valuable than any $2 United States Note with a brown seal, leading many people to think that the seal color is a factor in its value. The rarity of this note derives from the signature combination. Another was issued with the same date and same red seal, but with signatures of Allison and Gilfillan. Its value is less than one-tenth as much.

However, there are a few cases in which the seal color makes a great difference in value, so it should not be totally dismissed. The $1 United States Note of 1878 with a maroon seal is valuable, while the same note with a red seal—identical in all other respects—is worth sharply less.

The date appearing on a note can be a value factor, not just by indicating the note's age. There may be two or more variations of the note that are distinguished by the date. In the case of Federal Reserve Notes (the only notes still being printed), the district of origin can influence their value. In some series there were not as many printed for Kansas City or Dallas as for New York or Chicago, and the scarcer ones have gained an edge in collector appeal and value. This applies to an even greater extent among National Bank Notes, which involved literally thousands of local banks across the country.

It's safe to say that paper money should be carefully examined. When examined by a person who knows what he's looking for, there is little chance of a rarity slipping by undetected.

BUYING PAPER MONEY

Browsing in coin shops is the usual way in which beginners start buying paper money. Just about every coin dealer—and many stamp dealers—stock paper money to one degree or another, from a single display album with elementary material to vaults filled with literally millions of dollars worth of specimens. Be observant of condition when shopping from dealers' stocks. There is really no excuse for unsatisfactory purchases from shops—the buyer has ample opportunity for inspection. Don't buy in a rush. Get to know the dealer and become familiar with his grading practices. Some dealers will grade a specimen higher than another dealer, but this may be offset by the fact that they charge a lower price.

Bargains. Is it possible to get bargains in buying paper money? To the extent that prices vary somewhat from dealer to dealer, yes. But if you're talking about finding a note worth $100 selling at $50, this is unlikely to happen. The dealers are well aware of market values, and the slight price differences that do occur are merely the result of some dealers being overstocked on certain notes or, possibly, having made a very good "buy" from the public. What may appear to be a bargain will generally prove, on closer examination, to be a specimen in undesirable condition, such as a washed bill on which the color has faded.

Auction sales. Many coin auctions feature selections of paper money, and there are occasional sales (mostly of the postal-bid variety) devoted exclusively to it. There is much to be said for auction buying if you have some experience and know how to read an auction catalog.

Shows and conventions. Paper money is offered for sale at every coin show and exposition. These present excellent opportunities to buy, as the dealers exhibiting at such shows are generally out-of-towners whose stock you would not otherwise have a chance to examine. As many sellers are likely to be offering the same type of material, you have the opportunity to make price and condition comparisons before buying.

CARING FOR YOUR COLLECTION

Paper money is not at all difficult to care for, store, and display attractively. It consumes little space and, unlike many other collectors' items, runs no risk of breakage. Nevertheless, it is important that the hobbyist give some attention to maintenance, as a poorly kept collection soon becomes aimless clutter and provides little enjoyment.

There is not much question that albums are the favorite storage method of nearly all paper money enthusiasts. In the days before specially made albums with vinyl pocket-pages, collectors used ordinary scrapbooks and mounted their specimens with philatelic hinges or photo corners. This, of course, may still be done, but such collections do not have the advantage of displaying both sides of the notes. Furthermore, the use of gummed hinges may leave marks upon removal, whereas specimens may be removed and reinserted into vinyl-page albums without causing the slightest blemish. We especially recommend the albums and "currency wallet" sold by Anco Coin & Stamp Supply, PO Box 782, Florence, AL 35630.

Faded color. There is no known restorative for faded color.

Holes. It is suggested that no effort be undertaken to repair holes, as this will almost certainly result in a further reduction in value.

Missing corners. Missing corners can seldom be restored in a manner that is totally satisfactory. The best that can be done is to secure some paper of approximately the same color and texture, trim a small piece to the proper size, and glue it in place as described below. If a portion of printed matter is missing, this can be hand-drawn, in ink, after restoration. Obviously, this kind of repair is not carried out to "fool" anybody, but simply to give a damaged specimen a less objectionable appearance.

Repairs to paper money. Repair work on damaged or defaced paper money is carried out strictly for cosmetic purposes; to improve its physical appearance. Repairs, even if skillfully executed, will not enhance the value of a specimen, as it will still be classified as defective. Amateurish repair efforts can very possibly make matters worse.

Tears. Tears can be closed by brushing a very small quantity of clear-drying glue to both sides of the tear, placing the note between sheets of waxed kitchen paper, and setting it under a weight to dry. A dictionary of moderate size serves this function well. Allow plenty of drying time and handle gently thereafter.

Wrinkles. Wrinkles, creases, and the like can sometimes be improved by wetting the note (in plain water) and drying it between sheets of waxed paper beneath a reasonably heavy weight—five pounds or more. This should not be done with a modern or recent specimen if there is danger of losing crispness.

Many ills to which paper money falls prey result from not being housed in a suitable album, or any album at all. Framing and mounting present some risk, as the item may then be exposed to long periods of direct sunlight, almost sure to cause fading or "bleaching" of its color.

SELLING YOUR COLLECTION

Selling to a dealer. All dealers in paper money buy from the public, but not all buy every collection offered to them. Some are specialists and are interested only in collections within their fields of specialization. Some will not purchase (or even examine) collections worth under $100, or $500, or whatever their line of demarcation happens to be. Obviously, a valuable collection containing many hard-to-get notes in VF or UNC condition is easier to interest a dealer in than a beginner-type collection. If a dealer is interested enough to make an offer, this is no guarantee that another dealer would not offer more. In the case of a collection worth $50,000, offers from several dealers might vary by as much as $5,000. This is not an indication that the dealer making the lowest offer is unscrupulous. Dealers will pay as much as the material is worth to them, and one dealer may be overstocked on items that another badly needs. Or one dealer may have customers for certain material that another doesn't. For this reason it makes good sense, if you choose to sell to a dealer, to obtain several offers before accepting any. But should you sell to a dealer at all? The chief advantage is quick payment and reduced risk. The price may not be as high as would be obtained at auction, however, depending on the property's nature and pure luck.

Selling by auction. Auction selling presents uncertainties but at the same time offers the possibility of gaining a much better return than could be had by selling to a dealer. It is no easy matter deciding which route to follow. If your collection is better than average, you may be better advised to sell by auction. This will involve a waiting period of, generally, four to six months between consigning the collection and receiving settlement; over the summer months it may be longer. However, some auctioneers will give a cash advance, usually about 25 percent of the sum they believe the material is worth. In special circumstances a larger advance may be made, or the usual terms and conditions altered. One auctioneer paid $100,000 under a special contract, stipulating that the money was not to be returned regardless of the sale's outcome or even if no sale took place. But this was on a million-dollar collection. Auctioneers' commissions vary. The normal is 20 percent, but some houses take 10 percent from the buyer and 10 percent from the seller. This would appear to work to the seller's advantage, but such a practice may discourage bidding and result in lower sales prices.

Selling to other collectors. Unless the owner is personally acquainted with a large circle of collectors, this will likely involve running ads in periodicals and "playing dealer," which runs into some expense. Unless you offer material at very favorable prices, you are not apt to be as successful with your ads as are the established dealers, who have a reputation and an established clientele.

INVESTING

1. Buy only specimens in V.F. (Very Fine) or better condition.

2. Be sure the notes you buy are properly graded and priced in accordance with their grade.

3. Avoid Federal Reserve Notes of the past 30 years. These have been stockpiled by dealers to such an extent that their value is not likely to show dramatic increase.

4. For investment purposes it is usually wise to avoid the very highly specialized types of notes. Investment success depends on continued growth of the hobby, and most new collectors will buy the standard items.

5. Do not seek quick profits. It is rare for an investment profit on paper currency to occur in less than five years. When holding five years or longer, the possibility of a profit is much greater.

6. Notes recommended by their sellers as investments are sometimes the worst investments. Learn about the paper money market and make your own selections.

7. Do not invest more than you can afford. Tying up too much capital in investments of any kind can be hazardous.

GLOSSARY

BROKEN BANK NOTE (a.k.a. obsolete note)

Literally, a Broken Bank Note is a note issued by a "broken" bank—a bank that failed and whose obligations could therefore not be redeemed. It may be presumed, by those who recall passing of legislation establishing the Federal Deposit Insurance Corporation, that banks failed only in the financial panic of 1929. During the 19th century, bank failures were common, especially in western and southwestern states. These were generally small organizations set up in frontier towns which suffered either from mismanagement or a sudden decline in the town's fortunes. Some collectors make a specialty of Broken Bank Notes.

DEMAND NOTES

Demand Notes have the distinction of being the first official circulating paper currency of this country, issued in 1861. There are three denominations: $5, $10, and $20, each bearing its own design on front and back. Demand Notes arose out of the coinage shortage brought about by the Civil War. A total of $60,000,000 in Demand Notes was authorized to be printed, amounting to several million individual specimens. Though this was an extraordinary number for the time, it was small compared to modern output, and only a fraction of the total survived. These notes were signed not by any specially designated Treasury Department officers, but a battery of employees, each of whom was given authority to sign and affix his name by hand in a slow assembly-line process, two signatures to each note. Originally the spaces left blank for signatures were marked "Register of the Treasury" and "Treasurer of the United States." As the persons actually signing occupied neither of these offices, they were obliged to perpetually add "for the . . ." to their signatures. In an effort to relieve their tedium, fresh plates were prepared reading "For the Register of the Treasury" and "For the Treasurer of the United States," which required nothing but a signature. This created a rarity status for the earlier specimens, which are now very desirable collectors' items.

ENGRAVING

Engraving is the process by which designs are printed on U.S. paper money. Bank note engraving involves the use of a metal plate, traditionally steel, into which the design is cut with sharp instruments called "burins" or "gravers." Ink is smeared over the surface and allowed to work into the grooves or lines comprising the design. The ink is then cleaned away from raised portions (intended to show blank in the printing). The engraving is pressed against a sheet of moistened paper, and the ink left in these grooves transfers to the paper, resulting in a printed image. When done by modern rotary press, it's a fast-moving process.

FEDERAL RESERVE BANK NOTES

Federal Reserve Bank Notes were issued briefly in 1915 and 1918. Like National Bank Notes they were secured by bonds or securities placed on deposit by each Federal Reserve Bank with the U.S. government. While issued and redeemable by the member banks of the Federal Reserve system, these notes are secured by—and are obligations of—the government.

FEDERAL RESERVE NOTES

Federal Reserve Notes, the notes in current circulation, were authorized by the Federal Reserve Act of December 23, 1913. Issued under control of the Federal Reserve Board, these notes are released through twelve Federal Reserve Banks in various parts of the country. Originally they were redeemable in gold at the U.S. Treasury or "lawful money" (coins) at a Federal Reserve Bank. In 1934 the option of redemption for gold was removed.

FREAK AND ERROR NOTES

These are bills which, by virtue of error or accident, are in some respect different from normal specimens. See the chapter on Error or Freak Notes.

GOLD CERTIFICATES

When gold coinage became a significant medium of exchange, the government decided to hold aside quantities of it and issue paper notes redeemable by the Treasury Department. The first Gold Certificates for public circulation were released in 1882. The series lasted until the era of small-size currency, ending in 1928. In 1933 all were ordered returned to the Treasury Department for redemption, including those in possession of collectors. A new law in 1964 permitted their ownership by collectors, though they can no longer be redeemed for gold.

LARGE SIZE CURRENCY

Large Size currency is the term generally used to refer to U.S. notes issued up to 1929, which were somewhat larger in size than those printed subsequently. The increased size permitted more elaborate design, which seldom fails to endear Large Size currency to beginners. Some of the earlier examples (especially of the 1870s, 1880s, and 1890s) are works of art. Though economic considerations were mainly responsible for the switch to a reduced size, there is no doubt that today's notes are far more convenient to handle and carry. Large Size notes are sometimes referred to as "bedsheet notes."

NATIONAL BANK NOTES

This is the largest group of notes available to the collector. They were issued from 1863 to 1929 and present collecting potential that can only be termed vast. More than 14,000 banks issued notes, in all parts of the country. While the approach to collecting them is usually regional, sets and series can also be built up, virtually without end. The National Banking Act was instituted in 1863, during the Civil War, to permit chartered banks to issue and circulate their own currency. Printing was done at the U.S. Government Printing Office and the designs were all alike, differing only in names of the banks, state seals, bank signatures, and the bank's charter number. Each charter bank was limited to issuing currency up to 90 percent of the value of bonds that it kept on deposit with the government. Charters remained in force for twenty years and could be renewed for an additional twenty years. National Bank Notes circulated in the same fashion as conventional currency and, thanks to the bond-deposit system, gained public confidence. The financial panic of 1929, which brought ruin or near-ruin to many banks, put an end to National Bank Notes.

NATIONAL GOLD BANK NOTES

These notes were issued exclusively by California banks during the 1870s under the same terms as ordinary National Bank Notes, their values backed by bonds deposited with the government. Events surrounding their origins form a unique chapter in the history of American economy. Following the discoveries of substantial quantities of gold in California in the late 1840s, that metal soon became the chief medium of local exchange, largely because it was more readily available in that remote region than coinage. Later, when gold coins and tokens began to circulate heavily in California, banks became so swamped with them that they petitioned Washington for authority to issue Gold Notes that could be substituted for the actual coinage. On July 12, 1870, Congress voted favorably on this measure, giving the right to issue such notes to nine banks in California and one in Boston. The Boston bank, Kidder National Gold Bank, appears not to have exercised its right, as no Gold Notes of this institution have been recorded. The California banks wasted no time in exercising their authority, the result being a series of notes ranging from $5–$500. All were printed on yellow-toned paper so as to be instantly identifiable. The banks issuing these notes were permitted to redeem them in gold coins.

REFUNDING CERTIFICATES

Refunding Certificates, a sort of hybrid between currency and bonds or securities, were issued under a Congressional Act of February 26, 1879. These were notes with a $10 face value which could be spent and exchanged in the fashion of ordinary money but drew interest at the rate of 4 percent per year. The purposes behind Refunding Certificates were several. They were chiefly designed to encourage saving and thereby curb inflation, which even at that time was becoming a problem. Also, they provided a safe means of saving for persons who distrusted banks (safe so long as the certificates were not lost or stolen), and, probably more important, were readily obtainable in areas of the country not well served by banks. In 1907 the interest was halted. Their redemption value today, with interest, is $21.30.

SERIAL NUMBER

The serial number is the control number placed on all U.S. paper bills, appearing below left-center and above right-center. No two bills in the same series bear repetitive serial numbers. The use of serial numbers is not only an aid in counting and sorting bills as printed, but a deterrent to counterfeiting.

SIGNATURES

The inclusion of signatures of Treasury Department officials on our paper bills, a practice as old as our currency (1861), began as a mark of authorization and as a foil to counterfeiters. The belief was that the handwriting would be more difficult to copy than an engraved design. Persons whose signatures appear on notes did not always occupy the same office. From 1862 to 1923, the two signers were the Treasurer and the Register (or Registrar as it appears in old writings) of the Treasury. Subsequently, the Treasurer and the Secretary of the Treasury were represented. These signatures are of great importance to collectors, as some notes are relatively common with certain combinations of signatures and others are rare. A "series" collection is not considered complete until one obtains every existing combination, even though the specimens may be in other respects identical.

SILVER CERTIFICATES

Silver Certificates were authorized in 1878. America's economy was booming at that time, and the demand for silver coinage in day-to-day business transactions outdistanced the supply. Silver Certificates were not intended to replace coinage but to create a convenient medium of exchange, whereby the government held specific quantities of Silver Dollars (later bullion) and agreed to redeem the notes or certificates against them. In 1934 the Treasury Department ceased redemption of these notes in Silver Dollars, and on June 24, 1968, redemption in all forms was ended. The notes are still, however, legal tender at their face value. When printing of Silver Certificates was discontinued, a flurry of speculation arose and many persons began hoarding them. This was done not only in hope of eventual redemption for bullion but in the belief that such notes would become valuable to collectors. Though Silver Certificates are popular with hobbyists, they have not increased sufficiently in price to yield speculators any great profits—especially since many collectors saved specimens in circulated condition.

STAR NOTES

United States Notes, Silver Certificates, and Gold Certificates sometimes have a star or asterisk in place of the letter in front of the serial number. Federal Reserve Notes and Federal Reserve Bank Notes have it at the end of the serial number. These notes are known as "Star Notes."

When a note is mutilated or otherwise unfit for issue, it must be replaced. To replace it with a note of the same serial numbers would be impractical, and Star Notes are therefore substituted. Other than having their own special serial number and a star, these notes are the same as the others. On United States Notes and Silver Certificates, the star is substituted for the prefix letter; on Federal Reserve Notes, for the suffix letter. All defective notes are accounted for and destroyed by burning them in an incinerator.

Large stars after the serial number on the 1869 Series of United States Notes, and 1890 and 1891 Treasury Notes, do not signify replacement notes as are known in later and present-day Star Notes.

Serial numbers on early Large Size Notes were preceded by a letter and were ended by various odd characters or symbols. These characters are not known to have any significance, except to show that the number was terminated, and prevented any elimination or addition of digits. The suffix characters were replaced by alphabet letters on later issues of notes.

TREASURY OR COIN NOTES

Treasury Notes were authorized by Congress in 1890. Their official title was Coin Notes, as they could be redeemed for silver or gold coins. The series did not prove popular and was discontinued after the issue of 1891.

TREASURY SEAL

The Treasury Seal is the official emblem of the U.S. Treasury Department, which has appeared on all our currency since 1862. It is missing only from the early Demand Notes, issued in 1861, and some Fractional Currency. Two versions have been employed, distinguished readily by the fact that one (the original) bears a Latin inscription, while the current Treasury Seal is in English. The basic motif is the same, a badge displaying scales and a key. The original Seal, somewhat more decorative, was in use until 1968.

UNITED STATES NOTES

Also known as Legal Tender Notes, this substantial and ambitious series followed Demand Notes and constitutes the second earliest variety of U.S. paper currency. There are five distinct issues, running from 1862 to 1923. Though United States Notes are all "Large Size" and their designs not very similar to those in present use, they show in their successive stages the evolutionary advance from this nation's first efforts at paper money to its currency of today. The first issue is dated March 10, 1862. Denominations are $1, $2, $5, $10, $20, $50, $100, $500, $1,000, $5,000 and $10,000. Individuals portrayed included not only presidents but other government officials: Salmon P. Chase (Lincoln's Secretary of the Treasury), Daniel Webster, and Lewis and Clark. Some of the reverse designs are masterpieces of geometrical linework. A number of rarities are to be found among Legal Tender Notes, but in general the lower denominations can be collected without great expense.

WILDCAT NOTES

Wildcat Notes are the notes that were issued by so-called "wildcat banks" in the era of State Bank Notes before the Civil War. Numerous banks sprang up around the middle part of the 19th century, mostly in the west and southwest, operated by persons of questionable integrity. Some never had capital backing and were instituted purely as a front for confidence swindles. After issuing notes, the bank shut down, its directors disappeared, and owners of the notes were left with worthless paper. As news traveled slowly in those days, the same persons could move from town to town and work the scheme repeatedly. Notes issued by these banks, or any banks that became insolvent, are also called Broken Bank Notes. Apparently the origin of the term "wildcat" derives from public sentiment of the time, which held that owners of such banks had no greater trustworthiness than a wild animal. "Wildcat" may also refer to the rapid movement of swindling bank officials from one locality to another.

DEPARTMENT OF THE TREASURY, BUREAU OF ENGRAVING AND PRINTING

Reprinted with permission of the Department of the Treasury, Bureau of Printing and Engraving, Washington, D.C.

BUREAU FACTS

- Since October 1, 1877, all U.S. paper currency has been printed by the Bureau of Engraving and Printing, which began as a six-person operation using steam-powered presses in the Department of the Treasury's basement.
- Now 1,900 Bureau employees occupy 25 acres of floor space in two Washington, D.C. buildings flanking 14th Street. Currency and stamps are designed, engraved, and printed 24 hours a day, 5 days a week on 23 high-speed presses. An additional 600 Bureau employees are at the Western Currency Facility in Fort Worth, Texas, where currency is printed 24 hours a day, 5 days a week on 12 high-speed presses.
- In Fiscal Year 1999, at a cost of 4.5 cents each, the Bureau of Engraving and Printing produced for the Federal Reserve System a record 11.3 billion notes worth approximately $142 billion. Ninety-five percent will replace unfit notes, and five percent will support economic growth. At any one time, $200 million in notes may be in production.
- Of total production, notes currently produced are the $1 (48% of production time), $2 (1 %), $5 (9%), $10 (11%), $20 (19%), $50 (5%), and $100 (7%).
- The Bureau also prints White House invitations and some 500 engraved items, such as visa counterfoils, naturalization documents, commissions, and certificates for almost 75 federal departments and agencies.

TOURS

- The Bureau of Engraving and Printing is one of the most popular tourist stops in Washington with almost 500,000 visitors to the printing facility each year.
- Free 30-minute guided tours are offered Monday though Friday, 9:00 A.M.–2:00 P.M., except for federal holidays and the week between Christmas and the New Year. During the summer months (June–August), afternoon tours are given from 5:00 P.M.–6:50 P.M.
- Visitors can see press runs of 32-note currency sheets, the application of Federal Reserve and Treasury seals, and 4,000 note "bricks" being readied for distribution to Federal Reserve Banks.
- If you are planning a trip to Washington, please call our information number at (202) 874-3188 for updated information or program changes.

VISITORS' CENTER

- At the Visitors' Center, history, production, and counterfeit exhibits showcase interesting information about U.S. currency.
- Many unique items can be purchased at the sales counter. Items include uncut currency sheets of 32, 16, 8, or 4 $1, $2, and $5 notes; a premium portfolio containing a new series 1996 $20 note with a low serial number and one of the last previous series $20 notes; a deluxe single note in the series 1996 with a low serial number; $150 worth of shredded currency in plastic bags that are sold for $1.50; engraved collectors' prints; souvenir cards; and Department of the Interior Duck Stamps.
- If you are planning a trip to Washington, please call our information number at (202) 874-3188 for updated information or program changes.

MAIL ORDER SALES

- Persons wishing to receive notice of new Bureau products or to order by mail can write to the following address: Mail Order Sales, Bureau of Engraving and Printing, 14th and C Streets, SW, Room 513-M, Washington, D.C. 20228.
- Operators are available to take credit card orders for Bureau products at 1-800-456-3408, Monday through Friday, 7:30 A.M.–7:15 P.M.

INTERNET

The Bureau's **Internet address** is *www.bep.treas.gov/*. We also offer an **interactive website** at www.moneyfactory.com/.

THE FEDERAL RESERVE BANKS

Reprinted with permission of the Department of the Treasury, Bureau of Printing and Engraving, Washington, D.C.

The Federal Reserve System is divided into twelve Federal Reserve districts, in each of which is a Federal Reserve Bank. There are also twenty-four branches. Each district is designated by a number and the corresponding letter of the alphabet. The district numbers, the cities in which the twelve banks are located, and the letter symbols are:

1-A—Boston	5-E—Richmond	9-I—Minneapolis
2-B—New York	6-F—Atlanta	10-J—Kansas City
3-C—Philadelphia	7-G—Chicago	11-K—Dallas
4-D—Cleveland	8-H—St. Louis	12-L—San Francisco

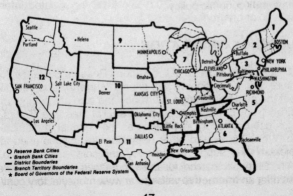

○ Reserve Bank Cities
• Branch Bank Cities
— District Boundaries
--- Branch Territory Boundaries
★ Board of Governors of the Federal Reserve System

FEDERAL RESERVE SYSTEM

The Federal Reserve System was created by the Federal Reserve Act, which was passed by Congress in 1913, in order to provide a safer and more flexible banking and monetary system. For approximately 100 years before the creation of the Federal Reserve, periodic financial panics had led to failures of a large number of banks, with associated business bankruptcies and general economic contractions. Following the studies of the National Monetary Commission, established by Congress a year after the particularly severe panic of 1907, several proposals were put forward for the creation of an institution designed to counter such financial disruptions. Following considerable debate, the Federal Reserve System was established. Its original purposes were to give the country an elastic currency, provide facilities for discounting commercial credits, and improve the supervision of the banking system.

ECONOMIC STABILITY AND GROWTH

From the inception of the Federal Reserve System, it was clear that these original purposes were aspects of broader national economic and financial objectives. Over the years, stability and growth of the economy, a high level of employment, stability in the purchasing power of the dollar, and a reasonable balance in transactions with foreign countries have come to be recognized as primary objectives of governmental economic policy.

CURRENCY CIRCULATION

An important function of the Federal Reserve System is to ensure that the economy has enough currency and coin to meet the public's demand. Currency and coin are put into or retired from circulation by the Federal Reserve Banks, which use depository institutions as the channel of distribution. When banks and other depository institutions need to replenish their supply of currency and coin—for example, when the public's need for cash increases around holiday shopping periods—depository institutions order the cash from the Federal Reserve Bank or Branch in their area, and the face value of that cash is charged to their accounts at the Federal Reserve. When the public's need for currency and coin declines, depository institutions return excess cash to the Federal Reserve Bank, which in turn credits their accounts.

UNFIT AND COUNTERFEIT NOTES

The Federal Reserve Banks and the U.S. Department of the Treasury share responsibility for maintaining the physical quality of U.S. paper currency in circulation. Each day, millions of dollars of deposits to Reserve Banks by depository institutions are carefully scrutinized. The Reserve Banks are responsible for receiving, verifying, authenticating, and storing currency and shipping it as needed. Currency in good condition is stored for later distribution. Worn or mutilated notes are removed from circulation and destroyed. Counterfeit notes are forwarded to the U.S. Secret Service, an agency of the Treasury Department.

FEDERAL RESERVE NOTES

Virtually all currency in circulation is in the form of Federal Reserve Notes, which are printed by the Bureau of Engraving and Printing of the U.S. Treasury. The Reserve Banks are currently authorized to issue notes in denominations of $1, $2, $5, $10, $20, $50, and $100. Coins are produced by the Treasury's U.S. Mint.

CASH TRANSFERS

Currency and coin are used primarily for small transactions. In the aggregate, such transactions probably account for only a small proportion of the value of all transfers of funds.

32-SUBJECT SHEET LAYOUT

All U.S. currency is now printed with 32 subjects (notes) to a large sheet. The first printing is the greenback. The second printing is the face of the note, in black. This includes the portrait and border, the series year, the check letter and quadrant number, two signatures, and the face plate number. The sheet is then cut in half vertically for the third printing. This includes the black Federal Reserve seal, the four Federal Reserve district numbers, the green Treasury seal, and two green serial numbers.

The 32-subject sheet is divided into four quarters called quadrants for numbering and other controls. Each quadrant has its own numbering sequence for the eight notes, with serial numbers advancing by 20,000 to the next note. The quadrant number and check letter in the upper left section indicate the first, second, third, or fourth quadrant and the position of the note in the quadrant. In the lower right corner the position letter is shown again with a plate number. On the back of the note the same small number in the lower right is the back plate number.

FIRST QUADRANT				THIRD QUADRANT			
A1		E1		A3		E3	
A00000001A	A100	A00080001A	E100	A00320001A	A100	A00400001A	E100
B1		F1		B3		F3	
A00020001A	B100	A00100001A	F100	A00340001A	B100	A00420001A	F100
C1		G1		C3		G3	
A00040001A	C100	A00120001A	G100	A00360001A	C100	A00440001A	G100
D1		H1		D3		H3	
A00060001A	D100	A00140001A	H100	A00380001A	D100	A004600001A	H100
A2		E2		A4		E4	
A00160001A	A100	A00240001A	E100	A00480001A	A100	A005600001A	E100
B2		F2		B4		F4	
A00180001A	B100	A00260001A	F100	A00500001A	B100	A00580001A	F100
C2		G2		C4		G4	
A00200001A	C100	A00280001A	G100	A0050001A	C100	A00600001A	G100
D2		H2		D4		H4	
A00220001A	D100	A00300001A	H100	A00540001A	D100	A00620001A	H100
SECOND QUADRANT				FOURTH QUADRANT			

NUMBERING SYSTEM

The system of numbering paper money must be adequate to accommodate a large volume of notes. For security and accountability purposes, no two notes of any one class, denomination, and series may have the same serial number. The two serial numbers on each note have a full complement of eight digits and an alphabetical prefix and suffix letter. When necessary, ciphers are used at the left of the number to make a total of eight digits.

Whenever a numbering sequence is initiated for United States Notes or Silver Certificates, the first note is numbered A 00 000 001 A; the second A 00 000 002 A; the hundredth A 00 000 100 A; the thousandth A 00 001 000 A; and so on through A 99 999 999 A. The suffix letter A will remain the same until a total of twenty-five groups, or "blocks," of 99 999 999 notes are numbered, each group having a different prefix letter of the alphabet from A to Z. The letter "O" is omitted, either as a prefix or as a suffix, because of its similarity to zero. The 100 000 000th note in each group will be a Star Note, since eight digits are the maximum in the mechanical operation of numbering machines.

At this point, the suffix letter changes to B for the next twenty-five groups of 99 999 999 notes, and proceeds in the same manner as the suffix letter A. A total of 62,500,000,000 notes could be numbered before a duplication of serial numbers would occur. However, it has never been required to number that many notes of any one class, denomination, and series.

The Federal Reserve Notes printed for the twelve districts are numbered in the same progression as United States Notes and Silver Certificates, except that a specific alphabetical letter identifies a specific Federal Reserve district. The letter identifying each district is used as a prefix letter at the beginning of the serial numbers on all Federal Reserve Notes and does not change. Only the suffix letter changes in the serial numbers on Federal Reserve currency.

PORTRAITS AND
BACK DESIGN ON
SMALL SIZE NOTES

DENOMINATION	PORTRAIT	BACK DESIGN
$1	Washington	Great Seal of the United States
$2	Jefferson	Monticello
$5	Lincoln	Lincoln Memorial
$10	Hamilton	United States Treasury
$20	Jackson	The White House
$50	Grant	United States Capitol
$100	Franklin	Independence Hall
$500	McKinley	Five Hundred
$1000	Cleveland	One Thousand
$5000	Madison	Five Thousand
$10,000	Chase	Ten Thousand
$100,000	Wilson	One Hundred Thousand

DATING U.S. CURRENCY

Unlike coins, the date is not changed each year on U.S. currency.

The date appearing on all notes, large or small, is that of the year in which the design was first approved or issued. For instance, Large Size $1 United States Notes of the Series 1880 were issued with the same date until the new Series 1917 was issued. There was no further date change until the Series 1923.

The same rule applies to Small Size Notes. However, in this case a letter is added after the date to designate or indicate a minor change in the main design or probably a change in one or both of the signatures. For example: the $1 Silver Certificate of 1935 was changed to 1935-A because of a change in the size of the tiny plate numbers appearing in the lower right corners of the face and back of the note. It was changed again from 1935-A to 1935-B in 1945 when the signatures of Julian/Morganthau were changed to Julian/Vinson. Subsequent changes in signatures continued in the 1935 Series to the year 1963 when the signatures of Smith/Dillon terminated the issue with the Series 1935-H. Therefore, these notes were issued for twenty-eight years bearing the date 1935.

NEW TREASURY SEAL

FORMER DESIGN:
The former design had the Latin inscription *Thesaur. Amer. Septent. Sigil.,* which has several translations. It was the Seal of the North American Treasury.

NEW DESIGN:
This new design drops the Latin and states THE DEPARTMENT OF THE TREASURY, 1789. First used on the $100 Note of the Series 1966.

GRADES AND CONDITIONS
OF PAPER MONEY

CONDITION

The physical condition of a note or bill plays an important role in determining its value. There are many notes that have no premium value beyond face value in ordinary condition but are valuable or moderately valuable when uncirculated. Even in the case of scarce early specimens, the price given for an Average example is generally much less than that commanded by Fine or Very Fine condition.

Defects encountered in paper money include:

Creases, folds, wrinkles. Generally the characteristic that distinguishes uncirculated notes from those that almost—but not quite—qualify for such designation is a barely noticeable crease running approximately down the center vertically, resulting from the note being folded for insertion into a wallet or billfold. It may be possible, through manipulation or storage beneath a heavy weight, to remove evidence of the crease; but the knowledge that it once existed cannot be obliterated.

Discoloration. Discoloration is not as easy to recognize as most defects, but it must be classed as one. A distinction should be made between notes printed from underinked rollers and those which originally were normally colored but became "washed out." Sometimes washing is indeed the cause; a well-intentioned collector will bathe a note, attempting to clean it, with the result that its color is no longer strong. This should not happen if warm water is used, without strong cleanser. Atmospheric conditions may play some part in discoloration.

Foxing. Fox spots may sometimes be observed on old notes, especially those of the pre-1890 era, just as on old paper in general. They seem more common to foreign currency than American, but their presence on our notes is certainly not rare. These are tiny brownish-red dots, caused by an infestation of lice attacking the paper fibers.

Holes. Holes are more likely to be encountered in early paper money than specimens of recent origin. In early years it was customary for Federal Reserve Banks to use wire clips in making up bundles of notes for distribution to banking organizations, and these clips or staples often pierced the bills. Another common occurrence years ago was the practice of shop clerks and cashiers in general to impale notes upon holders consisting of nails mounted on stands.

Missing pieces. Missing pieces is a highly undesirable defect which, except in the case of rare specimens, renders the item valueless to collectors. Even if only a blank unprinted corner is torn away, this is called a missing-piece note and hardly anyone will give it a second glance.

Stains. Notes sometimes become stained with ink or other liquids. If the specimen is commonplace and easily obtainable in Very Fine or Uncirculated condition, it will be worthless with any kind of stain. In a note of moderate value, its price will be hurt to a greater or lesser degree depending on the stain's intensity, size, nature, and the area it touches. A stain in an outer margin or at a corner is not so objectionable as one occurring at the center or across a signature or serial number. Ink stains, because of their strong color, are generally deemed the worst, but bad staining can also be caused by oil, crayon, "magic marker," and food substances. Pencil markings, which frequently are found on bank notes, will yield to ordinary erasing with a piece of soft "art-gum" worked gently over the surface and brushed away with an artist's camel-hair brush. Most other stains cannot be so easily removed. With ink there is no hope, as any caustic sufficiently strong to remove the ink will also injure the printing and possibly eat through the paper as well. Oil stains can sometimes be lightened, though not removed, by sprinkling the note on both sides (even if the stain shows only on one) with talcum powder or other absorbent powder, placing it between sheets of waxed kitchen paper, and leaving it beneath a heavy weight for several days in a room where the humidity is not unduly high.

Tears. Tears in notes are very common defects, which may be minute or run nearly the whole length of the bill. As a rule the paper on which American currency is printed is fairly rugged and will not tear as readily as most ordinary paper, but given careless or hurried handling anything is possible. An old worn note is more apt to tear in handling than a new one. Repaired tears are more common in the world of paper money collecting than may be generally supposed. A clean tear—one which does not involve loss of surface—can be patched so as to become virtually unnoticed, unless examined against a light or through a strong magnifying glass. X-ray examination will reveal repairs when all else fails.

CONDITION GRADES

The following condition standards have been used throughout this book and, with slight variations depending upon individual interpretation, are generally current in the trade.

Uncirculated—UNC. A specimen that for all appearances has not been handled or passed through general circulation; a crisp fresh note in "bank" condition. There may be minor blemishes, such as a finger smudge or pinhole, but if these are in any respect severe the condition merits description as "Almost Uncirculated." There is not much satisfaction to be taken in a note fresh and crisp that has gaping holes and fingerprints. Obviously, an 1870 Uncirculated note should not be expected to match a 1970 in appearance or feel.

*Uncirculated—***Unc.** An uncirculated "Star Note."

Almost Uncirculated—A.U. In the case of modern or semimodern notes, this is generally taken to mean a specimen that shows no evidence of having passed through general circulation but, because of some detraction, fails to measure up to a rating of Uncirculated. The problem may be finger smudges, counting crinkles, a light crease, a fold along one or more of the corners, or pinholes. But if more than one of these impairments is present, the item would surely not deserve a classification of Almost Uncirculated.

Extremely Fine—X.F. A note exhibiting little evidence of wear from handling, but not so perfect or near-perfect as to qualify for a rating of Uncirculated or Almost Uncirculated.

On a used note issued before 1900 there may be clear evidence of circulation, but no disfiguring marks.

Very Fine—V.F. A Very Fine note has experienced some circulation but escaped without "being mangled." It is still clean and crisp, and its creases are not offensive.

Fine—F. Here the scale begins sliding down. It is obvious that, being the fifth in rank of condition grades, Fine notes are quite a good deal removed from Uncirculated. They have been handed around pretty thoroughly and suffered the normal consequences, but still are without serious blemishes such as tears, missing corners, serious stains, or holes.

Very Good—V.G. A well-circulated note bearing evidence of much folding, creasing, and wrinkling. It may possibly be lightly stained, smudged, or pin punctured, but major defects—such as a torn-off corner—would drop it into an even lower category.

Good—G. Heavily circulated, worn notes that are possibly stained or scribbled on, edges could be frayed or "dog-eared." There may be holes larger than pin punctures, but not on the central portion of design. This is the lowest grade of condition acceptable to a collector, and only when nothing better is available. Unless very rare, such specimens are considered space-fillers only.

Average Buying Prices—A.B.P. The Average Buying Prices given here are the approximate sums paid by retail dealers for specimens in Good condition. As selling prices vary, so do buying prices, and, in fact, they usually vary a bit more.

RECORD KEEPING

For your convenience, we suggest you use the following record-keeping system to note condition of your paper money in the checklist box:

| ☒ FAIR | ☒ VERY GOOD | ☐ VERY FINE | ☒ ALMOST UNC |
| ☑ GOOD | ⊟ FINE | ☒ EXTREMELY FINE | ■ UNCIRCULATED |

ABOUT THE PRICES
IN THIS BOOK

Prices are compiled from offerings made by dealers and from auction sale results. In all cases (except for the Average Buying Price) the prices are retail selling prices. While prices are current at the time of publication, the market can be influenced by buying or selling trends, causing prices to change. All prices, except in the case of seldom-offered rarities, are averages, calculated from numerous sales. The actual prices charged by any individual currency dealer may be slightly higher or lower than those indicated in this book. In any given sale various factors play a role, such as whether the seller is overstocked on notes of that type.

HOW TO USE THIS BOOK

The *Official Blackbook Price Guide to United States Paper Money* provides a convenient reference to prices of all standard U.S. currency, old and new, as well as many unusual issues.

Notes are divided into section by denomination. Within each section can be found the various series of notes for that denomination. The series are arranged chronologically and will vary slightly from section to section, as some notes were issued in one series and not in another. An index page is provided at the beginning of each section.

To familiarize yourself with the various currency terms, the following illustration might be helpful:

To price a note correctly, it is necessary that it be accurately identified and graded. The illustrations will aid in identification, and a grading guide has been provided. In the case of some notes, particularly very old ones, the value depends upon minor details. In all such cases these details have been clearly noted.

Listings include the following information:

Date. This is the "series date," as it appears on the note, and may bear no relation whatsoever to the year in which the note was actually issued. The date of actual issue is not of importance to collectors. If the series date on the note carries a suffix letter, such as 1935A, it will be so indicated in the listing.

Seal. The color of the Treasury Seal will be noted, along with other information if relevant. The following abbreviations are also used: Sm.—small, Lg.—large; w/r—with rays, w/s—with scallops.

Signatures. All U.S. notes carry two signatures, and the names of each signer are given for every note listed. If different signature combinations exist for your note, be sure you refer to the correct signature combination. The listings will show you whether there is just one set of signatures for that note or more than one.

Type. In a small minority of cases, notes were issued in more than one type. For example, a slight change was made in the paper or printing. All recorded types are identified in the listings.

Issuing Bank. This information is provided for Federal Reserve Notes and Federal Reserve Bank Notes only. Check the Federal Reserve seal on your note to identify the issuing bank. In some instances there is a difference in value depending on where the note originated. Space prevents us from listing the numerous local banks issuing National Bank Notes.

A.B.P. The first price column is the A.B.P. or Average Buying Price. This is the approximate sum being paid by dealers for a specimen in the lowest listed grade of condition. The lowest listed grade of condition is the column next to the A.B.P. If the next column is headed "Good," the A.B.P. is for a specimen in Good condition. In all cases the A.B.P. includes the face value of the note. This is an important consideration insofar as U.S. notes, regardless of their age or physical condition, can still be spent as legal tender.

Current Selling Prices. The current selling prices are given in two or three different grades of condition, as indicated at the top of each price column. Different groups of notes are priced in different condition grades, owing to market availability. Some are virtually unobtainable in Uncirculated condition, so it would be pointless to give such a price. Others are of no premium value in less than V.F., hence V.F. is the lowest grade shown.

ONE DOLLAR NOTES

ORDER OF ISSUE

63

ONE DOLLAR NOTES (1862) UNITED STATES NOTES
(ALSO KNOWN AS LEGAL TENDER NOTES)
(Large Size)

Face Design: Portrait of Salmon Portland Chase (1808–73), Secretary of the Treasury under Lincoln, red Treasury Seal, signatures of Chittenden and Spinner, lower right.

Back Design: Large circle center with legal tender obligation.

SERIES	SIGNATURES	SEAL	A.B.P.	GOOD	V. FINE	UNC.
1862	Chittenden-Spinner					
☐Type I, National Bank Note, American Bank						
Note without monogram		Red	175.00	245.00	950.00	2000.00
☐Type II, National Bank Note, American Bank						
Note with monogram ABNCO		Red	80.00	125.00	550.00	1450.00
☐Type III, National Bank Note, National Bank						
Note without monogram		Red	80.00	115.00	600.00	1485.00
☐Type IV, National Bank Note, National Bank						
Note with monogram ABNCO		Red	80.00	115.00	550.00	1450.00

ONE DOLLAR NOTES (1869) UNITED STATES NOTES
(ALSO KNOWN AS LEGAL TENDER NOTES)
(Large Size)

Face Design: Portrait of President Washington in the center, large red seal to the right. Scene of Columbus in sight of land to left; also called "Rainbow Note" because of the many colors used in printing. Black ink for main design, red seal and serial numbers, green background for the serial number, green shading in upper-half and blue tint in paper left of portrait to deter counterfeiting.

Back Design: Green, ONE DOLLAR and ONE over "1" center, letters U.S. interwoven to left. Legal tender obligation to right of center.

SERIES	SIGNATURES	SEAL	A.B.P.	GOOD	V. FINE	UNC.
☐1869	Allison-Spinner	Red	60.00	115.00	650.00	1750.00
☐1869	Allison-Spinner Water Mark Paper		75.00	145.00	1100.00	2250.00

ONE DOLLAR NOTES (1874–1917)
UNITED STATES NOTES
(ALSO KNOWN AS LEGAL TENDER NOTES)
(Large Size)

Back Design: Large green "X" with UNITED STATES OF AMERICA in the center. Legal tender obligation and counterfeiting warning to right.
Face Design: No blue or green shading and tinting.

SERIES	SIGNATURES	SEAL	A.B.P.	GOOD	V. FINE	UNC.
☐1874	Allison-Spinner	Sm. Red	45.00	60.00	325.00	1250.00
☐1875	Allison-New	Sm. Red	35.00	55.00	300.00	960.00
☐1875	Same Series A	Sm. Red	95.00	210.00	775.00	2450.00
☐1875	Same Series B	Sm. Red	100.00	235.00	800.00	2475.00
☐1875	Same Series C	Sm. Red	115.00	260.00	830.00	2595.00
☐1875	Same Series D	Sm. Red	155.00	285.00	875.00	2595.00
☐1875	Same Series E	Sm. Red	175.00	310.00	1075.00	2700.00
☐1875	Allison-Wyman	Sm. Red	40.00	60.00	250.00	925.00
☐1878	Allison-Gilfillan	Sm. Red	40.00	60.00	250.00	900.00
☐1878	Allison-Gilfillan Water Marked Paper	45.00	85.00	425.00	1400.00
☐1880	Scofield-Gilfillan	Lg. Brown	30.00	60.00	250.00	850.00
☐1880	Bruce-Gilfillan	Lg. Brown	30.00	55.00	250.00	875.00
☐1880	Bruce-Wyman	Lg. Brown	30.00	55.00	250.00	850.00
☐1880	Rosecrans-Huston	Lg. Red	100.00	220.00	900.00	2800.00
☐1880	Rosecrans-Huston	Lg. Brown	80.00	160.00	825.00	2700.00
☐1880	Rosecrans-Nebeker	Lg. Brown	80.00	160.00	825.00	2700.00
☐1880	Rosecrans-Nebeker	Sm. Red	35.00	50.00	200.00	725.00
☐1880	Tillman-Morgan	Sm. Red	35.00	50.00	200.00	725.00
☐1917	Tehee-Burke	Sm. Red	25.00	34.00	75.00	250.00

Sm.—Small Seal, Lg.—Large Seal
*This note with signatures of Burke and Elliott is an error issue. The regular procedure was to have the signature of the Register of the Treasury on the left, and that of the Treasurer to the right. The signatures were transposed in this instance.

SERIES	SIGNATURES	SEAL	A.B.P.	GOOD	V. FINE	UNC.
☐1917	Elliott-Burke	Sm. Red	20.00	25.00	70.00	250.00
☐1917	Burke-Elliott*	Sm. Red	60.00	87.00	350.00	925.00
☐1917	Elliott-White	Sm. Red	20.00	25.00	70.00	250.00
☐1917	Speelman-White	Sm. Red	20.00	25.00	70.00	250.00

ONE DOLLAR NOTES (1923) UNITED STATES NOTES
(ALSO KNOWN AS LEGAL TENDER NOTES)
(Large Size)

Face Design: Portrait of President Washington in center. Red seal to left, red "1" to the right, red serial numbers.

Back Design: UNITED STATES OF AMERICA and ONE DOLLAR in center. Figures "1" to right and left. This was the last issue of Large Size ONE DOLLAR United States Notes. The last series of Large Size Notes was kept in use until 1929 when the first issue of Small Size Notes was released.

SERIES	SIGNATURES	SEAL	A.B.P.	GOOD	V. FINE	UNC.
☐1923	Speelman-White	Red	25.00	35.00	100.00	425.00

ONE DOLLAR NOTES (1928) UNITED STATES NOTES
(ALSO KNOWN AS LEGAL TENDER NOTES)
(Small Size)

Face Design: Red seal to left—red serial numbers, large ONE to right. This is the only issue of the $1 United States Note, Small Size. At the present time only the $100 United States Note is current.

Back Design: Large ONE in center with ONE DOLLAR overprint, back printed in green.

SERIES	SIGNATURES	SEAL	A.B.P.	GOOD	V. FINE	UNC.	★UNC.
☐1928	Woods-Woodin	Red	25.00	35.00	90.00	350.00	4500.00

*Star Notes: Damaged or unsatisfactory notes were replaced at the Bureau of Engraving with new notes bearing a star (★) in place of the first letter and preceding the serial no. Example: *12345678A

ONE DOLLAR NOTES (1863–1875)
NATIONAL BANK NOTES
FIRST CHARTER PERIOD (Large Size)

Face Design: Name of National Bank top center, maidens at altar below.

Back Design: Landing of Pilgrims center, State Seal of state issuing bank to left, eagle and flag.

SERIES	SIGNATURES	SEAL	A.B.P.	GOOD	V. FINE	UNC.
□Original*	Colby-Spinner	Red w/r	50.00	85.00	425.00	1450.00
□Original*	Jeffries-Spinner	Red w/r	120.00	400.00	1275.00	2900.00
□Original*	Allison-Spinner	Red w/r	50.00	75.00	425.00	1425.00
□1875	Allison-New	Red w/s	50.00	75.00	425.00	1425.00
□1875	Allison-Wyman	Red w/s	50.00	75.00	425.00	1425.00
□1875	Allison-Gilfillan	Red w/s	50.00	75.00	425.00	1425.00
□1875	Scofield-Gilfillan	Red w/s	50.00	75.00	425.00	1425.00

w/r—with Rays, w/s—with Scallops
*Early notes of the First Charter Period did not have the series imprinted on them. They are known by the date on the bill which was usually the date of charter or organization, or as the Original Series. These notes had a seal with rays or small notches. In 1875 the series was imprinted in red, and the seal was changed to have scallops around the border. The charter number was added to later issues of notes of the original series and to all notes of the 1875 series.

ONE DOLLAR NOTES (1886) SILVER CERTIFICATES
(Large Size)

SERIES	SIGNATURES	SEAL	A.B.P.	GOOD	V. FINE	UNC.
☐1886	Rosecrans-Jordan	Sm. Red	65.00	95.00	385.00	1225.00
☐1886	Rosecrans-Hyatt	Sm. Red	65.00	95.00	385.00	1225.00
☐1886	Rosecrans-Hyatt	Lg. Red	65.00	95.00	385.00	1225.00
☐1886	Rosecrans-Huston	Lg. Red	65.00	95.00	385.00	1225.00
☐1886	Rosecrans-Huston	Lg. Brown	65.00	105.00	400.00	1250.00
☐1886	Rosecrans-Nebeker	Lg. Brown	66.00	105.00	400.00	1250.00
☐1886	Rosecrans-Nebeker	Sm. Red	67.00	110.00	450.00	1550.00

ONE DOLLAR NOTES (1891) SILVER CERTIFICATES
(Large Size)
Back Design
Face Design:
Same as 1886
note.

SERIES	SIGNATURES	SEAL	A.B.P.	GOOD	V. FINE	UNC.
☐1891	Rosecrans-Nebeker	Sm. Red	65.00	90.00	325.00	1050.00
☐1891	Tillman-Morgan	Sm. Red	65.00	90.00	325.00	1000.00

ONE DOLLAR NOTES (1896) SILVER CERTIFICATES
(Large Size)

Face Design: History instructing youth. To the right, panoramic view of the Capitol and Washington Monument. Constitution on tablet, names of famous Americans on top and side borders.

Back Design: Portrait of Martha Washington to left and President Washington to right with large numeral "1" in center.

There is a story that when this note was issued people objected to it because they said No. "1" (ONE) shouldn't stand between George and Martha Washington. The set consists of $1, $2, and $5 denominations. They all have very beautiful engravings, and they are truly the most beautiful notes ever issued by our government. They were first released in 1896 and replaced by a new issue in 1899. They were short-lived because of objections to the unclad female on the $5 Note.

SERIES	SIGNATURES	SEAL	A.B.P.	GOOD	V. FINE	UNC.
☐1896	Tillman-Morgan	Red	70.00	95.00	450.00	1400.00
☐1896	Bruce-Roberts	Red	70.00	95.00	450.00	1400.00

ONE DOLLAR NOTES (1899) SILVER CERTIFICATES
(Large Size)

Face Design: Eagle on flag and Capitol background over portraits of Presidents Lincoln and Grant.

Back Design

SERIES	SIGNATURES	SEAL	A.B.P.	GOOD	V. FINE	UNC.
	SERIES OF 1899 (above upper right serial number)					
☐1899	Lyons-Roberts	Blue	30.00	45.00	110.00	320.00
	SERIES OF 1899 (below upper right serial number)					
☐1899	Lyons-Roberts	Blue	20.00	30.00	105.00	295.00
☐1899	Lyons-Treat	Blue	24.00	33.00	100.00	300.00
☐1899	Vernon-Treat	Blue	22.00	30.00	100.00	300.00
☐1899	Vernon-McClung	Blue	22.00	30.00	95.00	295.00
	SERIES OF 1899 (vertical to right of blue seal)					
☐1899	Napier-McClung	Blue	22.00	30.00	90.00	265.00
☐1899	Napier-Thompson	Blue	35.00	55.00	260.00	1100.00
☐1899	Parker-Burke	Blue	22.00	30.00	85.00	275.00
☐1899	Teehee-Burke	Blue	22.00	30.00	85.00	275.00
☐1899	Elliott-Burke	Blue	20.00	27.00	85.00	270.00
☐1899	Elliott-White	Blue	20.00	27.00	85.00	270.00

SERIES	SIGNATURES	SEAL	A.B.P.	GOOD	V. FINE	UNC.
☐1899	Speelman-White	Blue	20.00	30.00	80.00	260.00

ONE DOLLAR NOTES (1923) SILVER CERTIFICATES
(Large Size)

Face Design: Portrait of President Washington in center, blue seal left, blue 1 DOLLAR right, blue numbers.

Back Design: Same as 1923 note.

SERIES	SIGNATURES	SEAL	A.B.P.	GOOD	V. FINE	UNC.
☐1923	Speelman-White	Blue	14.00	18.00	35.00	85.00
☐1923	Woods-White	Blue	14.00	19.00	37.00	88.00
☐1923	Woods-Tate	Blue	18.00	26.00	78.00	310.00

ONE DOLLAR NOTES (1928) SILVER CERTIFICATES
(Small Size)

Face Design: Portrait of President Washington, blue seal to
the left, ONE to right, blue seal and numbers. ONE SILVER DOL-
LAR under portrait.

Back Design

First issue of Series 1928. U.S. paper money was reduced
in 1928 from the old Large Size to the size presently in use.
This was mostly an economy measure. Unlike Large Size
Notes, the Small Notes have a letter designation after the
date to denote a minor change in design or change of one
or both signatures.

SERIES	SIGNATURES	SEAL	A.B.P.	GOOD	V. FINE	UNC.	★UNC.
☐1928	Tate-Mellon	Blue	4.00	7.00	14.00	50.00	500.00
☐1928A	Woods-Mellon	Blue	4.00	7.00	14.00	50.00	450.00
☐1928B	Woods-Mills	Blue	4.00	7.00	14.00	50.00	515.00
☐1928C	Woods-Woodin	Blue	25.00	35.00	95.00	500.00	5250.00
☐1928D	Julian-Woodin	Blue	20.00	30.00	80.00	350.00	2500.00
☐1928E	Julian-Morgenthau	Blue	75.00	125.00	425.00	1600.00	12550.00

ONE DOLLAR NOTES (1934) SILVER CERTIFICATES
(Small Size)

Face Design: Portrait of President Washington, blue "1" to
left. ONE and blue seal to right. ONE DOLLAR IN SILVER under
portrait.
Back Design: Same as 1928 note.

SERIES	SIGNATURES	SEAL	A.B.P.	GOOD	V. FINE	UNC.	★UNC.
☐1934	Julian-Morgenthau	Blue	6.00	8.00	17.00	68.00	580.00

ONE DOLLAR NOTES (1935) SILVER CERTIFICATES
(Small Size)

Face Design: Portrait of President Washington in center.
Gray "1" to left, blue seal right, and blue numbers. ONE DOL-
LAR IN SILVER under portrait.

The following notes are without IN GOD WE TRUST on back.

SERIES	SIGNATURES	SEAL	A.B.P.	GOOD	V. FINE	UNC.	★UNC.
☐1935	Julian-Morgenthau	Blue	3.00	4.00	9.00	35.00	360.00
☐1935A	Julian-Morgenthau	Blue	2.00	3.50	4.00	10.00	110.00
☐1935A	Julian-Morgenthau	Brown	5.00	8.00	22.00	110.00	1250.00

This note was a special issue for use in war zones in the Pacific area during
World War II. Brown serial numbers and HAWAII stamped on front and back.

ONE DOLLAR NOTES (1935) SILVER CERTIFICATES
(Small Size)

SERIES SIGNATURES	SEAL	A.B.P.	GOOD	V. FINE	UNC.	★UNC.
☐ 1935A Julian-Morgenthau	Yellow	5.00	8.00	22.00	130.00	1250.00

The above note was a special issue for use in war zones in the North African and European areas during World War II. Blue serial numbers and yellow seal.

☐ 1935A Julian-Morgenthau	Blue	10.00	16.00	42.00	200.00	8200.00

Red "R" between the Treasury Seal and signature of Morgenthau. This was an experimental issue to test wearing qualities of differently treated paper.

☐ 1935A Julian-Morgenthau	Blue	10.00	15.00	40.00	195.00	7750.00

Above note with red "S" between Treasury Seal and signature of Morgenthau. Experimental issue "R" was for regular paper, "S" for special paper.

☐ 1935B Julian-Vinson	Blue	2.00	2.50	5.50	16.00	150.00
☐ 1935C Julian-Snyder	Blue	2.00	2.50	5.50	14.00	45.00
☐ 1935D Clark-Snyder	Blue	2.00	2.25	3.50	11.00	32.00

Wide design on back. This and all notes of 1935 prior to this have the wide design. See Fig I.

☐ 1935D Clark-Snyder	Blue	2.00	2.25	3.50	11.00	36.00

Narrow design on back. This and all $1 Notes following have narrow design. See Fig. II.

ONE DOLLAR NOTES (1935) SILVER CERTIFICATES
(Small Size)

SERIES	SIGNATURES	SEAL	A.B.P.	GOOD	V. FINE	UNC.	★UNC.
☐1935E	Priest-Humphrey	Blue	1.80	2.25	3.25	10.00	17.00
☐1935F	Priest-Anderson	Blue	1.80	2.25	3.50	10.50	17.00
☐1935G	Smith-Dillon	Blue	1.80	2.25	3.50	11.50	24.00

IN GOD WE TRUST added. All notes following have the motto.

☐1935G	Smith-Dillon	Blue	1.80	2.25	3.75	22.00	58.00
☐1935H	Granahan-Dillon	Blue	1.80	2.25	3.25	10.00	20.00

ONE DOLLAR NOTES (1957) SILVER CERTIFICATES
(Small Size)

The following three notes are the last issue of the $1 Silver Certificates. The reason for the change in series from 1935H to 1957 was due to printing improvements. The 1935 Series, up until the issue of Clark and Snyder, was printed in sheets of twelve subjects to a sheet. During the term of Clark and Snyder notes were printed eighteen subjects to a sheet. Starting with Series 1957, new high-speed rotary presses were installed and notes were printed thirty-two subjects to a sheet.

SERIES	SIGNATURES	SEAL	A.B.P.	GOOD	V. FINE	UNC.	★UNC.
☐1957	Priest-Anderson	Blue	1.45	1.75	2.15	5.50	11.00
☐1957A	Smith-Dillon	Blue	1.45	1.75	2.15	6.50	11.50
☐1957B	Granahan-Dillon	Blue	1.45	1.75	2.15	6.00	11.00

The redemption of Silver Certificates by the U.S. Treasury Department ended on June 24, 1968. These notes are now worth only their face value, plus the numismatic value to collectors. Notes in used condition are not regarded as collectors' items.

ONE DOLLAR NOTES (1890)
TREASURY OR COIN NOTES

(Large Size)

Face Design: Portrait of Stanton, Secretary of War during the Civil War.

Back Design: Green large ornate ONE. Entire back is beautifully engraved.

SERIES	SIGNATURES	SEAL	A.B.P.	GOOD	V. FINE	UNC.
☐1890	Rosecrans-Huston	Brown	70.00	110.00	825.00	2900.00
☐1890	Rosecrans-Nebeker	Brown	70.00	110.00	825.00	2900.00
☐1890	Rosecrans-Nebeker	Red	70.00	110.00	800.00	2900.00

ONE DOLLAR NOTES (1891)
TREASURY OR COIN NOTES
(Large Size)

Face Design: Is similar to 1890 note.

Back Design: More unengraved area, numerous ONES and "1"s.

SERIES	SIGNATURES	SEAL	A.B.P.	GOOD	V. FINE	UNC.
☐1891	Rosecrans-Nebeker	Red	52.00	75.00	250.00	800.00
☐1891	Tillman-Morgan	Red	52.00	75.00	250.00	800.00
☐1891	Bruce-Roberts	Red	50.00	75.00	250.00	800.00

ONE DOLLAR NOTES (1918)
FEDERAL RESERVE BANK NOTES

(Large Size)

Face Design: Portrait of President Washington, signature to left of center. Bank and city center, blue seal to right. Signatures of government officials above. Signatures of bank officials below. Federal Reserve district letter and numbers in four corners.

Back Design: Flying eagle and flag in center. All are Series 1918 and have blue seals and blue numbers.

BANK	GOV'T SIGNATURES	BANK SIGNATURES	A.B.P.	GOOD	V. FINE	UNC.
☐ Boston	Teehee-Burke	Bullen-Morss	24.00	34.00	80.00	210.00
☐ Boston	Teehee-Burke	Willet-Morss	24.00	34.00	95.00	375.00
☐ Boston	Elliot-Burke	Willet-Morss	24.00	34.00	80.00	210.00

BANK	GOV'T SIGNATURES	BANK SIGNATURES	A.B.P.	GOOD	V. FINE	UNC.
☐ New York	Teehee-Burke	Sailer-Strong	24.00	32.00	80.00	210.00
☐ New York	Teehee-Burke	Hendricks-Strong	24.00	32.00	80.00	210.00
☐ New York	Elliott-Burke	Hendricks-Strong	24.00	32.00	80.00	210.00
☐ Philadelphia	Teehee-Burke	Hardt-Passmore	24.00	32.00	80.00	210.00
☐ Philadelphia	Teehee-Burke	Dyer-Passmore	24.00	32.00	80.00	210.00
☐ Philadelphia	Elliott-Burke	Dyer-Passmore	39.00	54.00	235.00	765.00
☐ Philadelphia	Elliott-Burke	Dyer-Norris	24.00	32.00	80.00	210.00
☐ Cleveland	Teehee-Burke	Baxter-Fancher	24.00	32.00	80.00	210.00
☐ Cleveland	Teehee-Burke	Davis-Fancher	24.00	32.00	85.00	215.00
☐ Cleveland	Elliott-Burke	Davis-Fancher	24.00	32.00	80.00	215.00
☐ Richmond	Teehee-Burke	Keesee-Seay	24.00	32.00	80.00	210.00
☐ Richmond	Elliott-Burke	Keesee-Seay	24.00	32.00	85.00	215.00
☐ Atlanta	Teehee-Burke	Pike-McCord	24.00	32.00	80.00	210.00
☐ Atlanta	Teehee-Burke	Bell-McCord	39.00	54.00	260.00	815.00
☐ Atlanta	Teehee-Burke	Bell-Wellborn	37.00	54.00	235.00	715.00
☐ Atlanta	Elliott-Burke	Bell-Wellborn	24.00	32.00	85.00	215.00
☐ Chicago	Teehee-Burke	McCloud-McDougal	24.00	32.00	80.00	210.00
☐ Chicago	Teehee-Burke	Cramer-McDougal	24.00	32.00	85.00	215.00
☐ Chicago	Elliott-Burke	Cramer-McDougal	24.00	32.00	80.00	210.00
☐ St. Louis	Teehee-Burke	Attebery-Wells	24.00	32.00	80.00	210.00
☐ St. Louis	Teehee-Burke	Attebery-Biggs	39.00	54.00	235.00	765.00

BANK	GOV'T SIGNATURES	BANK SIGNATURES	A.B.P.	GOOD	V. FINE	UNC.
☐ St. Louis	Elliott-Burke	Attebery-Biggs				
			39.00	54.00	235.00	665.00
☐ St. Louis	Elliott-Burke	White-Biggs				
			24.00	32.00	85.00	215.00
☐ Minneapolis	Teehee-Burke	Cook-Wold				
			27.00	32.00	85.00	215.00
☐ Minneapolis	Teehee-Burke	Cook-Young				
			104.00	204.00	460.00	1065.00
☐ Minneapolis	Elliott-Burke	Cook-Young				
			25.00	34.00	85.00	265.00
☐ Kansas City	Teehee-Burke	Anderson-Miller				
			24.00	32.00	80.00	215.00
☐ Kansas City	Elliott-Burke	Anderson-Miller				
			24.00	32.00	80.00	215.00
☐ Kansas City	Elliott-Burke	Helm-Miller				
			24.00	32.00	80.00	215.00
☐ Dallas	Teehee-Burke	Talley-VanZandt				
			24.00	32.00	80.00	210.00
☐ Dallas	Elliott-Burke	Talley-VanZandt				
			34.00	48.00	135.00	315.00
☐ Dallas	Elliott-Burke	Lawder-VanZandt				
			24.00	32.00	80.00	210.00
☐ San Francisco	Teehee-Burke	Clerk-Lynch				
			24.00	32.00	85.00	210.00
☐ San Francisco	Teehee-Burke	Clerk-Calkins				
			34.00	49.00	135.00	415.00
☐ San Francisco	Elliott-Burke	Clerk-Calkins				
			34.00	47.00	110.00	310.00
☐ San Francisco	Elliott-Burke	Ambrose-Calkins				
			24.00	32.00	85.00	215.00

ONE DOLLAR NOTES (1963)
FEDERAL RESERVE NOTES

(Small Size)

Face Design: Portrait of President Washington in center, black Federal Reserve seal with city and district letter to left, green Treasury Seal to right. Green serial numbers, Federal Reserve numbers in four corners.
Back Design: Same as all $1 Notes from 1935.

SERIES OF 1963, GRANAHAN-DILLON, GREEN SEAL

DISTRICT	A.B.P.	UNC.	★UNC.	DISTRICT	A.B.P.	UNC.	★UNC.
☐1A Boston	1.85	4.75	6.50	☐7G Chicago	1.80	4.75	6.50
☐2B New York	1.85	4.75	6.50	☐8H St. Louis	1.80	4.75	6.50
☐3C Philadelphia	1.85	4.75	6.50	☐9I Minneapolis	1.80	4.75	6.50
☐4D Cleveland	1.85	4.75	6.50	☐10J Kansas City	1.80	4.75	6.50
☐5E Richmond	1.85	4.75	6.50	☐11K Dallas	1.80	4.75	6.50
☐6F Atlanta	1.85	4.75	6.50	☐12L San Francisco	1.80	4.75	6.50

The Dallas note of this series as shown, with the letter "K" in the black seal and the number "11" in the four corners, does not have any more significance or value than any other notes with their respective district letter and corresponding number.

A false rumor was circulated several years ago that the "K" was for Kennedy, the "11" was for November (the month in which he was assassinated), and that the note was issued by the Dallas Bank to commemorate the occasion. The entire story is apocryphal.

This note is in no way associated with the late President Kennedy. The notes were authorized by the Act of June 4, 1963. This was five months before Kennedy was assassinated. The Federal Reserve district for Dallas is K-11.

SERIES OF 1963A, GRANAHAN-FOWLER, GREEN SEAL

DISTRICT	A.B.P.	UNC.	★UNC.	DISTRICT	A.B.P.	UNC.	★UNC.
☐1A Boston	1.75	4.25	4.75	☐7G Chicago	1.75	4.25	4.75
☐2B New York	1.75	4.25	4.75	☐8H St. Louis	1.75	4.25	4.75
☐3C Philadelphia	1.75	4.25	4.75	☐9I Minneapolis	1.75	4.25	4.75
☐4D Cleveland	1.75	4.25	4.75	☐10J Kansas City	1.75	4.25	4.75
☐5E Richmond	1.75	4.25	4.75	☐11K Dallas	1.75	4.25	4.75
☐6F Atlanta	1.75	4.25	4.75	☐12L San Francisco	1.75	4.25	4.75

ONE DOLLAR NOTES (1963-B) FEDERAL RESERVE (WITH SIGNATURE OF JOSEPH W. BARR)
(Small Size)

Joseph W. Barr served as Secretary of the Treasury from December 20, 1968, to January 20, 1969, filling the unexpired term of Henry H. Fowler. His signature appears on the $1 Federal Reserve Notes of the Series of 1963-B only.

During the one-month term of Joseph W. Barr, about 471 million notes were printed with his signature. These notes were for the following Federal Reserve Banks.

	REGULAR NUMBERS	A.B.P.	UNC.	★UNC.	STAR NUMBERS	A.B.P.	UNC.	★UNC.
☐2B New York	123,040,000	1.75	4.75	5.50	3,680,000	2.00	4.75	5.50
☐5E Richmond	93,600,000	1.75	4.75	5.50	3,040,000	2.00	4.75	5.50
☐7G Chicago	91,040,000	1.75	4.75	5.50	2,400,000	2.00	4.75	5.50
☐10J Kansas City	44,800,000	1.75	4.75	5.50	None Printed	2.00	4.75	5.50
☐12L San Francisco	106,400,000	1.75	4.75	5.50	3,040,000	2.00	4.75	5.50

ONE DOLLAR NOTES (1969)
FEDERAL RESERVE NOTES
(WORDING IN GREEN, TREASURY SEAL
CHANGED FROM LATIN TO ENGLISH)

FORMER DESIGN:
The former design had
the Latin inscription:
*"Thesaur. Amer.
Septent. Sigil.,"*
which has several
translations. It was
the Seal of the North
American Treasury.

NEW DESIGN:
This new design
drops the Latin and
states *"The Department
of The Treasury, 1789."*
First used on the $100
Note of the
Series 1966.

ONE DOLLAR NOTES (1969)
FEDERAL RESERVE NOTES
(Small Size)

SERIES OF 1969, SIGNATURES OF ELSTON-KENNEDY, GREEN SEAL

BANK	A.B.P.	V.FINE	UNC.	★UNC.	BANK	A.B.P.	V.FINE	UNC.	★UNC.
☐ Boston	—	1.25	3.25	4.25	☐ Chicago	—	1.25	3.25	4.35
☐ New York	—	1.25	3.25	4.25	☐ St. Louis	—	1.25	3.25	4.35
☐ Philadelphia	—	1.25	3.25	4.25	☐ Minneapolis	—	1.25	3.25	4.35
☐ Cleveland	—	1.25	3.25	4.25	☐ Kansas City	—	1.25	3.25	4.35
☐ Richmond	—	1.25	3.25	4.25	☐ Dallas	—	1.25	3.25	4.35
☐ Atlanta	—	1.25	3.25	4.25	☐ San Francisco	—	1.25	3.25	4.35

SERIES OF 1969A, SIGNATURES OF KABIS-CONNALLY, GREEN SEAL

BANK	A.B.P.	V.FINE	UNC.	★UNC.	BANK	A.B.P.	V.FINE	UNC.	★UNC.
☐ Boston	—	1.25	3.25	5.25	☐ Chicago	—	1.25	3.25	5.45
☐ New York	—	1.25	3.25	5.25	☐ St. Louis	—	1.25	3.25	5.45
☐ Philadelphia	—	1.25	3.25	5.25	☐ Minneapolis	—	1.25	3.25	5.45
☐ Cleveland	—	1.25	3.25	5.25	☐ Kansas City	—	1.25	3.25	5.45
☐ Richmond	—	1.25	3.25	5.25	☐ Dallas	—	1.25	3.25	5.45
☐ Atlanta	—	1.25	3.25	5.25	☐ San Francisco	—	1.25	3.25	5.45

SERIES OF 1969B, SIGNATURES OF BANUELOS-CONNALLY, GREEN SEAL

BANK	A.B.P.	V.FINE	UNC.	★UNC.	BANK	A.B.P.	V.FINE	UNC.	★UNC.
☐ Boston	—	1.15	3.00	4.10	☐ Chicago	—	1.15	3.00	4.10
☐ New York	—	1.15	3.00	4.10	☐ St. Louis	—	1.15	3.00	4.10
☐ Philadelphia—		1.15	3.00	4.10	☐ Minneapolis	—	1.15	3.00	4.10
☐ Cleveland	—	1.15	3.00	4.10	☐ Kansas City	—	1.15	3.00	4.10
☐ Richmond	—	1.15	3.00	4.10	☐ Dallas	—	1.15	3.00	4.10
☐ Atlanta	—	1.15	3.00	4.10	☐ San Francisco	—	1.15	3.00	4.10

SERIES OF 1969C, SIGNATURES OF BANUELOS-SHULTZ, GREEN SEAL

BANK	A.B.P.	V.FINE	UNC.	★UNC.	BANK	A.B.P.	V.FINE	UNC.	★UNC.
☐ Boston	—	1.15	3.00	6.10	☐ Chicago	—	1.15	3.00	6.10
☐ New York	—	1.15	3.00	6.10	☐ St. Louis	—	1.15	3.00	6.10
☐ Philadelphia—		1.15	3.00	6.10	☐ Minneapolis	—	1.15	3.00	6.10
☐ Cleveland	—	1.15	3.00	6.10	☐ Kansas City	—	1.15	3.00	6.10
☐ Richmond	—	1.15	3.00	6.10	☐ Dallas	—	1.15	3.00	6.10
☐ Atlanta	—	1.15	3.00	6.10	☐ San Francisco	—	1.15	3.00	6.10

SERIES OF 1969D, SIGNATURES OF BANUELOS-SHULTZ, GREEN SEAL

BANK	A.B.P.	V.FINE	UNC.	★UNC.	BANK	A.B.P.	V.FINE	UNC.	★UNC.
☐ Boston	—	1.15	3.00	4.10	☐ Chicago	—	1.15	3.00	4.10
☐ New York	—	1.15	3.00	4.10	☐ St. Louis	—	1.15	3.00	4.10
☐ Philadelphia—		1.15	3.00	4.10	☐ Minneapolis	—	1.15	3.00	4.10
☐ Cleveland	—	1.15	3.00	4.10	☐ Kansas City	—	1.15	3.00	4.10
☐ Richmond	—	1.15	3.00	4.10	☐ Dallas	—	1.15	3.00	4.10
☐ Atlanta	—	1.15	3.00	4.10	☐ San Francisco—		1.15	3.00	4.10

SERIES OF 1974, SIGNATURES OF NEFF-SIMON, GREEN SEAL

BANK	A.B.P.	V.FINE	UNC.	★UNC.	BANK	A.B.P.	V.FINE	UNC.	★UNC.
☐ Boston	—	1.15	2.50	4.10	☐ Chicago	—	1.15	2.50	4.10
☐ New York	—	1.15	2.50	4.10	☐ St. Louis	—	1.15	2.50	4.10
☐ Philadelphia—		1.15	2.50	4.10	☐ Minneapolis	—	1.15	2.50	4.10
☐ Cleveland	—	1.15	2.50	4.10	☐ Kansas City	—	1.15	2.50	4.10
☐ Richmond	—	1.15	2.50	4.10	☐ Dallas	—	1.15	2.50	4.10
☐ Atlanta	—	1.15	2.50	4.10	☐ San Francisco—		1.15	2.50	4.10

SERIES OF 1977, SIGNATURES OF MORTON-BLUMENTHAL, GREEN SEAL

BANK	A.B.P.	V.FINE	UNC.	★UNC.	BANK	A.B.P.	V.FINE	UNC.	★UNC.
☐ Boston	—	1.15	2.50	4.10	☐ Chicago	—	1.15	2.50	4.10
☐ New York	—	1.15	2.50	4.10	☐ St. Louis	—	1.15	2.50	4.10
☐ Philadelphia—		1.15	2.50	4.10	☐ Minneapolis	—	1.15	2.50	4.10
☐ Cleveland	—	1.15	2.50	4.10	☐ Kansas City	—	1.15	2.50	4.10
☐ Richmond	—	1.15	2.50	4.10	☐ Dallas	—	1.15	2.50	4.10
☐ Atlanta	—	1.15	2.50	4.10	☐ San Francisco—		1.15	2.50	4.10

SERIES OF 1977A, SIGNATURES OF MORTON-MILLER, GREEN SEAL

BANK	A.B.P.	V.FINE	UNC.	★UNC.	BANK	A.B.P.	V.FINE	UNC.	★UNC.
☐ Boston	—	1.10	2.50	4.10	☐ Chicago	—	1.10	2.50	4.10
☐ New York	—	1.10	2.50	4.10	☐ St. Louis	—	1.10	2.50	4.10
☐ Philadelphia	—	1.10	2.50	4.10	☐ Minneapolis	—	1.10	2.50	4.10
☐ Cleveland	—	1.10	2.50	4.10	☐ Kansas City	—	1.10	2.50	4.10
☐ Richmond	—	1.10	2.50	4.10	☐ Dallas	—	1.10	2.50	4.10
☐ Atlanta	—	1.10	2.50	4.10	☐ San Francisco	—	1.10	2.50	4.10

SERIES OF 1981, SIGNATURES OF BUCHANAN-REGAN, GREEN SEAL

BANK	A.B.P.	V.FINE	UNC.	★UNC.	BANK	A.B.P.	V.FINE	UNC.	★UNC.
☐ Boston	—	1.10	2.50	4.10	☐ Chicago	—	1.10	2.50	4.10
☐ New York	—	1.10	2.50	4.10	☐ St. Louis	—	1.10	2.50	4.10
☐ Philadelphia	—	1.10	2.50	4.10	☐ Minneapolis	—	1.10	2.50	4.10
☐ Cleveland	—	1.10	2.50	4.10	☐ Kansas City	—	1.10	2.50	4.10
☐ Richmond	—	1.10	2.50	4.10	☐ Dallas	—	1.10	2.50	4.10
☐ Atlanta	—	1.10	2.50	4.10	☐ San Francisco	—	1.10	2.50	4.10

SERIES OF 1981A, SIGNATURES OF ORTEGA-REGAN, GREEN SEAL
★Notes not issued for all banks

BANK	A.B.P.	V.FINE	UNC.	★UNC.	BANK	A.B.P.	V.FINE	UNC.	★UNC.
☐ Boston	—	1.10	3.00	4.10	☐ Chicago	—	1.10	3.00	4.10
☐ New York	—	1.10	3.00	4.10	☐ St. Louis	—	1.10	3.00	4.10
☐ Philadelphia	—	1.10	3.00	4.10	☐ Minneapolis	—	1.10	3.00	4.10
☐ Cleveland	—	1.10	3.00	4.10	☐ Kansas City	—	1.10	3.00	4.10
☐ Richmond	—	1.10	3.00	4.10	☐ Dallas	—	1.10	3.00	4.10
☐ Atlanta	—	1.10	3.00	4.10	☐ San Francisco	—	1.10	3.00	4.10

SERIES OF 1981A or 1985 (REVERSE #129 LEFT), SIGNATURES OF ORTEGA-REGAN, GREEN SEAL

BANK	A.B.P.	V.FINE	UNC.	★UNC.	BANK	A.B.P.	V.FINE	UNC.	★UNC.
☐ Boston	—	26.00	42.00	—	☐ Chicago	—	26.00	42.00	—
☐ New York	—	26.00	42.00	—	☐ St. Louis	—	26.00	42.00	—
☐ Philadelphia	—	26.00	42.00	—	☐ Minneapolis	—	26.00	42.00	—
☐ Cleveland	—	26.00	42.00	—	☐ Kansas City	—	26.00	42.00	—
☐ Richmond	—	26.00	42.00	—	☐ Dallas	—	26.00	42.00	—
☐ Atlanta	—	26.00	42.00	—	☐ San Francisco	—	26.00	42.00	—

SERIES OF 1985, SIGNATURES OF ORTEGA-BAKER, GREEN SEAL
★Notes not issued for all banks

BANK	A.B.P.	V.FINE	UNC.	★UNC.	BANK	A.B.P.	V.FINE	UNC.	★UNC.
☐ Boston	—	1.10	2.50	4.10	☐ Chicago	—	1.10	2.50	4.10
☐ New York	—	1.10	2.50	4.10	☐ St. Louis	—	1.10	2.50	4.10
☐ Philadelphia	—	1.10	2.50	4.10	☐ Minneapolis	—	1.10	2.50	4.10
☐ Cleveland	—	1.10	2.50	4.10	☐ Kansas City	—	1.10	2.50	4.10
☐ Richmond	—	1.10	2.50	4.10	☐ Dallas	—	1.10	2.50	4.10
☐ Atlanta	—	1.10	2.50	4.10	☐ San Francisco	—	1.10	2.50	4.10

SERIES OF 1985 (REVERSE #129 LEFT), SIGNATURES OF ORTEGA-BAKER, GREEN SEAL

BANK	A.B.P.	V.FINE	UNC.	★UNC.	BANK	A.B.P.	V.FINE	UNC.	★UNC.
☐ Boston	—	25.00	36.00	—	☐ Chicago	—	25.00	36.00	—
☐ New York	—	25.00	36.00	—	☐ St. Louis	—	25.00	36.00	—
☐ Philadelphia	—	25.00	36.00	—	☐ Minneapolis	—	25.00	36.00	—
☐ Cleveland	—	25.00	36.00	—	☐ Kansas City	—	25.00	36.00	—
☐ Richmond	—	25.00	36.00	—	☐ Dallas	—	25.00	36.00	—

SERIES OF 1988, SIGNATURES OF ORTEGA-BRADY, GREEN SEAL

★Notes not issued for all banks

BANK	A.B.P.	V.FINE	UNC.	★UNC.	BANK	A.B.P.	V.FINE	UNC.	★UNC.
☐ Boston	—	1.10	3.00	6.00	☐ Chicago	—	1.10	3.00	6.00
☐ New York	—	1.10	3.00	6.00	☐ St. Louis	—	1.10	3.00	6.00
☐ Philadelphia	—	1.10	3.00	6.00	☐ Minneapolis	—	1.10	3.00	6.00
☐ Cleveland	—	1.10	3.00	6.00	☐ Kansas City	—	1.10	3.00	6.00
☐ Richmond	—	1.10	3.00	6.00	☐ Dallas	—	1.10	3.00	6.00
☐ Atlanta	—	1.10	3.00	6.00	☐ San Francisco	—	1.10	3.00	6.00

SERIES OF 1988A, SIGNATURES OF VILLALPANDO-BRADY, GREEN SEAL

★Notes not issued for all banks

BANK	A.B.P.	V.FINE	UNC.	★UNC.	BANK	A.B.P.	V.FINE	UNC.	★UNC.
☐ Boston	—	1.10	2.50	3.00	☐ Chicago	—	1.10	2.50	3.00
☐ New York	—	1.10	2.50	3.00	☐ St. Louis	—	1.10	2.50	3.00
☐ Philadelphia	—	1.10	2.50	3.00	☐ Minneapolis	—	1.10	2.50	3.00
☐ Cleveland	—	1.10	2.50	3.00	☐ Kansas City	—	1.10	2.50	3.00
☐ Richmond	—	1.10	2.50	3.00	☐ Dallas	—	1.10	2.50	3.00
☐ Atlanta	—	1.10	2.50	3.00	☐ San Francisco	—	1.10	2.50	3.00

SERIES OF 1993, SIGNATURES OF WITHROW-BENTSEN, GREEN SEAL

★Notes not issued for all banks

BANK	A.B.P.	V.FINE	UNC.	★UNC.	BANK	A.B.P.	V.FINE	UNC.	★UNC.
☐ Boston	—	1.10	2.50	3.00	☐ Chicago	—	1.10	2.50	3.00
☐ New York	—	1.10	2.50	3.00	☐ St. Louis	—	1.10	2.50	3.00
☐ Philadelphia	—	1.10	2.50	3.00	☐ Minneapolis	—	1.10	2.50	3.00
☐ Cleveland	—	1.10	2.50	3.00	☐ Kansas City	—	1.10	2.50	3.00
☐ Richmond	—	1.10	2.50	3.00	☐ Dallas	—	1.10	2.50	3.00
☐ Atlanta	—	1.10	2.50	3.00	☐ San Francisco	—	1.10	2.50	3.00

SERIES OF 1995, SIGNATURES OF WITHROW-RUBIN, GREEN SEAL

★Notes not issued for all banks

BANK	A.B.P.	V.FINE	UNC.	★UNC.	BANK	A.B.P.	V.FINE	UNC.	★UNC.
☐ Boston	—	1.10	2.50	4.00	☐ Chicago	—	1.10	2.50	4.00
☐ New York	—	1.10	2.50	4.00	☐ St. Louis	—	1.10	2.50	4.00
☐ Philadelphia	—	1.10	2.50	4.00	☐ Minneapolis	—	1.10	2.50	4.00
☐ Cleveland	—	1.10	2.50	4.00	☐ Kansas City	—	1.10	2.50	4.00
☐ Richmond	—	1.10	2.50	4.00	☐ Dallas	—	1.10	2.50	4.00
☐ Atlanta	—	1.10	2.50	4.00	☐ San Francisco	—	1.10	2.50	4.00

TWO DOLLAR NOTES

TWO DOLLAR NOTES (1862) UNITED STATES NOTES
(ALSO KNOWN AS LEGAL TENDER NOTES)
(Large Size)

Face Design: Portrait of Alexander Hamilton (1754–1804), cloverleaf "2"s in upper corners, medallion with "II" in lower left, medallion with "1, 2, 3" right of portrait.

Back Design: "2" in each corner, with "2" motif repeated in scallop circles around obligation; back is printed green.

SERIES	SIGNATURES	SEAL	A.B.P.	GOOD	V. FINE	UNC.
☐ 1862	Chittenden-Spinner					
	Type I, American Banknote Company vertical in left border	Red	100.00	155.00	1000.00	2500.00
☐ 1862	Chittenden-Spinner					
	Type II, National Banknote Company vertical in left border	Red	100.00	145.00	985.00	2450.00

TWO DOLLAR NOTES (1869) UNITED STATES NOTES
(ALSO KNOWN AS LEGAL TENDER NOTES)
(Large Size)

Face Design: Portrait of President Jefferson to left, Capitol in center, large red seal to right.

Back Design: Roman "II" left, arabic "2" center, TWO right. This is the companion note to the $1 "Rainbow Note".

SERIES	SIGNATURES	SEAL	A.B.P.	GOOD	V. FINE	UNC.
☐1869	Allison-Spinner	Red	90.00	155.00	875.00	3400.00
☐1869	Allison-Spinner	Water Mark Paper	110.00	200.00	1325.00	4100.00

TWO DOLLAR NOTES (1874) UNITED STATES NOTES
(ALSO KNOWN AS LEGAL TENDER NOTES)
(Large Size)

Face Design: Portrait of President Jefferson; same as 1869 note.

Back Design: Completely revised.

SERIES	SIGNATURES	SEAL	A.B.P.	GOOD	V. FINE	UNC.
☐1874	Allison-Spinner	Red	55.00	100.00	650.00	1850.00
☐1875	Allison-New	Red	60.00	100.00	850.00	2250.00
☐Series A	Allison-New	Red	170.00	310.00	1550.00	5550.00
☐Series B	Allison-New	Red	170.00	310.00	1500.00	5300.00
☐1875	Allison-Wyman	Red	70.00	125.00	650.00	1500.00
☐1878	Allison-Gilfillan	Red	60.00	95.00	550.00	1400.00
☐1878	Scofield-Gilfillan	Red	850.00	1100.00	2750.00	5550.00
☐1880	Scofield-Gilfillan	Brown	32.00	43.00	250.00	950.00
☐1880	Bruce-Gilfillan	Brown	32.00	43.00	240.00	925.00
☐1880	Bruce-Wyman	Brown	32.00	43.00	200.00	925.00
☐1880	Rosecrans-Huston	Red	250.00	500.00	1200.00	4300.00
☐1880	Rosecrans-Huston	Brown	350.00	1200.00	2100.00	4700.00
☐1880	Rosecrans-Nebeker	Red	30.00	45.00	170.00	700.00
☐1880	Tillman-Morgan	Red	30.00	47.00	170.00	700.00

SERIES	SIGNATURES	SEAL	A.B.P.	GOOD	V. FINE	UNC.
☐1917	Teehee-Burke	Red	18.00	25.00	77.00	265.00
☐1917	Elliott-Burke	Red	18.00	25.00	77.00	265.00
☐1917	Elliott-White	Red	18.00	25.00	77.00	265.00
☐1917	Speelman-White	Red	18.00	25.00	77.00	265.00

TWO DOLLAR NOTES (1928) UNITED STATES NOTES (ALSO KNOWN AS LEGAL TENDER NOTES)
(Small Size)

Face Design: Portrait of President Jefferson, red seal left, TWO right, red serial numbers.

Back Design: Jefferson Home—Monticello.

SERIES	SIGNATURES	SEAL	A.B.P.	GOOD	V. FINE	UNC.	★UNC.
☐1928	Tate-Mellon	Red	4.00	9.00	15.00	70.00	550.00
☐1928A	Woods-Mellon	Red	8.00	15.00	45.00	375.00	5100.00
☐1928B	Woods-Mills	Red	26.00	52.00	125.00	900.00	15100.00
☐1928C	Julian-Morgenthau	Red	4.00	6.50	15.00	135.00	1100.00
☐1928D	Julian-Morgenthau	Red	3.50	5.00	10.00	42.00	275.00
☐1928E	Julian-Vinson	Red	3.50	6.00	16.00	90.00	5250.00
☐1928F	Julian-Snyder	Red	3.50	4.00	10.00	40.00	280.00
☐1928G	Clark-Snyder	Red	3.50	4.00	10.00	32.00	270.00

TWO DOLLAR NOTES (1953) UNITED STATES NOTES
(ALSO KNOWN AS LEGAL TENDER NOTES)
(Small Size)

Face Design: Portrait of President Jefferson, gray "2" to left, red seal to right over TWO.
Back Design: Same as 1928 note.

SERIES	SIGNATURES	SEAL	A.B.P.	GOOD	V. FINE	UNC.	★UNC.
☐1953	Priest-Humphrey	Red	2.50	3.25	4.50	15.00	35.00
☐1953A	Priest-Anderson	Red	2.50	3.25	4.50	13.00	45.00
☐1953B	Smith-Dillon	Red	2.50	3.25	4.00	12.00	35.00
☐1953C	Granahan-Dillon	Red	2.50	3.25	4.00	13.00	60.00

Back Design: IN GOD WE TRUST on back.
Face Design: Same as previous note.

SERIES	SIGNATURES	SEAL	A.B.P.	GOOD	V. FINE	UNC.	★UNC.
☐1963	Granahan-Dillon	Red	2.25	3.00	5.00	9.00	17.00
☐1963A	Granahan-Fowler	Red	2.25	3.00	5.00	9.00	23.00

Production of $2 United States Notes was discontinued on August 10, 1966.

TWO DOLLAR NOTES (1875) NATIONAL BANK NOTES
FIRST CHARTER PERIOD (Large Size)

Face Design: This note is known as the "Lazy Two Note" due to the unusual "lying down" shape of the "2" shown on the face. Liberty with flag and red seal.

Back Design: Sir Walter Raleigh in England, 1585, exhibiting corn and smoking tobacco from America, State Seal, and eagle.

SERIES	SIGNATURES	SEAL	A.B.P.	GOOD	V. FINE	UNC.
☐Original	Colby-Spinner	Red	200.00	450.00	1750.00	5100.00
☐Original	Jeffries-Spinner	Red	225.00	900.00	1900.00	5350.00
☐Original	Allison-Spinner	Red	200.00	450.00	1750.00	5100.00
☐1875	Allison-New	Red	200.00	450.00	1750.00	5100.00
☐1875	Allison-Wyman	Red	200.00	450.00	1750.00	5100.00
☐1875	Allison-Gilfillan	Red	200.00	450.00	1750.00	5100.00
☐1875	Scofield-Gilfillan	Red	200.00	450.00	1750.00	5100.00

TWO DOLLAR NOTES (1886) SILVER CERTIFICATES
(Large Size)

Face Design: General Hancock portrait left. Treasury Seal to the right of center.

Back Design: "2" left and right, very ornate engraving, obligation in center of note. Note is printed in green.

SERIES	SIGNATURES	SEAL	A.B.P.	GOOD	V. FINE	UNC.
☐1886	Rosecrans-Jordan	Red	95.00	125.00	775.00	1725.00
☐1886	Rosecrans-Hyatt	Sm.Red	95.00	125.00	775.00	1725.00
☐1886	Rosecrans-Hyatt	Lg.Red	95.00	125.00	775.00	1725.00
☐1886	Rosecrans-Huston	Red	95.00	125.00	775.00	1725.00
☐1886	Rosecrans-Huston	Brown	95.00	125.00	775.00	1725.00

TWO DOLLAR NOTES (1891) SILVER CERTIFICATES
(Large Size)

Face Design: Portrait of William Windom, Secretary of the
Treasury 1881–84 and 1889–91, red seal right.

Back Design: "2" left and right, scalloped design center
with obligation, printed in green.

SERIES	SIGNATURES	SEAL	A.B.P.	GOOD	V. FINE	UNC.
☐1891	Rosecrans-Nebeker	Red	95.00	140.00	750.00	2475.00
☐1891	Tillman-Morgan	Red	95.00	140.00	750.00	2475.00

TWO DOLLAR NOTES (1896) SILVER CERTIFICATES
(Large Size)

Face Design: Science presenting Steam and Electricity to Industry and Commerce.

Back Design: Portraits of Robert Fulton and Samuel F.B. Morse.

This is the second note of the popular Educational Series.

SERIES	SIGNATURES	SEAL	A.B.P.	GOOD	V. FINE	UNC.
☐1896	Tillman-Morgan	Red	140.00	190.00	900.00	2600.00
☐1896	Bruce-Roberts	Red	140.00	190.00	900.00	2600.00

TWO DOLLAR NOTES (1899) SILVER CERTIFICATES
(Large Size)

Face Design: Portrait of President Washington between figures of Trade and Agriculture, blue "2" left, blue seal right.

Back Design

SERIES	SIGNATURES	SEAL	A.B.P.	GOOD	V. FINE	UNC.
☐1899	Lyons-Roberts	Blue	60.00	85.00	225.00	900.00
☐1899	Lyons-Treat	Blue	60.00	85.00	225.00	900.00
☐1899	Vernon-Treat	Blue	60.00	85.00	225.00	900.00
☐1899	Vernon-McClung	Blue	60.00	85.00	225.00	900.00
☐1899	Napier-McClung	Blue	60.00	85.00	225.00	900.00
☐1899	Napier-Thompson	Blue	65.00	105.00	345.00	1305.00
☐1899	Parker-Burke	Blue	60.00	85.00	225.00	900.00
☐1899	Teehee-Burke	Blue	60.00	85.00	225.00	900.00
☐1899	Elliott-Burke	Blue	60.00	85.00	225.00	900.00
☐1899	Speelman-White	Blue	60.00	85.00	225.00	900.00

TWO DOLLAR NOTES (1890-1891)
TREASURY OR COIN NOTES
(Large Size)

Face Design: Portrait of General James McPherson.

Back Design: Large TWO center, over obligation. Large "2" on engraved background right. Intricate engraving, printed green.

SERIES	SIGNATURES	SEAL	A.B.P.	GOOD	V. FINE	UNC.
☐1890	Rosecrans-Huston	Brown	175.00	225.00	1600.00	5250.00
☐1890	Rosecrans-Nebeker	Brown	175.00	225.00	1600.00	5250.00
☐1890	Rosecrans-Nebeker	Red	175.00	225.00	1600.00	5250.00

TWO DOLLAR NOTES (1890-1891)
TREASURY OR COIN NOTES
(Large Size) **NOTE NO. 30**
Face Design: Similar to 1890–1891 note.
Back Design: Revised.

SERIES	SIGNATURES	SEAL	A.B.P.	GOOD	V. FINE	UNC.
☐1891	Rosecrans-Nebeker	Red	75.00	115.00	650.00	2050.00
☐1891	Tillman-Morgan	Red	75.00	115.00	650.00	2050.00
☐1891	Bruce-Roberts	Red	75.00	115.00	650.00	2050.00

TWO DOLLAR NOTES (1918)
FEDERAL RESERVE BANK NOTES

(Large Size)

Face Design: Portrait of President Jefferson to left, name of
bank in center, blue seal to the right, blue numbers, Federal
Reserve district letter and number in four corners.

Back Design: American battleship of World War I.

TWO DOLLAR NOTES (1918)
FEDERAL RESERVE BANK NOTES
(Large Size)

BANK	GOV'T SIGNATURES	BANK SIGNATURES	A.B.P.	GOOD	V. FINE	UNC.
☐ Boston	Teehee-Burke	Bullen-Morss	85.00	135.00	325.00	1000.00
☐ Boston	Teehee-Burke	Willet-Morss	85.00	135.00	375.00	1100.00
☐ Boston	Elliot-Burke	Willet-Morss	85.00	135.00	325.00	1000.00
☐ New York	Teehee-Burke	Sailer-Strong	85.00	135.00	325.00	1000.00
☐ New York	Teehee-Burke	Hendricks-Strong	85.00	135.00	325.00	1000.00
☐ New York	Elliott-Burke	Hendricks-Strong	85.00	135.00	325.00	1000.00
☐ Philadelphia	Teehee-Burke	Hardt-Passmore	85.00	135.00	325.00	1000.00
☐ Philadelphia	Teehee-Burke	Dyer-Passmore	85.00	135.00	375.00	1100.00
☐ Philadelphia	Elliott-Burke	Dyer-Passmore	85.00	135.00	825.00	1875.00
☐ Philadelphia	Elliott-Burke	Dyer-Norris	85.00	135.00	325.00	1000.00
☐ Cleveland	Teehee-Burke	Baxter-Francher	85.00	135.00	325.00	1000.00
☐ Cleveland	Teehee-Burke	Davis-Francher	85.00	135.00	375.00	1100.00
☐ Cleveland	Elliott-Burke	Davis-Francher	85.00	135.00	325.00	1000.00
☐ Richmond	Teehee-Burke	Keesee-Seay	85.00	135.00	325.00	1000.00
☐ Richmond	Elliott-Burke	Keesee-Seay	85.00	135.00	400.00	1125.00
☐ Atlanta	Teehee-Burke	Pike-McCord	85.00	135.00	375.00	1100.00
☐ Atlanta	Teehee-Burke	Bell-McCord	85.00	135.00	825.00	1875.00
☐ Atlanta	Elliott-Burke	Bell-Wellborn	85.00	135.00	775.00	1725.00
☐ Chicago	Teehee-Burke	McCloud-McDougal	85.00	135.00	325.00	1000.00

BANK	GOV'T SIGNATURES	BANK SIGNATURES	A.B.P.	GOOD	V. FINE	UNC.
☐ Chicago	Teehee-Burke	Cramer-McDougal	85.00	135.00	375.00	1100.00
☐ Chicago	Elliott-Burke	Cramer-McDougal	85.00	135.00	325.00	1000.00
☐ St. Louis	Teehee-Burke	Attebery-Wells	85.00	135.00	325.00	1000.00
☐ St. Louis	Teehee-Burke	Attebery-Biggs	85.00	135.00	575.00	1550.00
☐ St. Louis	Elliott-Burke	Attebery-Biggs	85.00	135.00	575.00	1550.00
☐ St. Louis	Elliott-Burke	White-Biggs	85.00	135.00	650.00	1500.00
☐ Minneapolis	Teehee-Burke	Cook-Wold	85.00	135.00	375.00	1050.00
☐ Minneapolis	Elliott-Burke	Cook-Young	85.00	135.00	475.00	1175.00
☐ Kansas City	Teehee-Burke	Anderson-Miller	85.00	135.00	325.00	1050.00
☐ Kansas City	Elliott-Burke	Helm-Miller	85.00	135.00	400.00	1175.00
☐ Dallas	Teehee-Burke	Talley-VanZandt	85.00	135.00	350.00	1050.00
☐ Dallas	Elliott-Burke	Talley-VanZandt	85.00	135.00	375.00	1175.00
☐ San Francisco	Teehee-Burke	Clerk-Lynch	85.00	135.00	400.00	1175.00
☐ San Francisco	Elliott-Burke	Clerk-Calkins	85.00	135.00	400.00	1175.00
☐ San Francisco	Elliott-Burke	Ambrose-Calkins	85.00	135.00	400.00	1175.00

TWO DOLLAR NOTES (1976)
FEDERAL RESERVE NOTES
(Small Size)

Face Design: Portrait of President Jefferson.

Back Design: Signing of the Declaration of Independence.

SERIES OF 1995, GREEN SEAL

DISTRICT	A.B.P.	UNC.	★UNC.	DISTRICT	A.B.P.	UNC.	★UNC.
☐1A Boston	2.15	3.25	7.25	☐7G Chicago	2.50	3.25	6.25
☐2B New York	2.15	3.25	7.25	☐8H St. Louis	2.50	3.25	6.25
☐3C Philadelphia	2.15	3.25	7.25	☐9I Minneapolis	2.50	3.25	6.25
☐4D Cleveland	2.15	3.25	7.25	☐10J Kansas City	2.50	3.25	6.25
☐5E Richmond	2.15	3.25	7.25	☐11K Dallas	2.50	3.25	6.25
☐6F Atlanta	2.15	3.25	7.25	☐12L San Francisco	2.50	3.25	6.25

SERIES OF 1976, NEFF-SIMON, GREEN SEAL

DISTRICT	A.B.P.	UNC.	★UNC.	DISTRICT	A.B.P.	UNC.	★UNC.
☐1A Boston	3.00	6.25	9.50	☐7G Chicago	3.00	6.25	9.25
☐2B New York	3.00	6.25	9.50	☐8H St. Louis	3.00	6.25	9.25
☐3C Philadelphia	3.00	6.25	9.50	☐9I Minneapolis	3.00	6.25	9.25
☐4D Cleveland	3.00	6.25	9.50	☐10J Kansas City	3.00	6.25	9.25
☐5E Richmond	3.00	6.25	9.50	☐11K Dallas	3.00	6.25	9.25
☐6F Atlanta	3.00	6.25	9.50	☐12L San Francisco	3.00	6.25	9.25

FIVE DOLLAR NOTES

ORDER OF ISSUE

FIVE DOLLAR NOTES (1861) DEMAND NOTES
(Large Size)

Face Design: Left, Statue of America by Crawford atop
United States Capitol. Center, numeral "5" in green. Right,
portrait of Alexander Hamilton, statesman, first Secretary of
the Treasury.

Back Design: Numerous small "5"s in ovals. This note has
no Treasury Seal. The signatures are those of Treasury
Department employees who signed for officials.

CITY	A.B.P.	GOOD	V. GOOD
☐Boston (I)	900.00	1650.00	3250.00
☐New York (I)	900.00	1650.00	3250.00
☐Philadelphia (I)	900.00	1650.00	3250.00
☐Cincinnati (I)	2550.00	8050.00	16,550.00
☐St. Louis (I)	2550.00	8050.00	16,550.00
☐Boston (II)	500.00	650.00	1150.00
☐New York (II)	500.00	650.00	1150.00
☐Philadelphia (II)	500.00	650.00	1150.00
☐Cincinnati (II)	3050.00	6050.00	12,050.00
☐St. Louis (II)	3050.00	6050.00	12,050.00

FIVE DOLLAR NOTES (1875–1907)
UNITED STATES NOTES
(ALSO KNOWN AS LEGAL TENDER NOTES)
(Large Size)

Back Design: First Obligation.

Back Design: Second Obligation

SERIES	SIGNATURES	SEAL	A.B.P.	GOOD	V. FINE	UNC.
☐1862	Crittenden-Spinner*	Red	70.00	105.00	565.00	1450.00
☐1862	Crittenden-Spinner**	Red	70.00	100.00	565.00	1450.00
☐1863	Crittenden-Spinner**	Red	70.00	105.00	565.00	1450.00

*First Obligation
**Second Obligation

FIVE DOLLAR NOTES (1869) UNITED STATES NOTES
(ALSO KNOWN AS LEGAL TENDER NOTES)
(Large Size)

Face Design: Portrait of President Jackson on left. Pioneer and family in center.

Back Design: Color, green. This is a companion note to the $1 and $2 Notes of 1869 "Rainbow Notes."

SERIES	SIGNATURES	SEAL	A.B.P.	GOOD	V. FINE	UNC.
☐1869	Allison-Spinner	Red	90.00	125.00	525.00	1600.00
☐1869	Allison-Spinner	Water Marked Paper	95.00	150.00	1025.00	2100.00

FIVE DOLLAR NOTES (1875–1907)
UNITED STATES NOTES
(ALSO KNOWN AS LEGAL TENDER NOTES)
(Large Size)

Back Design: Revised.
Face Design: Similar to 1869 note.

SERIES	SIGNATURES	SEAL	A.B.P.	GOOD	V. FINE	UNC.
☐1875	Allison-New	Red	65.00	100.00	270.00	950.00
☐1875A	Allison-New	Red	85.00	130.00	620.00	1850.00
☐1875B	Allison-New	Red	65.00	90.00	345.00	925.00
☐1875	Allison-Wyman	Red	70.00	90.00	320.00	1050.00
☐1878	Allison-Gilfillan	Red	60.00	75.00	360.00	1000.00
☐1880	Scofield-Gilfillan	Brown	300.00	700.00	3400.00	7000.00
☐1880	Bruce-Gilfillan	Brown	95.00	150.00	725.00	2100.00
☐1880	Bruce-Wyman	Brown	60.00	100.00	325.00	900.00
☐1880	Bruce-Wyman	Red	65.00	110.00	395.00	1600.00
☐1880	Rosecrans-Jordan	Red	60.00	105.00	375.00	1200.00
☐1880	Rosecrans-Hyatt	Red	325.00	725.00	3425.00	7050.00
☐1880	Rosecrans-Huston	Red	60.00	125.00	600.00	1650.00
☐1880	Rosecrans-Huston	Brown	88.00	175.00	645.00	1850.00
☐1880	Rosecrans-Nebeker	Brown	50.00	125.00	445.00	1350.00
☐1880	Rosecrans-Nebeker	Red	35.00	55.00	220.00	850.00
☐1880	Tillman-Morgan	Red	35.00	55.00	200.00	650.00
☐1880	Bruce-Roberts	Red	30.00	42.00	180.00	775.00
☐1880	Lyons-Roberts	Red	50.00	80.00	800.00	2025.00
☐1907	Vernon-Treat	Red	25.00	40.00	185.00	775.00
☐1907	Vernon-McClung	Red	25.00	40.00	185.00	775.00
☐1907	Napier-McClung	Red	25.00	38.00	135.00	525.00
☐1907	Napier-Thompson	Red	45.00	100.00	290.00	700.00
☐1907	Parker-Burke	Red	25.00	38.00	135.00	500.00
☐1907	Teehee-Burke	Red	25.00	38.00	155.00	500.00
☐1907	Elliott-Burke	Red	25.00	38.00	155.00	525.00

SERIES	SIGNATURES	SEAL	A.B.P.	GOOD	V. FINE	UNC.
☐1907	Elliott-White	Red	30.00	40.00	160.00	460.00
☐1907	Speelman-White	Red	30.00	38.00	120.00	405.00
☐1907	Woods-White	Red	30.00	40.00	160.00	460.00

FIVE DOLLAR NOTES (1928) UNITED STATES NOTES (ALSO KNOWN AS LEGAL TENDER NOTES)

(Small Size)

Face Design: Portrait of President Lincoln center. Red seal to left, red serial numbers.

Back Design: Lincoln Memorial in Washington, D.C.

SERIES	SIGNATURES	SEAL	A.B.P	GOOD	V. FINE	UNC.	★UNC.
☐1928	Woods-Mellon	Red	6.50	8.50	15.00	85.00	250.00
☐1928A	Woods-Mills	Red	6.50	8.50	20.00	115.00	1825.00
☐1928B	Julian-Morgenthau	Red	6.50	8.50	15.00	50.00	375.00
☐1928C	Julian-Morgenthau	Red	6.50	8.50	15.00	50.00	325.00
☐1928D	Julian-Vinson	Red	6.50	8.50	34.00	330.00	1525.00
☐1928E	Julian-Snyder	Red	6.50	8.50	15.00	44.50	400.00
☐1928F	Clark-Snyder	Red	6.50	8.50	15.00	60.00	275.00

FIVE DOLLAR NOTES (1953–1963)
UNITED STATES NOTES
(Small Size)

Face Design: Similar to previous note. Portrait of President Lincoln center. Red seal is moved to the right, red numbers.
Back Design: Similar to 1928 note.

SERIES	SIGNATURES	SEAL	A.B.P.	GOOD	V. FINE	UNC.	★UNC.
☐1953	Priest-Humphrey	Red	6.00	7.50	11.00	41.00	105.00
☐1953A	Priest-Anderson	Red	6.00	7.50	13.00	26.00	50.00
☐1953B	Smith-Dillon	Red	6.00	7.50	11.00	27.00	60.00
☐1953C	Granahan-Dillon	Red	6.00	7.50	11.00	32.00	70.00

FIVE DOLLAR NOTES (1953-1963)
UNITED STATES NOTES
(ALSO KNOWN AS LEGAL TENDER NOTES)
(Small Size)

Back Design: The following notes have IN GOD WE TRUST on the back.
Face Design: Similar to 1953–1963 note.

SERIES	SIGNATURES	SEAL	A.B.P.	GOOD	V. FINE	UNC.	★UNC.
☐1963	Granahan-Dillon	Red	6.00	7.50	12.00	21.00	27.00

Production of $5 United States Notes ended in 1967.

FIVE DOLLAR NOTES (1863-1875)
NATIONAL BANK NOTES
FIRST CHARTER PERIOD (Large Size)

Face Design: The Columbus Note. The face shows Columbus in sight of land and Columbus with an Indian princess.

Back Design: Christopher Columbus landing at San Salvador, 1492. Also the State Seal left, and American eagle right.

SERIES	SIGNATURES	SEAL	A.B.P.	GOOD	V. FINE	UNC.
☐Original Chittenden-Spinner		Red	70.00	105.00	500.00	1410.00
☐Original Colby-Spinner		Red	70.00	105.00	500.00	1360.00
☐Original Jeffries-Spinner		Red	195.00	525.00	1625.00	3710.00
☐Original Allison-Spinner		Red	70.00	100.00	500.00	1410.00
☐1875	Allison-New	Red	70.00	100.00	500.00	1360.00
☐1875	Allison-Wyman	Red	70.00	100.00	500.00	1360.00
☐1875	Allison-Gilfillan	Red	70.00	100.00	500.00	1360.00
☐1875	Scofield-Gilfillan	Red	70.00	100.00	500.00	1360.00
☐1875	Bruce-Gilfillan	Red	70.00	100.00	500.00	1360.00
☐1875	Bruce-Wyman	Red	70.00	100.00	500.00	1360.00
☐1875	Bruce-Jordan	Red		EXTREMELY RARE		
☐1875	Rosecrans-Huston	Red	70.00	100.00	500.00	1360.00
☐1875	Rosecrans-Jordan	Red	70.00	100.00	500.00	1360.00

FIVE DOLLAR NOTES (1882) NATIONAL BANK NOTES
SECOND CHARTER PERIOD (Large Size)

First Issue (Brown seal and brown backs)
Face Design: Portrait of President Garfield left. Name of bank
and city center, brown seal to right. Brown charter number.

Back Design: Brown border design similar to previous note.
Center oval now has the bank's charter number in green.
The top signatures are those of the Treasury officials.
Bottom signatures, usually handwritten or probably rubber-
stamped, are bank officials.

SERIES	SIGNATURES	SEAL	A.B.P.	GOOD	V. FINE	UNC.
☐1882	Bruce-Gilfillan	Brown	60.00	80.00	300.00	900.00
☐1882	Bruce-Wyman	Brown	60.00	80.00	300.00	900.00
☐1882	Bruce-Jordan	Brown	60.00	80.00	300.00	900.00
☐1882	Rosecrans-Jordan	Brown	60.00	80.00	300.00	900.00
☐1882	Rosecrans-Hyatt	Brown	60.00	80.00	300.00	900.00
☐1882	Rosecrans-Huston	Brown	60.00	80.00	300.00	900.00
☐1882	Rosecrans-Nebeker	Brown	60.00	80.00	300.00	900.00
☐1882	Rosecrans-Morgan	Brown	85.00	180.00	425.00	1250.00
☐1882	Tillman-Morgan	Brown	60.00	80.00	300.00	900.00
☐1882	Tillman-Roberts	Brown	60.00	80.00	300.00	900.00
☐1882	Bruce-Roberts	Brown	60.00	80.00	300.00	900.00
☐1882	Lyons-Roberts	Brown	60.00	80.00	300.00	900.00
☐1882	Lyons-Treat		(Unknown in any collection)			
☐1882	Vernon-Treat	Brown	60.00	95.00	300.00	900.00

FIVE DOLLAR NOTES (1882) NATIONAL BANK NOTES
SECOND CHARTER PERIOD, Second Issue (Large Size)

Face Design: Similar to preceding portrait of President Garfield.

Back Design: Back is now green with date "1882–1908" in center.

SERIES	SIGNATURES	SEAL	A.B.P.	GOOD	V. FINE	UNC.
☐1882	Rosecrans-Huston	Blue	55.00	85.00	280.00	825.00
☐1882	Rosecrans-Nebeker	Blue	55.00	85.00	280.00	825.00
☐1882	Rosecrans-Morgan	Blue	115.00	225.00	815.00	1900.00
☐1882	Tillman-Morgan	Blue	55.00	85.00	280.00	825.00
☐1882	Tillman-Roberts	Blue	55.00	85.00	280.00	825.00
☐1882	Bruce-Roberts	Blue	55.00	85.00	280.00	825.00
☐1882	Lyons-Roberts	Blue	55.00	85.00	280.00	825.00
☐1882	Vernon-Treat	Blue	55.00	85.00	280.00	825.00
☐1882	Vernon-McClung	Blue				RARE
☐1882	Napier-McClung	Blue	90.00	275.00	915.00	1800.00

FIVE DOLLAR NOTES (1882) NATIONAL BANK NOTES
SECOND CHARTER PERIOD, Third Issue (Large Size)

Face Design: Same as 1882 note. Blue seal.

Back Design: Similar to 1882 Second Issue note. FIVE DOLLARS replaces "1882–1908."

SERIES	SIGNATURES	SEAL	A.B.P.	GOOD	V. FINE	UNC.
☐1882	Tillman-Morgan	Blue	70.00	100.00	400.00	1325.00
☐1882	Tillman-Roberts	Blue	70.00	100.00	400.00	1425.00
☐1882	Bruce-Roberts	Blue	70.00	100.00	400.00	1325.00
☐1882	Lyons-Roberts	Blue	70.00	100.00	400.00	1425.00
☐1882	Vernon-Treat	Blue	70.00	100.00	400.00	1325.00
☐1882	Napier-McClung	Blue	70.00	100.00	400.00	1325.00
☐1882	Teehee-Burke	Blue		EXTREMELY RARE		

FIVE DOLLAR NOTES (1902) NATIONAL BANK NOTES
THIRD CHARTER PERIOD (Large Size)

First Issue (Red seal and charter numbers.)
Face Design: Portrait of President Harrison left, name of bank and city center, Treasury Seal to right, red seal and charter number.

Back Design: Landing of Pilgrims.

SERIES	SIGNATURES	SEAL	A.B.P.	GOOD	V. FINE	UNC.
☐1902	Lyons-Roberts	Red	60.00	90.00	275.00	975.00
☐1902	Lyons-Treat	Red	60.00	90.00	275.00	975.00
☐1902	Vernon-Treat	Red	60.00	90.00	275.00	975.00

FIVE DOLLAR NOTES (1902) NATIONAL BANK NOTES
THIRD CHARTER PERIOD (Large Size)
SECOND ISSUE

SERIES	SIGNATURES	SEAL	A.B.P.	GOOD	V. FINE	UNC.
☐1902	Lyons-Roberts	Blue	17.00	27.00	85.00	375.00
☐1902	Lyons-Treat	Blue	17.00	27.00	85.00	375.00
☐1902	Vernon-Treat	Blue	17.00	27.00	85.00	375.00
☐1902	Vernon-McClung	Blue	17.00	27.00	85.00	375.00
☐1902	Napier-McClung	Blue	17.00	27.00	85.00	375.00
☐1902	Napier-Thompson	Blue	25.00	38.00	95.00	500.00
☐1902	Napier-Burke	Blue	17.00	27.00	85.00	375.00
☐1902	Parker-Burke	Blue	17.00	27.00	85.00	375.00
☐1902	Teehee-Burke	Blue	17.00	27.00	100.00	375.00

FIVE DOLLAR NOTES (1902) NATIONAL BANK NOTES
THIRD CHARTER PERIOD (Large Size)
Third Issue (Blue seal and numbers.)
   The following notes do not have date of "1902–1908" on the back.

SERIES	SIGNATURES	SEAL	A.B.P.	GOOD	V. FINE	UNC.
□1902	Lyons-Roberts	Blue	18.00	27.00	78.00	325.00
□1902	Lyons-Treat	Blue	18.00	27.00	78.00	325.00
□1902	Vernon-Treat	Blue	18.00	27.00	78.00	325.00
□1902	Vernon-McClung	Blue	18.00	27.00	78.00	325.00
□1902	Napier-McClung	Blue	18.00	27.00	78.00	325.00
□1902	Napier-Thompson	Blue	18.00	27.00	78.00	325.00
□1902	Napier-Burke	Blue	18.00	27.00	78.00	325.00
□1902	Parker-Burke	Blue	18.00	27.00	78.00	325.00
□1902	Teehee-Burke	Blue	18.00	27.00	78.00	325.00
□1902	Elliott-Burke	Blue	18.00	27.00	78.00	325.00
□1902	Elliott-White	Blue	18.00	27.00	78.00	325.00
□1902	Speelman-White	Blue	18.00	27.00	78.00	325.00
□1902	Woods-White	Blue	18.00	27.00	78.00	325.00
□1902	Woods-Tate	Blue	18.00	27.00	78.00	325.00
□1902	Jones-Woods	Blue	65.50	94.00	188.00	525.00

FIVE DOLLAR NOTES (1929) NATIONAL BANK NOTES
(Small Size)

TYPE I

TYPE II

Face Design: Portrait of President Lincoln in center, name of bank to left, brown seal to the right. Type I—charter number in black. Type II—similar; charter number added in brown.

Back Design: Lincoln Memorial.

SERIES	SIGNATURES	SEAL	A.B.P.	GOOD	V. FINE	UNC.
□1929	Type I Jones-Woods	Brown	8.50	12.00	29.00	110.00
□1929	Type II Jones-Woods	Brown	8.50	14.00	29.00	115.00

FIVE DOLLAR NOTES (1870)
NATIONAL GOLD BANK NOTES
(Large Size)

Face Design: Vignettes of Columbus sighting land.
Presentation of an Indian princess. Red seal. Signatures,
Allison-Spinner.

Back Design: California State Seal left, gold coins center,
American eagle right.

DATE	BANK	CITY	A.B.P.	GOOD	V. GOOD
☐1870 First National Gold Bank		San Francisco	460.00	670.00	1300.00
☐1872 National Gold Bank and Trust Co.		San Francisco	460.00	670.00	1300.00
☐1872 National Gold Bank of D.O. Mills and Co.		Sacramento	580.00	820.00	1700.00
☐1873 First National Gold Bank		Santa Barbara	580.00	820.00	1700.00
☐1873 First National Gold Bank		Stockton	580.00	870.00	2100.00
☐1874 Farmers National Gold Bank		San Jose	580.00	870.00	2100.00

FIVE DOLLAR NOTES (1886–1891)
SILVER CERTIFICATES

(Large Size)

Face Design: Portrait of President Grant.

Back Design: Five silver dollars.

SERIES	SIGNATURES	SEAL	A.B.P.	GOOD	V. FINE	UNC.
☐1886	Rosecrans-Jordan	Red	165.00	235.00	1500.00	4200.00
☐1886	Rosecrans-Hyatt	Sm. Red	165.00	235.00	1500.00	4200.00
☐1886	Rosecrans-Hyatt	Lg. Red	165.00	235.00	1500.00	4200.00
☐1886	Rosecrans-Huston	Lg. Red	165.00	235.00	1500.00	4200.00
☐1886	Rosecrans-Huston	Brown	165.00	235.00	1500.00	4200.00
☐1886	Rosecrans-Nebeker	Brown	165.00	235.00	1500.00	4200.00
☐1886	Rosecrans-Nebeker	Sm. Red	180.00	250.00	1650.00	4700.00

FIVE DOLLAR NOTES (1891) SILVER CERTIFICATES
(Large Size)

Face Design: Similar to previous note.

Back Design: Revised.

SERIES	SIGNATURES	SEAL	A.B.P.	GOOD	V. FINE	UNC.
☐1891	Rosecrans-Nebeker	Red	85.00	135.00	775.00	3250.00
☐1891	Tillman-Morgan	Red	85.00	135.00	775.00	3050.00

FIVE DOLLAR NOTES (1896) SILVER CERTIFICATES
(Large Size)

Face Design: Portraits of General Grant and General Sheridan.

Back Design: Five females representing Electricity as the dominant force in the world.

This was the last note of the popular Education Series.

SERIES	SIGNATURES	SEAL	A.B.P.	GOOD	V. FINE	UNC.
☐1896	Tillman-Morgan	Red	190.00	300.00	1700.00	6200.00
☐1896	Bruce-Roberts	Red	190.00	300.00	1700.00	6200.00
☐1896	Lyons-Roberts	Red	190.00	300.00	1700.00	6200.00

FIVE DOLLAR NOTES (1899) SILVER CERTIFICATES
(Large Size)

Face Design: Portrait of Indian chief.

Back Design: Green "V" and "5."

SERIES	SIGNATURES	SEAL	A.B.P.	GOOD	V. FINE	UNC.
☐1899	Lyons-Roberts	Blue	165.00	225.00	640.00	1700.00
☐1899	Lyons-Treat	Blue	165.00	225.00	640.00	1700.00
☐1899	Vernon-Treat	Blue	165.00	225.00	640.00	1700.00
☐1899	Vernon-McClung	Blue	165.00	225.00	640.00	1700.00
☐1899	Napier-McClung	Blue	165.00	225.00	640.00	1700.00
☐1899	Napier-Thompson	Blue	165.00	250.00	940.00	2600.00
☐1899	Parker-Burke	Blue	165.00	225.00	640.00	1700.00
☐1899	Teehee-Burke	Blue	165.00	225.00	640.00	1700.00
☐1899	Elliott-Burke	Blue	165.00	225.00	640.00	1700.00
☐1899	Elliott-White	Blue	165.00	225.00	640.00	1700.00
☐1899	Speelman-White	Blue	165.00	225.00	640.00	1700.00

FIVE DOLLAR NOTES (1923) SILVER CERTIFICATES
(Large Size)

Face Design: Portrait of President Lincoln in oval, nickname "Porthole Note," blue seal left, blue "5" right.

Back Design: Obverse of Great Seal of the United States.

SERIES	SIGNATURES	SEAL	A.B.P.	GOOD	V. FINE	UNC.
☐1923	Speelman-White	Blue	125.00	190.00	700.00	1750.00

FIVE DOLLAR NOTES (1934) SILVER CERTIFICATES
(Small Size)

First Issue (Small size of $5 Silver Certificates 1934.)
Face Design: Portrait of President Lincoln, blue "5" to left, blue seal to right.

Back Design: All Small Size $5 Notes have the same back design.

SERIES	SIGNATURES	SEAL	A.B.P.	GOOD	V. FINE	UNC.	★UNC.
☐1934	Julian-Morgenthau	Blue	6.00	8.00	13.00	38.00	300.00
☐1934A	Julian-Morgenthau	Blue	6.00	8.00	10.00	24.00	135.00
☐1934A	Julian-Morgenthau	Yellow	6.50	8.00	25.00	225.00	500.00

This note, with yellow Treasury Seal, was a Special Issue during World War II for military use in combat areas of North Africa and Europe.

SERIES	SIGNATURES	SEAL	A.B.P.	GOOD	V. FINE	UNC.	★UNC.
☐1934B	Julian-Vinson	Blue	6.00	8.00	20.00	60.00	250.00
☐1934C	Julian-Synder	Blue	6.00	8.00	11.00	29.00	125.00
☐1934D	Clark-Snyder	Blue	6.00	8.00	11.00	27.00	75.00

FIVE DOLLAR NOTES (1953) SILVER CERTIFICATES
(Small Size)

Face Design: The following notes are similar to the previous note. The face design has been revised. Gray "5" replaces blue "5" to left of Lincoln. Blue seal is slightly smaller.

Back Design: Same as previous note.

SERIES	SIGNATURES	SEAL	A.B.P.	GOOD	V. FINE	UNC.	★UNC.
☐1953	Priest-Humphrey	Blue	6.25	7.25	10.00	26.00	50.00
☐1953A	Priest-Anderson	Blue	6.25	7.25	10.00	21.00	25.00
☐1953B	Smith-Dillon	Blue	6.25	7.25	10.00	23.00	3000.00

Production of $5 Silver Certificates ended in 1962.

FIVE DOLLAR NOTES (1890) TREASURY OR COIN NOTES
(Large Size)

Face Design: Portrait of General George Henry Thomas (1816–70), the "Rock of Chickamauga."

Back Design:

SERIES	SIGNATURES	SEAL	A.B.P.	GOOD	V. FINE	UNC.
☐1890	Rosecrans-Huston	Brown	110.00	170.00	925.00	3500.00
☐1890	Rosecrans-Nebeker	Brown	110.00	170.00	925.00	3700.00
☐1890	Rosecrans-Nebeker	Red	110.00	170.00	925.00	3500.00

Back Design: Second Issue

SERIES	SIGNATURES	SEAL	A.B.P.	GOOD	V.FINE	UNC.
☐1891	Rosecrans-Nebeker	Red	75.00	125.00	500.00	1550.00
☐1891	Tillman-Morgan	Red	75.00	125.00	500.00	1550.00
☐1891	Bruce-Roberts	Red	75.00	125.00	500.00	1550.00
☐1891	Lyons-Roberts	Red	75.00	125.00	500.00	1550.00

FIVE DOLLAR NOTES (1914)
FEDERAL RESERVE NOTES

(Large Size)

Face Design: Portrait of President Lincoln center, Federal Reserve Seal left, Treasury Seal right.

Back Design: Scene of Columbus in sight of land left, landing of Pilgrims right.

SERIES OF 1914, RED TREASURY SEAL AND RED NUMBERS

SERIES BANK	SIGNATURES	SEAL	A.B.P.	GOOD	V. FINE	UNC.
☐1914 Boston	Burke-McAdoo	Red	24.00	37.00	235.00	1550.00
☐1914 New York	Burke-McAdoo	Red	24.00	37.00	150.00	1475.00
☐1914 Philadelphia	Burke-McAdoo	Red	24.00	37.00	170.00	1525.00
☐1914 Cleveland	Burke-McAdoo	Red	24.00	37.00	160.00	1500.00
☐1914 Richmond	Burke-McAdoo	Red	24.00	37.00	185.00	1550.00
☐1914 Atlanta	Burke-McAdoo	Red	24.00	37.00	175.00	1500.00
☐1914 Chicago	Burke-McAdoo	Red	24.00	37.00	160.00	1475.00
☐1914 St. Louis	Burke-McAdoo	Red	24.00	37.00	185.00	1500.00
☐1914 Minneapolis	Burke-McAdoo	Red	24.00	37.00	235.00	1850.00
☐1914 Kansas City	Burke-McAdoo	Red	24.00	37.00	160.00	1500.00
☐1914 Dallas	Burke-McAdoo	Red	24.00	37.00	235.00	1575.00
☐1914 San Francisco	Burke-McAdoo	Red	24.00	37.00	260.00	1650.00

FIVE DOLLAR NOTES (1914)
FEDERAL RESERVE NOTES

SERIES OF 1914, BLUE TREASURY SEAL AND BLUE NUMBERS

SERIES BANK	SIGNATURES	SEAL	A.B.P.	GOOD	V. FINE	UNC.
☐1914 Boston	Burke-McAdoo	Blue	15.00	40.00	80.00	180.00
☐1914 Boston	Burke-Glass	Blue	15.00	40.00	95.00	225.00
☐1914 Boston	Burke-Huston	Blue	15.00	40.00	70.00	140.00
☐1914 Boston	White-Mellon	Blue	15.00	40.00	70.00	135.00
☐1914 New York	Burke-McAdoo	Blue	15.00	40.00	70.00	140.00
☐1914 New York	Burke-Glass	Blue	15.00	40.00	80.00	180.00
☐1914 New York	Burke-Huston	Blue	15.00	40.00	70.00	140.00
☐1914 New York	White-Mellon	Blue	15.00	40.00	70.00	135.00
☐1914 Philadelphia	Burke-McAdoo	Blue	15.00	40.00	95.00	225.00
☐1914 Philadelphia	Burke-Glass	Blue	15.00	40.00	95.00	225.00
☐1914 Philadelphia	Burke-Huston	Blue	15.00	40.00	70.00	140.00

SERIES BANK	SIGNATURES	SEAL	A.B.P.	GOOD	V. FINE	UNC.
☐1914 Philadelphia	White-Mellon	Blue	15.00	22.50	70.00	135.00
☐1914 Cleveland	Burke-McAdoo	Blue	15.00	22.50	80.00	180.00
☐1914 Cleveland	Burke-Glass	Blue	15.00	22.50	120.00	290.00
☐1914 Cleveland	Burke-Huston	Blue	15.00	22.50	70.00	140.00
☐1914 Cleveland	White-Mellon	Blue	15.00	22.50	70.00	135.00
☐1914 Richmond	Burke-McAdoo	Blue	15.00	22.50	70.00	140.00
☐1914 Richmond	Burke-Glass	Blue	15.00	22.50	120.00	290.00
☐1914 Richmond	Burke-Huston	Blue	15.00	22.50	70.00	250.00
☐1914 Richmond	White-Mellon	Blue	15.00	22.50	70.00	240.00
☐1914 Atlanta	Burke-McAdoo	Blue	15.00	22.50	120.00	290.00
☐1914 Atlanta	Burke-Glass	Blue	15.00	22.50	280.00	540.00
☐1914 Atlanta	Burke-Huston	Blue	15.00	22.50	90.00	225.00
☐1914 Atlanta	White-Mellon	Blue	15.00	22.50	70.00	140.00
☐1914 Chicago	Burke-McAdoo	Blue	15.00	22.50	120.00	290.00
☐1914 Chicago	Burke-Glass	Blue	15.00	22.50	70.00	135.00
☐1914 Chicago	Burke-Huston	Blue	15.00	22.50	70.00	135.00
☐1914 Chicago	White-Mellon	Blue	15.00	22.50	70.00	135.00
☐1914 St. Louis	Burke-McAdoo	Blue	15.00	22.50	90.00	225.00
☐1914 St. Louis	Burke-Glass	Blue	15.00	24.00	72.00	160.00
☐1914 St. Louis	Burke-Huston	Blue	15.00	22.50	71.00	150.00
☐1914 St. Louis	White-Mellon	Blue	15.00	22.50	70.00	140.00
☐1914 Minneapolis	Burke-McAdoo	Blue	15.00	24.00	90.00	225.00
☐1914 Minneapolis	Burke-Glass	Blue	15.00	24.00	120.00	265.00
☐1914 Minneapolis	Burke-Huston	Blue	15.00	22.50	80.00	180.00
☐1914 Minneapolis	White-Mellon	Blue	15.00	22.50	70.00	150.00
☐1914 Kansas City	Burke-McAdoo	Blue	15.00	22.50	80.00	180.00
☐1914 Kansas City	Burke-Glass	Blue	15.00	24.00	90.00	225.00
☐1914 Kansas City	Burke-Huston	Blue	15.00	22.50	70.00	180.00
☐1914 Kansas City	White-Mellon	Blue	15.00	22.50	70.00	135.00
☐1914 Dallas	Burke-McAdoo	Blue	15.00	22.50	125.00	265.00
☐1914 Dallas	Burke-Glass	Blue	15.00	25.00	120.00	235.00
☐1914 Dallas	Burke-Huston	Blue	15.00	22.50	120.00	230.00
☐1914 Dallas	White-Mellon	Blue	15.00	22.50	75.00	150.00
☐1914 San Francisco	Burke-McAdoo	Blue	15.00	22.50	130.00	275.00
☐1914 San Francisco	Burke-Glass	Blue	15.00	24.00	180.00	340.00
☐1914 San Francisco	Burke-Huston	Blue	15.00	22.50	110.00	265.00
☐1914 San Francisco	White-Mellon	Blue	15.00	22.50	70.00	140.00

FIVE DOLLAR NOTES (1928)
FEDERAL RESERVE NOTES

(Small Size)

Face Design: Portrait of President Lincoln center, black Federal Reserve Seal with numeral for district in center. City of issuing bank in seal circle. Green Treasury Seal to right.
Back Design: Similar to 1935 note. Lincoln Memorial in Washington, D.C.

SERIES OF 1928,
SIGNATURES OF TATE AND MELLON, GREEN SEAL

BANK	A.B.P.	GOOD	V.FINE	UNC.	★UNC.	BANK	A.B.P.	GOOD	V.FINE	UNC.	★UNC.
☐ Boston	10.00	13.00	30.00	125.00	925.00	☐ Chicago	8.50	12.00	30.00	125.00	950.00
☐ New York	10.00	13.00	30.00	125.00	925.00	☐ St. Louis	8.50	12.00	30.00	130.00	950.00
☐ Philadelphia	10.00	13.00	30.00	125.00	925.00	☐ Minneapolis	8.50	12.00	125.00	510.00	950.00
☐ Cleveland	10.00	13.00	30.00	125.00	925.00	☐ Kansas City	8.50	12.00	30.00	130.00	950.00
☐ Richmond	10.00	13.00	30.00	125.00	925.00	☐ Dallas	8.50	12.00	30.00	140.00	950.00
☐ Atlanta	10.00	13.00	30.00	125.00	925.00	☐ San Francisco	8.50	12.00	30.00	215.00	950.00

SERIES OF 1928A,
SIGNATURES OF WOODS-MELLON, GREEN SEAL

BANK	A.B.P.	GOOD	V.FINE	UNC.	★UNC.	BANK	A.B.P.	GOOD	V.FINE	UNC.	★UNC.
☐ Boston	8.00	12.00	23.00	120.00	775.00	☐ Chicago	8.00	12.00	23.00	120.00	775.00
☐ New York	8.00	12.00	23.00	120.00	775.00	☐ St. Louis	8.00	12.00	25.00	135.00	775.00
☐ Philadelphia	8.00	12.00	23.00	120.00	775.00	☐ Minneapolis	8.00	12.00	27.00	285.00	1025.00
☐ Cleveland	8.00	12.00	23.00	120.00	775.00	☐ Kansas City	8.00	12.00	25.00	135.00	775.00
☐ Richmond	8.00	12.00	50.00	145.00	775.00	☐ Dallas	8.00	12.00	50.00	145.00	775.00
☐ Atlanta	8.00	12.00	23.00	120.00	775.00	☐ San Francisco	8.00	12.00	25.00	135.00	775.00

SERIES OF 1928B,
SIGNATURES OF WOODS-MELLON, GREEN SEAL

The black Federal Reserve Seal now has a letter for district in place of the numeral.

BANK	A.B.P.	GOOD	V.FINE	UNC.	★UNC.	BANK	A.B.P.	GOOD	V.FINE	UNC.	★UNC.
☐ Boston	7.00	10.00	20.00	80.00	325.00	☐ Chicago	7.00	10.00	20.00	80.00	325.00
☐ New York	7.00	10.00	20.00	80.00	325.00	☐ St. Louis	7.00	10.00	20.00	80.00	325.00
☐ Philadelphia	7.00	10.00	20.00	80.00	325.00	☐ Minneapolis	7.00	10.00	20.00	80.00	325.00
☐ Cleveland	7.00	10.00	20.00	80.00	325.00	☐ Kansas City	7.00	10.00	20.00	80.00	325.00
☐ Richmond	7.00	10.00	20.00	80.00	325.00	☐ Dallas	7.00	10.00	20.00	80.00	325.00
☐ Atlanta	7.00	10.00	20.00	80.00	325.00	☐ San Francisco	7.00	10.00	20.00	80.00	325.00

SERIES OF 1928C,
SIGNATURES OF WOODS-WOODIN, GREEN SEAL

BANK	A.B.P.	GOOD	V.FINE	UNC.	★UNC.	BANK	A.B.P.	GOOD	V.FINE	UNC.	★UNC.
☐ Cleveland	205.00	410.00	850.00	1900.00	RARE	☐ San Francisco					
☐ Atlanta	80.00	110.00	400.00	1475.00	RARE		205.00	410.00	850.00	1900.00	RARE

SERIES OF 1928D,
SIGNATURES OF WOODS-MILLS, GREEN SEAL

BANK	A.B.P.	GOOD	V.FINE	UNC.	★UNC.
☐ Atlanta	255.00	410.00	750.00	2450.00	RARE

FIVE DOLLAR NOTES (1934)
FEDERAL RESERVE NOTES
SERIES OF 1934,
JULIAN-MORGENTHAU, GREEN SEAL

"Redeemable in Gold" was removed from obligation over Federal Reserve Seal. Also, the green Treasury Seal on this note is known in a light and dark color. The light seal is worth about 10–20 percent more in most cases.

BANK	A.B.P.	V.FINE	UNC.	★UNC.	BANK	A.B.P.	V.FINE	UNC.	★UNC.
☐ Boston	8.00	13.00	50.00	170.00	☐ St. Louis	8.00	13.00	40.00	170.00
☐ New York	8.00	13.00	40.00	170.00	☐ Minneapolis	8.00	13.00	40.00	170.00
☐ Philadelphia	8.00	13.00	40.00	170.00	☐ Kansas City	8.00	13.00	40.00	170.00
☐ Cleveland	8.00	13.00	40.00	170.00	☐ Dallas	8.00	13.00	50.00	170.00
☐ Richmond	8.00	13.00	40.00	170.00	☐ San Francisco	8.00	13.00	40.00	170.00
☐ Atlanta	8.00	13.00	40.00	170.00	☐ San Francisco*	20.00	75.00	575.00	1600.00
☐ Chicago	8.00	13.00	40.00	170.00					

*This note has brown Treasury Seal and is surprinted HAWAII. For use in Pacific area of operations during World War II.

(Small Size)

Note—1934A (Julian-Morgenthau) is surprinted HAWAII. It was used in the Pacific area during World War II.

SERIES OF 1934A, JULIAN-MORGENTHAU, GREEN SEAL

BANK	A.B.P.	V.FINE	UNC.	★UNC.	BANK	A.B.P.	V.FINE	UNC.	★UNC.
☐ Boston	7.00	12.00	40.00	260.00	☐ Atlanta	7.00	12.00	40.00	260.00
☐ New York	7.00	12.00	40.00	260.00	☐ Chicago	7.00	12.00	40.00	260.00
☐ Philadelphia	7.00	12.00	40.00	260.00	☐ St. Louis	7.00	12.00	40.00	260.00
☐ Cleveland	7.00	12.00	40.00	260.00	☐ San Francisco	7.00	12.00	40.00	260.00
☐ Richmond	7.00	12.00	40.00	260.00	☐ Hawaii*	20.00	70.00	550.00	800.00

*This note has brown Treasury Seal and is surprinted HAWAII. For use in Pacific area of operations during World War II.
(Small Size)

SERIES OF 1934B,
SIGNATURES OF JULIAN-VINSON, GREEN SEAL

BANK	A.B.P.	V.FINE	UNC.	★UNC.	BANK	A.B.P.	V.FINE	UNC.	★UNC.
☐ Boston	7.00	12.00	55.00	210.00	☐ Chicago	6.00	11.00	55.00	235.00
☐ New York	7.00	12.00	55.00	210.00	☐ St. Louis	6.00	11.00	55.00	235.00
☐ Philadelphia	7.00	12.00	55.00	210.00	☐ Minneapolis	6.00	11.00	55.00	235.00
☐ Cleveland	7.00	12.00	55.00	210.00	☐ Kansas City	75.00	150.00	600.00	1100.00
☐ Richmond	7.00	12.00	40.00	210.00	☐ Dallas			NOT ISSUED	
☐ Atlanta	7.00	12.00	50.00	210.00	☐ San Francisco	6.00	11.00	50.00	210.00

SERIES OF 1934C,
SIGNATURES OF JULIAN-SNYDER, GREEN SEAL

BANK	A.B.P.	V.FINE	UNC.	★UNC.	BANK	A.B.P.	V.FINE	UNC.	★UNC.
☐ Boston	7.00	11.00	65.00	135.00	☐ Chicago	7.00	10.00	55.00	135.00
☐ New York	7.00	11.00	55.00	135.00	☐ St. Louis	7.00	10.00	55.00	135.00
☐ Philadelphia	7.00	11.00	55.00	135.00	☐ Minneapolis	7.00	10.00	55.00	135.00
☐ Cleveland	7.00	11.00	55.00	135.00	☐ Kansas City	7.00	10.00	55.00	135.00
☐ Richmond	7.00	11.00	55.00	655.00	☐ Dallas	7.00	10.00	55.00	135.00
☐ Atlanta	7.00	11.00	55.00	135.00	☐ San Francisco	7.00	10.00	55.00	135.00

SERIES OF 1934D,
SIGNATURES OF CLARK-SNYDER, GREEN SEAL

BANK	A.B.P.	V.FINE	UNC.	★UNC.	BANK	A.B.P.	V.FINE	UNC.	★UNC.
☐ Boston	6.50	9.00	75.00	160.00	☐ Chicago	6.50	9.00	70.00	170.00
☐ New York	6.50	9.00	65.00	160.00	☐ St. Louis	6.50	9.00	80.00	170.00
☐ Philadelphia	6.50	9.00	70.00	160.00	☐ Minneapolis	6.50	9.00	80.00	170.00
☐ Cleveland	6.50	9.00	70.00	160.00	☐ Kansas City	6.50	9.00	75.00	170.00
☐ Richmond	6.50	9.00	110.00	160.00	☐ Dallas	6.50	9.00	95.00	170.00
☐ Atlanta	40.00	80.00	200.00	160.00	☐ San Francisco	6.50	9.00	80.00	170.00

FIVE DOLLAR NOTES (1950)
FEDERAL RESERVE NOTES
BLACK FEDERAL RESERVE SEAL AND
GREEN TREASURY SEALS ARE NOW SMALLER
(Small Size)

SERIES OF 1950, SIGNATURES OF CLARK-SNYDER, GREEN SEAL

BANK	A.B.P.	V.FINE	UNC.	★UNC.	BANK	A.B.P.	V.FINE	UNC.	★UNC.
☐ Boston	6.00	20.00	60.00	155.00	☐ Chicago	6.00	20.00	45.00	115.00
☐ New York	6.00	20.00	50.00	155.00	☐ St. Louis	6.00	20.00	40.00	115.00
☐ Philadelphia	6.00	20.00	45.00	155.00	☐ Minneapolis	6.00	20.00	45.00	115.00
☐ Cleveland	6.00	20.00	40.00	405.00	☐ Kansas City	6.00	20.00	85.00	115.00
☐ Richmond	6.00	20.00	50.00	205.00	☐ Dallas	6.00	20.00	40.00	115.00
☐ Atlanta	6.00	20.00	40.00	405.00	☐ San Francisco	6.00	20.00	60.00	115.00

SERIES OF 1950A, SIGNATURES OF PRIEST-HUMPHERY, GREEN SEAL

BANK	A.B.P.	V.FINE	UNC.	★UNC.	BANK	A.B.P.	V.FINE	UNC.	★UNC.
☐ Boston	5.50	10.00	25.00	40.00	☐ Chicago	5.50	10.00	25.00	40.00
☐ New York	5.50	10.00	25.00	40.00	☐ St. Louis	5.50	10.00	25.00	40.00
☐ Philadelphia	5.50	10.00	25.00	40.00	☐ Minneapolis	5.50	10.00	25.00	50.00
☐ Cleveland	5.50	10.00	25.00	45.00	☐ Kansas City	5.50	10.00	25.00	60.00
☐ Richmond	5.50	10.00	25.00	40.00	☐ Dallas	5.50	10.00	25.00	60.00
☐ Atlanta	5.50	10.00	25.00	40.00	☐ San Francisco	5.50	10.00	25.00	50.00

SERIES OF 1950B, SIGNATURES OF PRIEST-ANDERSON, GREEN SEAL

BANK	A.B.P.	V.FINE	UNC.	★UNC.	BANK	A.B.P.	V.FINE	UNC.	★UNC.
☐ Boston	5.25	9.00	20.00	35.00	☐ Chicago	5.25	9.00	20.00	35.00
☐ New York	5.25	9.00	20.00	35.00	☐ St. Louis	5.25	9.00	20.00	35.00
☐ Philadelphia	5.25	9.00	20.00	35.00	☐ Minneapolis	5.25	10.00	22.00	35.00
☐ Cleveland	5.25	9.00	20.00	35.00	☐ Kansas City	5.25	10.00	22.00	35.00
☐ Richmond	5.25	9.00	20.00	35.00	☐ Dallas	5.25	9.00	20.00	40.00
☐ Atlanta	5.25	9.00	20.00	35.00	☐ San Francisco	5.25	9.00	20.00	35.00

SERIES OF 1950C, SIGNATURES OF SMITH-DILLON, GREEN SEAL

BANK	A.B.P.	V.FINE	UNC.	★UNC.	BANK	A.B.P.	V.FINE	UNC.	★UNC.
☐ Boston	5.25	9.00	20.00	35.00	☐ Chicago	5.25	9.00	20.00	35.00
☐ New York	5.25	9.00	20.00	75.00	☐ St. Louis	5.25	9.00	20.00	35.00
☐ Philadelphia	5.25	9.00	20.00	115.00	☐ Minneapolis	5.25	10.00	22.00	35.00
☐ Cleveland	5.25	9.00	20.00	35.00	☐ Kansas City	5.25	10.00	22.00	35.00
☐ Richmond	5.25	9.00	20.00	35.00	☐ Dallas	5.25	9.00	20.00	35.00
☐ Atlanta	5.25	9.00	20.00	35.00	☐ San Francisco	5.25	9.00	20.00	35.00

SERIES OF 1950D, SIGNATURES OF GRANAHAN-DILLON, GREEN SEAL

BANK	A.B.P.	V.FINE	UNC.	★UNC.	BANK	A.B.P.	V.FINE	UNC.	★UNC.
☐ Boston	5.25	9.00	30.00	70.00	☐ Chicago	5.25	9.00	20.00	55.00
☐ New York	5.25	9.00	20.00	50.00	☐ St. Louis	5.25	9.00	26.00	80.00
☐ Philadelphia	5.25	9.00	30.00	85.00	☐ Minneapolis	5.25	10.00	32.00	100.00
☐ Cleveland	5.25	9.00	22.00	75.00	☐ Kansas City	5.25	9.00	22.00	100.00
☐ Richmond	5.25	9.00	27.00	55.00	☐ Dallas	5.25	9.00	27.00	130.00
☐ Atlanta	5.25	9.00	27.00	75.00	☐ San Francisco	5.25	9.00	20.00	60.00

SERIES OF 1950E, SIGNATURES OF GRANAHAN-FOWLER, GREEN SEAL

BANK	A.B.P.	V.FINE	UNC.	★UNC.	BANK	A.B.P.	V.FINE	UNC.	★UNC.
					☐ Chicago	5.25	9.00	24.00	70.00
☐ New York	5.25	9.00	23.00	65.00					
					☐ San Francisco	5.25	9.00	26.00	65.00

FIVE DOLLAR NOTES (1963)
FEDERAL RESERVE NOTES
(IN GOD WE TRUST IS ADDED ON BACK)
SERIES OF 1963, SIGNATURES OF GRANAHAN-DILLON, GREEN SEAL

BANK	A.B.P.	V.FINE	UNC.	★UNC.	BANK	A.B.P.	V.FINE	UNC.	★UNC.
☐ Boston	—	8.00	26.00	47.00	☐ Chicago	—	8.00	17.00	42.00
☐ New York	—	8.00	17.00	27.00	☐ St. Louis	—	8.00	21.00	37.00
☐ Philadelphia	—	8.00	19.00	32.00	☐ Minneapolis	—	8.00	21.00	42.00
☐ Cleveland	—	8.00	17.00	32.00	☐ Kansas City	—	8.00	21.00	32.00
☐ Richmond	—	8.00	17.00	32.00	☐ Dallas	—	8.00	21.00	45.00
☐ Atlanta	—	8.00	19.00	37.00	☐ San Francisco	—	8.00	21.00	42.00

SERIES OF 1963A, SIGNATURES OF GRANAHAN-FOWLER, GREEN SEAL

BANK	A.B.P.	V.FINE	UNC.	★UNC.	BANK	A.B.P.	V.FINE	UNC.	★UNC.
☐ Boston	—	7.00	16.00	21.00	☐ Chicago	—	7.00	16.00	21.00
☐ New York	—	7.00	16.00	21.00	☐ St. Louis	—	7.00	16.00	21.00
☐ Philadelphia	—	7.00	16.00	21.00	☐ Minneapolis	—	7.00	16.00	21.00
☐ Cleveland	—	7.00	16.00	21.00	☐ Kansas City	—	7.00	16.00	21.00
☐ Richmond	—	7.00	16.00	21.00	☐ Dallas	—	7.00	16.00	21.00
☐ Atlanta	—	7.00	16.00	21.00	☐ San Francisco	—	7.00	16.00	21.00

FIVE DOLLAR NOTES (1969)
FEDERAL RESERVE NOTES
(WORDING IN GREEN TREASURY SEAL IS CHANGED FROM LATIN TO ENGLISH)

SERIES OF 1969, SIGNATURES OF ELSTON-KENNEDY, GREEN SEAL

BANK	A.B.P.	V.FINE	UNC.	★UNC.	BANK	A.B.P.	V.FINE	UNC.	★UNC.
☐ Boston	—	6.00	13.00	26.00	☐ Chicago	—	6.00	13.00	26.00
☐ New York	—	6.00	13.00	26.00	☐ St. Louis	—	6.00	13.00	26.00
☐ Philadelphia	—	6.00	13.00	26.00	☐ Minneapolis	—	6.00	13.00	26.00
☐ Cleveland	—	6.00	13.00	26.00	☐ Kansas City	—	6.00	13.00	26.00
☐ Richmond	—	6.00	13.00	26.00	☐ Dallas	—	6.00	13.00	26.00
☐ Atlanta	—	6.00	13.00	26.00	☐ San Francisco	—	6.00	13.00	26.00

SERIES OF 1969A, SIGNATURES OF KABIS-CONNALLY, GREEN SEAL

BANK	A.B.P.	V.FINE	UNC.	★UNC.	BANK	A.B.P.	V.FINE	UNC.	★UNC.
☐ Boston	—	6.00	21.00	41.00	☐ Chicago	—	6.00	21.00	32.00
☐ New York	—	6.00	21.00	31.00	☐ St. Louis	—	6.00	21.00	47.00
☐ Philadelphia	—	6.00	21.00	36.00	☐ Minneapolis	—	6.00	21.00	37.00
☐ Cleveland	—	6.00	21.00	41.00	☐ Kansas City	—	6.00	21.00	37.00
☐ Richmond	—	6.00	21.00	41.00	☐ Dallas	—	6.00	21.00	40.00
☐ Atlanta	—	6.00	21.00	41.00	☐ San Francisco	—	6.00	21.00	42.00

SERIES OF 1969B, SIGNATURES OF BANUELOS-CONNALLY, GREEN SEAL

BANK	A.B.P.	V.FINE	UNC.	★UNC.	BANK	A.B.P.	V.FINE	UNC.	★UNC.
☐ Boston	—	12.00	26.00	86.00	☐ Chicago	—	12.00	26.00	100.00
☐ New York	—	8.00	17.00	76.00	☐ St. Louis	—	12.00	26.00	95.00
☐ Philadelphia	—	12.00	26.00	91.00	☐ Minneapolis	—	12.00	26.00	105.00
☐ Cleveland	—	12.00	26.00	91.00	☐ Kansas City	—	12.00	26.00	105.00
☐ Richmond	—	12.00	26.00	91.00	☐ Dallas	—	12.00	26.00	105.00
☐ Atlanta	—	12.00	26.00	91.00	☐ San Francisco	—	12.00	26.00	105.00

SERIES OF 1969C, SIGNATURES OF BANUELOS-SHULTZ, GREEN SEAL

BANK	A.B.P.	V.FINE	UNC.	★UNC.	BANK	A.B.P.	V.FINE	UNC.	★UNC.
☐ Boston	—	6.00	12.00	30.00	☐ Chicago	—	6.00	12.00	30.00
☐ New York	—	6.00	12.00	30.00	☐ St. Louis	—	6.00	12.00	30.00
☐ Philadelphia	—	6.00	12.00	30.00	☐ Minneapolis	—	6.00	12.00	30.00
☐ Cleveland	—	6.00	12.00	30.00	☐ Kansas City	—	6.00	12.00	30.00
☐ Richmond	—	6.00	12.00	30.00	☐ Dallas	—	6.00	12.00	30.00
☐ Atlanta	—	6.00	12.00	30.00	☐ San Francisco	—	6.00	12.00	30.00

FIVE DOLLAR NOTES (1974)
FEDERAL RESERVE NOTES
SERIES OF 1974, SIGNATURES OF NEFF-SIMON, GREEN SEAL

BANK	A.B.P.	V.FINE	UNC.	★UNC.	BANK	A.B.P.	V.FINE	UNC.	★UNC.
☐ Boston	—	6.00	12.00	20.00	☐ Chicago	—	6.00	12.00	20.00
☐ New York	—	6.00	12.00	20.00	☐ St. Louis	—	6.00	12.00	20.00
☐ Philadelphia	—	6.00	12.00	20.00	☐ Minneapolis	—	7.00	14.00	20.00
☐ Cleveland	—	6.00	12.00	20.00	☐ Kansas City	—	7.00	14.00	20.00
☐ Richmond	—	6.00	12.00	20.00	☐ Dallas	—	7.00	14.00	20.00
☐ Atlanta	—	6.00	12.00	20.00	☐ San Francisco	—	6.00	12.00	20.00

FIVE DOLLAR NOTES (1977)
FEDERAL RESERVE NOTES
SERIES OF 1977, SIGNATURES OF MORTON-BLUMENTHAL, GREEN SEAL

★Notes not issued for all banks

BANK	A.B.P.	V.FINE	UNC.	★UNC.	BANK	A.B.P.	V.FINE	UNC.	★UNC.
☐ Boston	—	6.00	12.00	25.00	☐ Chicago	—	6.00	12.00	25.00
☐ New York	—	6.00	12.00	25.00	☐ St. Louis	—	6.00	12.00	25.00
☐ Philadelphia	—	6.00	12.00	25.00	☐ Minneapolis	—	7.00	14.00	25.00
☐ Cleveland	—	6.00	12.00	25.00	☐ Kansas City	—	7.00	14.00	25.00
☐ Richmond	—	6.00	12.00	25.00	☐ Dallas	—	7.00	14.00	25.00
☐ Atlanta	—	6.00	12.00	25.00	☐ San Francisco	—	6.00	12.00	25.00

SERIES OF 1977A, SIGNATURES OF MORTON-BLUMENTHAL, GREEN SEAL

BANK	A.B.P.	V.FINE	UNC.	★UNC.	BANK	A.B.P.	V.FINE	UNC.	★UNC.
☐ Boston	—	6.00	12.00	15.00	☐ Chicago	—	6.00	12.00	15.00
☐ New York	—	6.00	12.00	15.00	☐ St. Louis	—	6.00	12.00	15.00
☐ Philadelphia	—	6.00	12.00	15.00	☐ Minneapolis	—	6.00	12.00	15.00
☐ Cleveland	—	6.00	12.00	15.00	☐ Kansas City	—	6.00	12.00	15.00
☐ Richmond	—	6.00	12.00	15.00	☐ Dallas	—	6.00	12.00	15.00
☐ Atlanta	—	6.00	12.00	15.00	☐ San Francisco	—	6.00	12.00	15.00

FIVE DOLLAR NOTES (1981)
FEDERAL RESERVE NOTES
SERIES OF 1981, SIGNATURES OF BUCHANAN-REGAN, GREEN SEAL
★Notes not issued for all banks

BANK	A.B.P.	V.FINE	UNC.	★UNC.	BANK	A.B.P.	V.FINE	UNC.	★UNC.
☐ Boston	—	6.00	16.00	45.00	☐ Chicago	—	6.00	16.00	45.00
☐ New York	—	6.00	16.00	45.00	☐ St. Louis	—	6.00	16.00	45.00
☐ Philadelphia	—	6.00	16.00	45.00	☐ Minneapolis	—	7.00	16.00	45.00
☐ Cleveland	—	6.00	16.00	45.00	☐ Kansas City	—	7.00	16.00	45.00
☐ Richmond	—	6.00	16.00	45.00	☐ Dallas	—	7.00	16.00	45.00
☐ Atlanta	—	6.00	16.00	45.00	☐ San Francisco	—	6.00	16.00	45.00

SERIES OF 1981A, SIGNATURES OF ORTEGA-REGAN, GREEN SEAL
★Notes not issued for all banks

BANK	A.B.P.	V.FINE	UNC.	★UNC.	BANK	A.B.P.	V.FINE	UNC.	★UNC.
☐ Boston	—	6.00	12.00	40.00	☐ Chicago	—	6.00	12.00	40.00
☐ New York	—	6.00	12.00	40.00	☐ St. Louis	—	6.00	12.00	40.00
☐ Philadelphia	—	6.00	12.00	40.00	☐ Minneapolis	—	7.00	14.00	40.00
☐ Cleveland	—	6.00	12.00	40.00	☐ Kansas City	—	6.00	12.00	40.00
☐ Richmond	—	6.00	12.00	40.00	☐ Dallas	—	6.00	12.00	40.00
☐ Atlanta	—	6.00	12.00	40.00	☐ San Francisco	—	6.00	12.00	40.00

FIVE DOLLAR NOTES (1985)
FEDERAL RESERVE NOTES
SERIES OF 1985, SIGNATURES OF ORTEGA-BAKER, GREEN SEAL
★Notes not issued for all banks

BANK	A.B.P.	V.FINE	UNC.	★UNC.	BANK	A.B.P.	V.FINE	UNC.	★UNC.
☐ Boston	—	6.00	12.00	30.00	☐ Chicago	—	6.00	12.00	30.00
☐ New York	—	6.00	12.00	30.00	☐ St. Louis	—	6.00	12.00	30.00
☐ Philadelphia	—	6.00	12.00	30.00	☐ Minneapolis	—	6.00	12.00	30.00
☐ Cleveland	—	6.00	12.00	30.00	☐ Kansas City	—	6.00	12.00	30.00
☐ Richmond	—	6.00	12.00	30.00	☐ Dallas	—	6.00	12.00	30.00
☐ Atlanta	—	6.00	12.00	30.00	☐ San Francisco	—	6.00	12.00	30.00

FIVE DOLLAR NOTES (1988)
FEDERAL RESERVE NOTES
SERIES OF 1988, SIGNATURES OF ORTEGA-BRADY, GREEN SEAL

★Notes not issued for all banks

BANK	A.B.P.	V.FINE	UNC.	★UNC.	BANK	A.B.P.	V.FINE	UNC.	★UNC.
☐ Boston	—	6.00	15.00	18.00	☐ Chicago	—	6.00	15.00	18.00
☐ New York	—	6.00	15.00	18.00	☐ St. Louis	—	6.00	15.00	18.00
☐ Philadelphia	—	6.00	15.00	18.00	☐ Minneapolis	—	6.00	15.00	18.00
☐ Cleveland	—	6.00	15.00	18.00	☐ Kansas City	—	6.00	15.00	18.00
☐ Richmond	—	6.00	15.00	18.00	☐ Dallas	—	6.00	15.00	18.00
☐ Atlanta	—	6.00	15.00	18.00	☐ San Francisco	—	6.00	15.00	18.00

SERIES OF 1988A, SIGNATURES OF VILLALPANDO-BRADY, GREEN SEAL

★Notes not issued for all banks

BANK	A.B.P.	V.FINE	UNC.	★UNC.	BANK	A.B.P.	V.FINE	UNC.	★UNC.
☐ Boston	—	6.00	12.00	20.00	☐ Chicago	—	6.00	12.00	20.00
☐ New York	—	6.00	12.00	20.00	☐ St. Louis	—	6.00	12.00	20.00
☐ Philadelphia	—	6.00	12.00	20.00	☐ Minneapolis	—	6.00	12.00	20.00
☐ Cleveland	—	6.00	12.00	20.00	☐ Kansas City	—	6.00	12.00	20.00
☐ Richmond	—	6.00	12.00	20.00	☐ Dallas	—	6.00	12.00	20.00
☐ Atlanta	—	6.00	12.00	20.00	☐ San Francisco	—	6.00	12.00	20.00

FIVE DOLLAR NOTES (1993)
FEDERAL RESERVE NOTES
SERIES OF 1993, SIGNATURES OF WITHROW-BENTSEN, GREEN SEAL

★Notes not issued for all banks

BANK	A.B.P.	V.FINE	UNC.	★UNC.	BANK	A.B.P.	V.FINE	UNC.	★UNC.
☐ Boston	—	6.00	12.00	20.00	☐ Chicago	—	6.00	12.00	20.00
☐ New York	—	6.00	12.00	20.00	☐ St. Louis	—	6.00	12.00	20.00
☐ Philadelphia	—	6.00	12.00	20.00	☐ Minneapolis	—	6.00	12.00	20.00
☐ Cleveland	—	—	—	—	☐ Kansas City	—	6.00	12.00	20.00
☐ Richmond	—	6.00	12.00	20.00	☐ Dallas	—	6.00	12.00	20.00
☐ Atlanta	—	6.00	12.00	20.00	☐ San Francisco	—	6.00	12.00	20.00

FIVE DOLLAR NOTES (1995)
FEDERAL RESERVE NOTES
SERIES OF 1995, SIGNATURES OF WITHROW-RUBIN, GREEN SEAL
★Notes not issued for all banks

BANK	A.B.P.	V.FINE	UNC.	★UNC.	BANK	A.B.P.	V.FINE	UNC.	★UNC.
☐ Boston	—	6.00	8.00	20.00	☐ Chicago	—	6.00	8.00	20.00
☐ New York	—	6.00	8.00	20.00	☐ St. Louis	—	6.00	8.00	20.00
☐ Philadelphia	—	6.00	8.00	20.00	☐ Minneapolis	—	6.00	8.00	20.00
☐ Cleveland	—	6.00	8.00	20.00	☐ Kansas City	—	6.00	8.00	20.00
☐ Richmond	—	6.00	8.00	20.00	☐ Dallas	—	6.00	8.00	20.00
☐ Atlanta	—	6.00	8.00	20.00	☐ San Francisco	—	6.00	8.00	20.00

FIVE DOLLAR NOTES (1918)
FEDERAL RESERVE BANK NOTES
(ALL WITH BLUE SEAL AND BLUE SERIAL NUMBERS)
(Large Size)

Face Design: Portrait of President Lincoln with Reserve City in center.

Back Design: Same as 1914 note.

BANK	SERIES	GOV'T SIGNATURES	BANK SIGNATURES	A.B.P.	GOOD	V. FINE	UNC.
☐Boston	1918	Teehee-Burke	Bullen-Morse	30.00	45.00	185.00	750.00
☐New York	1918	Teehee-Burke	Hendricks-Strong	30.00	45.00	160.00	700.00
☐Philadelphia	1918	Teehee-Burke	Hardt-Passmore	30.00	45.00	185.00	800.00
☐Philadelphia	1918	Teehee-Burke	Dyer-Passmore	30.00	45.00	185.00	800.00
☐Cleveland	1918	Teehee-Burke	Dyer-Fancher	30.00	45.00	160.00	700.00
☐Cleveland	1918	Teehee-Burke	Davis-Fancher	30.00	45.00	210.00	900.00
☐Cleveland	1918	Elliott-Burke	Davis-Fancher	30.00	45.00	160.00	700.00
☐Atlanta	1915	Teehee-Burke	Bell-Wellborn	30.00	45.00	200.00	900.00
☐Atlanta	1915	Teehee-Burke	Pike-McCord	30.00	45.00	185.00	725.00
☐Atlanta	1918	Teehee-Burke	Pike-McCord	30.00	45.00	170.00	725.00
☐Atlanta	1918	Teehee-Burke	Bell-Wellborn	30.00	45.00	210.00	800.00

BANK	SERIES	GOV'T SIGNATURES	BANK SIGNATURES	A.B.P.	GOOD	V. FINE	UNC.
☐Atlanta	1918	Elliott-Burke	Bell-Wellborn				
				28.00	45.00	260.00	950.00
☐Chicago	1915	Teehee-Burke	McLallen-McDougal				
				28.00	45.00	175.00	700.00
☐Chicago	1918	Teehee-Burke	McCloud-McDougal				
				24.00	43.00	160.00	700.00
☐Chicago	1918	Teehee-Burke	Cramer-McDougal				
				24.00	43.00	260.00	950.00
☐St. Louis	1918	Teehee-Burke	Attebery-Wells				
				24.00	43.00	160.00	700.00
☐St. Louis	1918	Teehee-Burke	Attebery-Biggs				
				24.00	43.00	160.00	700.00
☐St. Louis	1918	Elliott-Burke	White-Biggs				
				24.00	43.00	160.00	700.00
☐Minneapolis	1918	Teehee-Burke	Cook-Wold				
				24.00	43.00	185.00	725.00
☐Kansas City	1915	Teehee-Burke	Anderson-Miller				
				28.00	45.00	175.00	700.00
☐Kansas City	1915	Teehee-Burke	Cross-Miller				
				28.00	45.00	195.00	700.00
☐Kansas City	1915	Teehee-Burke	Helm-Miller				
				28.00	45.00	260.00	950.00
☐Kansas City	1918	Teehee-Burke	Anderson-Miller				
				28.00	43.00	160.00	700.00
☐Kansas City	1918	Elliott-Burke	Helm-Miller				
				28.00	43.00	205.00	750.00
☐Dallas	1915	Teehee-Burke	Hoopes-VanZandt				
				28.00	45.00	185.00	750.00
☐Dallas	1915	Teehee-Burke	Talley-VanZandt				
				28.00	45.00	260.00	950.00
☐Dallas	1918	Teehee-Burke	Talley-VanZandt				
				28.00	43.00	195.00	800.00
☐San Francisco	1915	Teehee-Burke	Clerk-Lynch				
				28.00	45.00	185.00	775.00
☐San Francisco	1918	Teehee-Burke	Clerk-Lynch				
				28.00	43.00	260.00	950.00

FIVE DOLLAR NOTES (1929)
FEDERAL RESERVE BANK NOTES

(Small Size)
Face Design: Portrait of President Lincoln.
SERIES 1929, BROWN SEAL

BANK & CITY	SIGNATURES	A.B.P.	GOOD	V.FINE	UNC.	*UNC.
☐Boston	Jones-Woods	8.00	13.00	33.00	145.00	1850.00
☐New York	Jones-Woods	8.00	13.00	32.00	115.00	1550.00
☐Philadelphia	Jones-Woods	8.00	13.00	33.00	145.00	1850.00
☐Cleveland	Jones-Woods	8.00	13.00	33.00	135.00	1750.00
☐Atlanta	Jones-Woods	8.00	13.00	31.00	260.00	2050.00
☐Chicago	Jones-Woods	8.00	13.00	31.00	105.00	1500.00
☐St. Louis	Jones-Woods	8.00	13.00	211.00	955.00	3050.00
☐Minneapolis	Jones-Woods	8.00	13.00	71.00	310.00	2250.00
☐Kansas City	Jones-Woods	8.00	13.00	32.00	140.00	1800.00
☐Dallas	Jones-Woods	8.00	13.00	36.00	135.00	1750.00
☐San Francisco	Jones-Woods	140.00	230.00	825.00	3100.00	9950.00

TEN DOLLAR NOTES

TEN DOLLAR NOTES (1861) DEMAND NOTES
(NO TREASURY SEAL)

(Large Size)

Face Design: Portrait of President Lincoln left, female figure with sword and shield.

Back Design: Ornate designs of TEN.

PAYABLE AT	A.B.P.	GOOD	V. GOOD	FINE
☐Boston (I)	1000.00	1700.00	8000.00	RARE
☐New York (I)	1000.00	1700.00	8000.00	RARE
☐Philadelphia (I)	1000.00	1700.00	8000.00	RARE
☐Cincinnati (I)	740.00	2600.00	RARE	RARE
☐St. Louis (I)	1540.00	2600.00	RARE	RARE
☐Boston (II)	565.00	950.00	1400.00	3000.00
☐New York (II)	540.00	900.00	1400.00	3000.00
☐Philadelphia (II)	540.00	900.00	1400.00	3000.00
☐Cincinnati (II)	4200.00	7800.00	18,000.00	RARE
☐St. Louis (II)	4500.00	8200.00	25,000.00	RARE

TEN DOLLAR NOTES (1862–1863)
UNITED STATES NOTES
(ALSO KNOWN AS LEGAL TENDER NOTES)
(Large Size)

Back Design
Face Design: Similar to 1861 note.

SERIES	SIGNATURES	SEAL	A.B.P.	GOOD	V.FINE	UNC.
☐1862	Chittenden-Spinner*	Red	200.00	275.00	1200.00	5000.00
☐1862	Chittenden-Spinner**	Red	200.00	275.00	1200.00	5000.00
☐1863	Chittenden-Spinner**	Red	200.00	275.00	1200.00	5000.00

* First Obligation: Similar to 1875–1907 $5 note.
** Second Obligation: Shown above.

TEN DOLLAR NOTES (1869) UNITED STATES NOTES
(Large Size)

Face Design: Portrait of Daniel Webster left, presentation of Indian princess right. (This note is nicknamed "Jackass Note," because the EAGLE between the signatures resembles a donkey when it is held upside down.)

SERIES	SIGNATURES	SEAL	A.B.P.	GOOD	V.FINE	UNC.
☐1869	Allison-Spinner	Red	120.00	175.00	825.00	3300.00

TEN DOLLAR NOTES (1875–1880)
UNITED STATES NOTES
(Large Size)

Face Design: Similar to 1869 note.

Back Design: Revised.

SERIES	SIGNATURES	SEAL	A.B.P.	GOOD	V.FINE	UNC.
☐1875	Allison-New	Red	150.00	200.00	800.00	2950.00
☐Same as above, Series A		Red	150.00	200.00	1100.00	3000.00
☐1878	Allison-Gilfillan	Red	150.00	200.00	1100.00	2500.00
☐1880	Scofield-Gilfillan	Brown	150.00	200.00	850.00	1750.00
☐1880	Bruce-Gilfillan	Brown	150.00	140.00	650.00	1600.00
☐1880	Bruce-Wyman	Brown	150.00	140.00	650.00	1600.00
☐1880	Bruce-Wyman	Red Plain	100.00	140.00	700.00	2000.00
☐1880	Rosecrans-Jordan	Red Plain	100.00	130.00	750.00	2050.00
☐1880	Rosecrans-Hyatt	Red Plain	100.00	130.00	750.00	2050.00
☐1880	Rosecrans-Hyatt	Red Spikes	100.00	130.00	750.00	2050.00
☐1880	Rosecrans-Huston	Red Spikes	100.00	130.00	700.00	2050.00
☐1880	Rosecrans-Huston	Brown	150.00	200.00	900.00	2550.00
☐1880	Rosecrans-Nebeker	Brown	650.00	1000.00	4000.00	7550.00
☐1880	Rosecrans-Nebeker	Red	100.00	150.00	550.00	1500.00
☐1880	Tillman-Morgan	Red	100.00	150.00	550.00	1500.00

SERIES SIGNATURES	SEAL	A.B.P.	GOOD	V.FINE	UNC.
☐1880 Bruce-Roberts	Red	100.00	150.00	550.00	1500.00
☐1880 Lyons-Roberts	Red	100.00	150.00	550.00	1500.00

TEN DOLLAR NOTES (1901) UNITED STATES NOTES
(Large Size)

Face Design: American bison (buffalo) center, portrait of
Lewis left, portrait of Clark right.

Back Design: Female allegorical figure in arch.

SERIES	SIGNATURES	SEAL	A.B.P.	GOOD	V.FINE	UNC.
☐1901	Lyons-Roberts	Red	160.00	260.00	700.00	2600.00
☐1901	Lyons-Treat	Red	160.00	260.00	700.00	2600.00
☐1901	Vernon-Treat	Red	160.00	260.00	700.00	2600.00
☐1901	Vernon-McClung	Red	160.00	260.00	700.00	2600.00
☐1901	Napier-McClung	Red	160.00	260.00	700.00	2600.00
☐1901	Parker-Burke	Red	160.00	260.00	700.00	2600.00
☐1901	Teehee-Burke	Red	160.00	260.00	700.00	2600.00
☐1901	Elliott-White	Red	160.00	260.00	700.00	2600.00
☐1901	Speelman-White	Red	160.00	260.00	700.00	2600.00

TEN DOLLAR NOTES (1923) UNITED STATES NOTES
(Large Size)

Face Design: Portrait of President Jackson center, red seal left, red "X" to right.

Back Design

SERIES	SIGNATURES	SEAL	A.B.P.	GOOD	V.FINE	UNC.
☐1923	Speelman-White	Red	125.00	185.00	1200.00	3850.00

TEN DOLLAR NOTES (1863–1875)
NATIONAL BANK NOTES
FIRST CHARTER PERIOD (Large Size)

Face Design: Benjamin Franklin and kite left, name of bank and city center. Effigy of Liberty and eagle right.

Back Design: Border green, center black. DeSoto on horseback at Mississippi River.

SERIES	SIGNATURES	SEAL	A.B.P.	GOOD	V.FINE	UNC.
☐Original	Chittenden-Spinner	Red	125.00	175.00	725.00	2800.00
☐Original	Colby-Spinner	Red	125.00	175.00	725.00	2800.00
☐Original	Jeffries-Spinner	Red	385.00	525.00	1225.00	3300.00
☐Original	Allison-Spinner	Red	125.00	175.00	825.00	2900.00
☐1875	Allison-New	Red	125.00	175.00	825.00	2600.00
☐1875	Allison-Wyman	Red	125.00	175.00	850.00	2650.00
☐1875	Allison-Gilfillan	Red	125.00	175.00	800.00	2500.00
☐1875	Scofield-Gilfillan	Red	125.00	175.00	800.00	2500.00
☐1875	Bruce-Gilfillan	Red	125.00	175.00	825.00	2600.00
☐1875	Bruce-Wyman	Red	125.00	175.00	825.00	2600.00
☐1875	Rosecrans-Huston	Red	125.00	175.00	725.00	2600.00
☐1875	Rosecrans-Nebeker	Red	125.00	175.00	725.00	2600.00

TEN DOLLAR NOTES (1882) NATIONAL BANK NOTES
SECOND CHARTER PERIOD (Large Size)

First Issue (Brown seal and brown backs)
Face Design: Similar to 1863–1875 note.
Back Design: Similar to 1882 $5 note. Border in brown with green Charter Number.

SERIES	SIGNATURES	SEAL	A.B.P.	GOOD	V.FINE	UNC.
☐1882	Bruce-Gilfillan	Brown	45.00	75.00	335.00	1000.00
☐1882	Bruce-Wyman	Brown	45.00	75.00	335.00	1000.00
☐1882	Bruce-Jordan	Brown	45.00	75.00	335.00	1000.00
☐1882	Rosecrans-Jordan	Brown	45.00	75.00	335.00	1000.00
☐1882	Rosecrans-Hyatt	Brown	45.00	75.00	335.00	1000.00
☐1882	Rosecrans-Huston	Brown	45.00	75.00	335.00	1000.00
☐1882	Rosecrans-Nebeker	Brown	45.00	75.00	335.00	1000.00
☐1882	Rosecrans-Morgan	Brown	156.00	260.00	750.00	1200.00
☐1882	Tillman-Morgan	Brown	45.00	75.00	335.00	1000.00
☐1882	Tillman-Roberts	Brown	45.00	75.00	335.00	1000.00

SERIES	SIGNATURES	SEAL	A.B.P.	GOOD	V.FINE	UNC.
☐1882	Bruce-Roberts	Brown	46.00	75.00	335.00	1000.00
☐1882	Lyons-Roberts	Brown	46.00	75.00	335.00	1000.00
☐1882	Lyons-Treat	Brown	46.00	75.00	335.00	1000.00
☐1882	Vernon-Treat	Brown	46.00	75.00	335.00	1000.00

Second Issue (Blue seal, green back with date "1882–1908")
Face Design: Similar to 1863–1875 note.
Back Design: Similar to 1882 $5 Second Issue note.
(Large Size)

SERIES	SIGNATURES	SEAL	A.B.P.	GOOD	V.FINE	UNC.
☐1882	Rosecrans-Huston	Blue	46.00	80.00	290.00	825.00
☐1882	Rosecrans-Nebeker	Blue	46.00	80.00	290.00	825.00
☐1882	Rosecrans-Morgan	Blue	110.00	205.00	505.00	1175.00
☐1882	Tillman-Morgan	Blue	46.00	80.00	290.00	1175.00
☐1882	Tillman-Roberts	Blue	46.00	80.00	290.00	1175.00
☐1882	Bruce-Roberts	Blue	46.00	80.00	290.00	1175.00
☐1882	Lyons-Roberts	Blue	46.00	80.00	290.00	1175.00
☐1882	Vernon-Treat	Blue	46.00	80.00	290.00	1175.00
☐1882	Vernon-McClung	Blue	46.00	80.00	290.00	1175.00
☐1882	Napier-McClung	Blue	46.00	80.00	290.00	1175.00

TEN DOLLAR NOTES (1882) NATIONAL BANK NOTES
(Large Size)

Third Issue (Blue seal, green back with value in block letters)
Face Design: Similar to previous notes. (*see* 1863–1875 note).
Back Design: Similar to 1882 $500 Third Issue note.

SERIES	SIGNATURES	SEAL	A.B.P.	GOOD	V. FINE	UNC.
☐1882	Tillman-Roberts	Blue	50.00	125.00	450.00	2100.00
☐1882	Lyons-Roberts	Blue	50.00	125.00	450.00	2100.00
☐1882	Vernon-Treat	Blue	50.00	125.00	450.00	2100.00
☐1882	Napier-McClung	Blue	50.00	125.00	450.00	1900.00

These notes may exist with other signatures, but are very rare.

TEN DOLLAR NOTES (1902) NATIONAL BANK NOTES
THIRD CHARTER PERIOD (Large Size)

First Issue (Red seal and red Charter Numbers)
Face Design: Portrait of President McKinley left, name of
bank and city in center.

SERIES	SIGNATURES	SEAL	A.B.P.	GOOD	V.FINE	UNC.
☐1902	Lyons-Roberts	Red	65.00	110.00	315.00	1600.00
☐1902	Lyons-Treat	Red	65.00	110.00	315.00	1600.00
☐1902	Vernon-Treat	Red	65.00	110.00	315.00	1600.00

TEN DOLLAR NOTES (1902) NATIONAL BANK NOTES
THIRD CHARTER PERIOD (Large Size)

Second Issue (Blue seal and numbers, "1902–1908" on the
back)
Back Design: Same as 1882 Second Issue note. Date
1902–1908.
Face Design: Same as 1882 Third Issue note.

SERIES	SIGNATURES	SEAL	A.B.P.	GOOD	V.FINE	UNC.
☐1902	Lyons-Roberts	Blue	20.00	30.00	90.00	420.00
☐1902	Lyons-Treat	Blue	20.00	30.00	90.00	420.00
☐1902	Vernon-Treat	Blue	20.00	30.00	90.00	420.00
☐1902	Vernon-McClung	Blue	20.00	30.00	90.00	420.00

SERIES	SIGNATURES	SEAL	A.B.P.	GOOD	V.FINE	UNC.
☐1902	Napier-McClung	Blue	20.00	30.00	90.00	410.00

SERIES	SIGNATURES	SEAL	A.B.P.	GOOD	V.FINE	UNC.
☐1902	Napier-Thompson	Blue	25.00	40.00	155.00	760.00
☐1902	Napier-Burke	Blue	20.00	30.00	90.00	410.00
☐1902	Parker-Burke	Blue	20.00	30.00	90.00	410.00
☐1902	Teehee-Burke	Blue	20.00	30.00	90.00	410.00

Third Issue (Blue seal and numbers, without date on back.)

SERIES	SIGNATURES	SEAL	A.B.P.	GOOD	V.FINE	UNC.
☐1902	Lyons-Roberts	Blue	15.00	20.00	80.00	350.00
☐1902	Lyons-Treat	Blue	15.00	20.00	80.00	350.00
☐1902	Vernon-Treat	Blue	15.00	20.00	80.00	350.00
☐1902	Vernon-McClung	Blue	15.00	20.00	80.00	350.00
☐1902	Napier-McClung	Blue	15.00	20.00	80.00	350.00
☐1902	Napier-Thompson	Blue	15.00	24.00	90.00	660.00
☐1902	Napier-Burke	Blue	15.00	20.00	80.00	350.00
☐1902	Parker-Burke	Blue	15.00	20.00	80.00	350.00
☐1902	Teehee-Burke	Blue	15.00	20.00	80.00	350.00
☐1902	Elliott-Burke	Blue	15.00	20.00	80.00	350.00
☐1902	Elliott-White	Blue	15.00	20.00	80.00	350.00
☐1902	Speelman-White	Blue	15.00	20.00	80.00	350.00
☐1902	Woods-White	Blue	15.00	20.00	80.00	350.00
☐1902	Woods-Tate	Blue	15.00	20.00	80.00	350.00
☐1902	Jones-Woods	Blue	40.00	82.00	285.00	1110.00

TEN DOLLAR NOTES (1929) NATIONAL BANK NOTES (Small Size)

Face Design, Type I: Portrait of Hamilton center, name of bank left, brown seal right, Charter Number black.

Face Design, Type II: Charter Number added in brown.

Back Design: United States Treasury Building.

SERIES	SIGNATURES	SEAL	A.B.P.	GOOD	V.FINE	UNC.
☐1929, Type I Jones-Woods		Brown	12.00	16.00	32.00	110.00
☐1929, Type II Jones-Woods		Brown	12.00	16.00	32.00	115.00

TEN DOLLAR NOTES (1870-1875)
NATIONAL GOLD BANK NOTES
(Large Size)

Face Design: Similar to 1863–1875 First Charter Period note.

Back Design: State Seal left, gold coins center, American eagle right.

The following have signatures of Allison-Spinner and a red Treasury Seal.

DATE	BANK	CITY	A.B.P.	GOOD	V. GOOD
☐1870	First National Gold Bank	San Francisco	880.00	1600.00	3000.00
☐1872	National Gold Bank and Trust Co.	San Francisco	880.00	1600.00	3000.00
☐1872	National Gold Bank of D.O. Mills and Co.	Sacramento	950.00	1850.00	3300.00
☐1873	First National Gold Bank	Santa Barbara	1100.00	1950.00	3300.00
☐1873	First National Gold Bank	Stockton	1040.00	2150.00	3300.00
☐1874	Farmers Nat'l Gold Bank	San Jose	1040.00	2150.00	3300.00
☐1874	First National Gold Bank	Petaluma	1040.00	2150.00	6400.00
☐1875	First National Gold Bank	Oakland	1040.00	2150.00	7000.00

TEN DOLLAR NOTES (1880) SILVER CERTIFICATES
(Large Size)

Face Design: Portrait of Robert Morris left.

Back Design: Printed in black ink, SILVER in large letters.

SERIES	SIGNATURES	SEAL	A.B.P.	GOOD	V.FINE	UNC.
☐1880	Scofield-Gilfillan	Brown	300.00	450.00	1950.00	5500.00
☐1880	Bruce-Gilfillan	Brown	300.00	450.00	1950.00	5500.00
☐1880	Bruce-Wyman	Brown	300.00	450.00	2150.00	5500.00
☐1880	Bruce-Wyman	Red	350.00	500.00	3600.00	7500.00

TEN DOLLAR NOTES (1886) SILVER CERTIFICATES
(Large Size)

SERIES	SIGNATURES	SEAL	A.B.P.	GOOD	V.FINE	UNC.
☐1886	Rosencrans-Jordan	Sm. Red	255.00	430.00	2050.00	6800.00
☐1886	Rosecrans-Hyatt	Sm. Red	165.00	275.00	1550.00	5800.00
☐1886	Rosecrans-Hyatt	Lg. Red	155.00	275.00	1550.00	5800.00
☐1886	Rosecrans-Huston	Lg. Red	165.00	275.00	1550.00	5800.00
☐1886	Rosecrans-Huston	Lg. Brown	170.00	285.00	1550.00	5800.00
☐1886	Rosecrans-Nebeker	Lg. Brown	165.00	275.00	1550.00	5800.00
☐1886	Rosecrans-Nebeker	Sm. Red	305.00	455.00	2250.00	7300.00

TEN DOLLAR NOTES (1891–1908)
SILVER CERTIFICATES
(Large Size)

Face Design:
Same as 1886
note.
Back Design

SERIES	SIGNATURES	SEAL	A.B.P.	GOOD	V.FINE	UNC.
☐1891	Rosecrans-Nebeker	Red	95.00	175.00	785.00	2650.00
☐1891	Tillman-Morgan	Red	95.00	150.00	735.00	2550.00
☐1891	Bruce-Roberts	Red	95.00	175.00	785.00	2650.00
☐1891	Lyons-Roberts	Red	95.00	160.00	760.00	2600.00
☐1891	Vernon-Treat	Blue	95.00	160.00	760.00	2600.00
☐1891	Vernon-McClung	Blue	95.00	165.00	750.00	2615.00
☐1891	Parker-Burke	Blue	95.00	150.00	735.00	2550.00

TEN DOLLAR NOTES (1933) SILVER CERTIFICATES
(Small Size)

Face Design: Portrait of Alexander Hamilton center. Blue
seal to left, blue numbers.

Back Design: Green United States Treasury Building.

SERIES	SIGNATURES	SEAL	A.B.P.	GOOD	V.FINE	UNC.
☐1933	Julian-Woodin	Blue	1100.00	1500.00	4600.00	9500.00

TEN DOLLAR NOTES (1934) SILVER CERTIFICATES
(Small Size)

Face Design: Blue "10" to left of portrait, Treasury Seal is
now to right.
Back Design: Similar to 1933 issue.

TEN DOLLAR NOTES (1934) SILVER CERTIFICATES
(Small Size)

SERIES	SIGNATURES	SEAL	A.B.P.	GOOD	V.FINE	UNC.	★UNC.
☐1934	Julian-Morgenthau	Blue	13.00	16.00	27.00	100.00	1200.00
☐1934	Julian-Morgenthau	*Yellow	275.00	450.00	2600.00	12000.00	RARE
☐1934A	Julian-Morgenthau	Blue	13.00	17.00	27.00	155.00	975.00
☐1934A	Julian-Morgenthau	*Yellow	14.00	19.00	32.00	235.00	1300.00
☐1934B	Julian-Vinson	Blue	20.00	30.00	155.00	2100.00	8100.00
☐1934C	Julian-Snyder	Blue	13.00	16.00	28.00	95.00	375.00
☐1934D	Clark-Snyder	Blue	13.00	16.00	28.00	95.00	1075.00

* Silver Certificates with a yellow seal were a special issue for use in combat areas of North Africa and Europe during World War II.

TEN DOLLAR NOTES (1953) SILVER CERTIFICATES
(Small Size)

Face Design: Gray "10" to left of portrait. Treasury Seal is smaller.
Back Design: Back similar to previous note.

SERIES	SIGNATURES	SEAL	A.B.P.	GOOD	V.FINE	UNC.	★UNC.
☐1953	Priest-Humphrey	Blue	12.00	15.00	34.00	135.00	220.00
☐1953A	Priest-Anderson	Blue	12.00	18.00	37.00	275.00	260.00
☐1953B	Smith-Dillon	Blue	14.00	17.00	34.00	125.00	NONE

Regarding the 1953 note, there were 720,000 issued. This was the last issue of $10 Silver Certificates. These were not issued with IN GOD WE TRUST on the back. Production ended in 1962.

TEN DOLLAR (1879) REFUNDING CERTIFICATES

Face Design: Portrait of Benjamin Franklin.

Back Design: Large TEN, ornate cornucopia border.

SERIES	SIGNATURES	SEAL	A.B.P.	GOOD	V.FINE	UNC.
☐1879	Scofield-Gilfillan					
PAY TO ORDER		Red	500.00			VERY RARE
☐1879	Scofield-Gilfillan					
PAY TO BEARER		Red	450.00	800.00	2100.00	7700.00

TEN DOLLAR NOTES (1907) GOLD CERTIFICATES
(Large Size)

Face Design: Portrait of Hillegas center, yellow x left, yellow seal right, yellow numbers.

Back Design: The backs are a bright yellow color.

SERIES	SIGNATURES	SEAL	A.B.P.	GOOD	V.FINE	UNC.
☐1907	Vernon-Treat	Gold	37.00	55.00	155.00	925.00
☐1907	Vernon-McClung	Gold	37.00	55.00	155.00	850.00
☐1907	Napier-McClung	Gold	37.00	55.00	155.00	750.00
☐1907	Napier-Thompson	Gold	47.00	78.00	230.00	1250.00
☐1907	Parker-Burke	Gold	37.00	55.00	155.00	775.00
☐1907	Teehee-Burke	Gold	37.00	55.00	155.00	775.00
☐1922	Speelman-White	Gold	37.00	55.00	155.00	650.00

TEN DOLLAR NOTES (1928) GOLD CERTIFICATES
(Small Size)

Face Design: Portrait of Alexander Hamilton center, yellow seal to left, yellow numbers.

Back Design: Printed in green ink.

SERIES	SIGNATURES	SEAL	A.B.P.	GOOD	V.FINE	UNC.
☐1928	Woods-Mellon	Gold	18.00	25.00	70.00	450.00

TEN DOLLAR NOTES (1890) TREASURY OR COIN NOTES
(Large Size)

Face Design: Portrait of General Philip Sheridan.

Back Design:
Very ornate
large TEN.

SERIES	SIGNATURES	SEAL	A.B.P.	GOOD	V.FINE	UNC.
☐1890	Rosecrans-Huston	Lg. Brown	185.00	295.00	1450.00	4950.00
☐1890	Rosecrans-Nebeker	Lg. Brown	185.00	295.00	1450.00	4950.00
☐1890	Rosecrans-Nebeker	Sm. Red	185.00	295.00	1450.00	4950.00

TEN DOLLAR NOTES (1891) TREASURY OR COIN NOTES
(Large Size)

Face Design:
Same as 1890 note.
Back Design:
Ornate small
TEN.

SERIES	SIGNATURES	SEAL	A.B.P.	GOOD	V.FINE	UNC.
☐1891	Rosecrans-Nebeker	Sm. Red	110.00	165.00	850.00	3000.00
☐1891	Tillman-Morgan	Sm. Red	110.00	165.00	850.00	3000.00
☐1891	Bruce-Roberts	Sm. Red	110.00	165.00	850.00	3750.00

TEN DOLLAR NOTES (1914)
FEDERAL RESERVE NOTES
(Large Size)

Face Design: Portrait of President Jackson center, Federal Reserve Seal left, Treasury Seal right.

Back Design: Scenes of farming and industry.

The following have signatures of Burke-McAdoo, red seals and red serial numbers.

SERIES	BANK	SEAL	A.B.P.	GOOD	V.FINE	UNC.
☐1914	Boston	Red	27.00	40.00	190.00	975.00
☐1914	New York	Red	27.00	40.00	165.00	825.00
☐1914	Philadelphia	Red	27.00	38.00	170.00	845.00
☐1914	Cleveland	Red	27.00	38.00	190.00	975.00
☐1914	Richmond	Red	27.00	38.00	190.00	975.00
☐1914	Atlanta	Red	27.00	38.00	190.00	975.00
☐1914	Chicago	Red	27.00	38.00	165.00	825.00
☐1914	St. Louis	Red	27.00	38.00	170.00	835.00
☐1914	Minneapolis	Red	27.00	38.00	175.00	875.00
☐1914	Kansas City	Red	27.00	38.00	190.00	975.00
☐1914	Dallas	Red	27.00	38.00	170.00	845.00
☐1914	San Francisco	Red	27.00	38.00	190.00	975.00

TEN DOLLAR NOTES (1914)
FEDERAL RESERVE NOTES

(Large Size)

BANK	SIGNATURES	SEAL	A.B.P.	V.FINE	UNC.
☐ Boston	Burke-McAdoo	Blue	23.00	85.00	235.00
☐ Boston	Burke-Glass	Blue	23.00	185.00	360.00
☐ Boston	Burke-Huston	Blue	23.00	60.00	170.00
☐ Boston	White-Mellon	Blue	23.00	60.00	170.00
☐ New York	Burke-McAdoo	Blue	23.00	55.00	160.00
☐ New York	Burke-Glass	Blue	23.00	55.00	160.00
☐ New York	Burke-Huston	Blue	23.00	55.00	160.00
☐ New York	White-Mellon	Blue	23.00	55.00	160.00
☐ Philadelphia	Burke-McAdoo	Blue	23.00	85.00	235.00
☐ Philadelphia	Burke-Glass	Blue	23.00	85.00	235.00
☐ Philadelphia	Burke-Huston	Blue	23.00	60.00	170.00
☐ Philadelphia	White-Mellon	Blue	23.00	60.00	170.00
☐ Cleveland	Burke-McAdoo	Blue	23.00	75.00	210.00
☐ Cleveland	Burke-Glass	Blue	23.00	185.00	335.00
☐ Cleveland	Burke-Huston	Blue	23.00	55.00	160.00
☐ Cleveland	White-Mellon	Blue	23.00	55.00	160.00
☐ Richmond	Burke-McAdoo	Blue	23.00	100.00	260.00
☐ Richmond	Burke-Glass	Blue	23.00	100.00	270.00
☐ Richmond	Burke-Huston	Blue	23.00	60.00	170.00
☐ Richmond	White-Mellon	Blue	23.00	60.00	170.00
☐ Atlanta	Burke-McAdoo	Blue	23.00	100.00	270.00
☐ Atlanta	Burke-Glass	Blue	23.00	255.00	385.00
☐ Atlanta	Burke-Huston	Blue	23.00	85.00	235.00
☐ Atlanta	White-Mellon	Blue	23.00	60.00	170.00
☐ Chicago	Burke-McAdoo	Blue	23.00	55.00	160.00
☐ Chicago	Burke-Glass	Blue	22.00	55.00	160.00
☐ Chicago	Burke-Huston	Blue	22.00	55.00	160.00
☐ Chicago	White-Mellon	Blue	22.00	55.00	160.00
☐ St. Louis	Burke-McAdoo	Blue	23.00	57.00	165.00
☐ St. Louis	Burke-Glass	Blue	23.00	185.00	310.00
☐ St. Louis	Burke-Huston	Blue	23.00	55.00	160.00
☐ St. Louis	White-Mellon	Blue	23.00	55.00	160.00
☐ Minneapolis	Burke-McAdoo	Blue	23.00	85.00	235.00
☐ Minneapolis	Burke-Glass	Blue	23.00	57.00	165.00
☐ Minneapolis	Burke-Huston	Blue	23.00	57.00	165.00
☐ Minneapolis	White-Mellon	Blue	23.00	55.00	160.00
☐ Kansas City	Burke-McAdoo	Blue	23.00	57.00	165.00
☐ Kansas City	Burke-Glass	Blue	23.00	120.00	290.00

BANK	SIGNATURES	SEAL	A.B.P.	V.FINE	UNC.
☐ Kansas City	Burke-Huston	Blue	21.00	57.00	145.00
☐ Kansas City	White-Mellon	Blue	21.00	57.00	145.00
☐ Dallas	Burke-McAdoo	Blue	21.00	57.00	160.00
☐ Dallas	Burke-Glass	Blue	21.00	310.00	535.00
☐ Dallas	Burke-Huston	Blue	21.00	85.00	260.00
☐ Dallas	White-Mellon	Blue	21.00	100.00	285.00
☐ San Francisco	Burke-McAdoo	Blue	21.00	260.00	435.00
☐ San Francisco	Burke-Glass	Blue	21.00	210.00	360.00
☐ San Francisco	Burke-Huston	Blue	21.00	260.00	435.00
☐ San Francisco	White Mellon	Blue	21.00	57.00	160.00

TEN DOLLAR NOTES (1928–1928A)
FEDERAL RESERVE NOTES
(Small Size)

Face Design: Portrait of Alexander Hamilton center, black Federal Reserve Seal left, with number over green Treasury Seal to the right.

Back Design: United States Treasury Building.

SERIES OF 1928, SIGNATURES OF TATE-MELLON, GREEN SEAL

BANK	A.B.P.	V.FINE	UNC.	★UNC.	BANK	A.B.P.	V.FINE	UNC.	★UNC.
☐ Boston	13.00	23.00	120.00	900.00	☐ Chicago	16.00	25.00	120.00	925.00
☐ New York	13.00	23.00	105.00	900.00	☐ St. Louis	16.00	51.00	130.00	925.00
☐ Philadelphia	13.00	51.00	110.00	900.00	☐ Minneapolis	16.00	25.00	140.00	925.00
☐ Cleveland	13.00	23.00	110.00	900.00	☐ Kansas City	16.00	36.00	160.00	975.00

BANK	A.B.P.	V.FINE	UNC.	★UNC.	BANK	A.B.P.	V.FINE	UNC.	★UNC.
☐ Richmond	32.00	70.00	185.00	900.00	☐ Dallas	32.00	70.00	210.00	1300.00
☐ Atlanta	32.00	70.00	185.00	900.00	☐ San Francisco	37.00	40.00	135.00	1000.00

SERIES OF 1928A,
SIGNATURES OF WOODS-MELLON, GREEN SEAL

BANK	A.B.P.	V.FINE	UNC.	★UNC.	BANK	A.B.P.	V.FINE	UNC.	★UNC.
☐ Boston	55.00	85.00	200.00	525.00	☐ Chicago	50.00	100.00	215.00	535.00
☐ New York	55.00	85.00	200.00	525.00	☐ St. Louis	50.00	100.00	215.00	535.00
☐ Philadelphia	55.00	85.00	200.00	525.00	☐ Minneapolis	100.00	170.00	325.00	535.00
☐ Cleveland	55.00	85.00	200.00	525.00	☐ Kansas City	75.00	130.00	325.00	535.00
☐ Richmond	80.00	130.00	500.00	800.00	☐ Dallas	75.00	130.00	325.00	535.00
☐ Atlanta	55.00	85.00	200.00	525.00	☐ San Francisco	75.00	130.00	325.00	535.00

TEN DOLLAR NOTES (1928B-1928C)
FEDERAL RESERVE NOTES
(Small Size)

Face Design: Alexander Hamilton; black Federal Reserve Seal left, has letter instead of number.
Back Design: Same as 1928–1928A note.

SERIES OF 1928B,
SIGNATURES OF WOODS-MELLON, GREEN SEAL

BANK	A.B.P.	V.FINE	UNC.	★UNC.	BANK	A.B.P.	V.FINE	UNC.	★UNC.
☐ Boston	15.00	36.00	125.00	325.00	☐ Chicago	15.00	30.00	110.00	325.00
☐ New York	12.00	26.00	100.00	325.00	☐ St. Louis	15.00	30.00	110.00	325.00
☐ Philadelphia	15.00	36.00	125.00	325.00	☐ Minneapolis	25.00	50.00	150.00	325.00
☐ Cleveland	15.00	36.00	130.00	325.00	☐ Kansas City	15.00	30.00	105.00	325.00
☐ Richmond	20.00	40.00	135.00	325.00	☐ Dallas	25.00	50.00	160.00	325.00
☐ Atlanta	22.00	40.00	150.00	325.00	☐ San Francisco	22.00	45.00	150.00	325.00

SERIES OF 1928C,
SIGNATURES OF WOOD-MILLS, GREEN SEAL

BANK	A.B.P.	V.FINE	UNC.	★UNC.
☐New York	35.00	70.00	295.00	5000.00
☐Cleveland	75.00	150.00	500.00	5000.00
☐Richmond	250.00	1600.00	3500.00	8000.00
☐Chicago	40.00	80.00	300.00	5000.00

TEN DOLLAR NOTES (1934)
FEDERAL RESERVE NOTES

(Small Size)

SERIES OF 1934,
SIGNATURES OF JULIAN-MORGENTHAU, GREEN SEAL

BANK	A.B.P.	V.FINE	UNC.	★UNC.	BANK	A.B.P.	V.FINE	UNC.	★UNC.
☐ Boston	12.00	15.00	60.00	465.00	☐ Chicago	12.00	20.00	75.00	365.00
☐ New York	12.00	20.00	75.00	365.00	☐ St. Louis	12.00	20.00	80.00	465.00
☐ Philadelphia	12.00	20.00	80.00	465.00	☐ Minneapolis	12.00	20.00	85.00	465.00
☐ Cleveland	12.00	20.00	80.00	465.00	☐ Kansas City	12.00	20.00	80.00	365.00
☐ Richmond	12.00	20.00	80.00	465.00	☐ Dallas	12.00	20.00	80.00	465.00
☐ Atlanta	12.00	20.00	80.00	465.00	☐ San Francisco	12.00	20.00	80.00	465.00

The green Treasury Seal on this note is known in a light and dark color. The light seal is worth about 10–20 percent more in most cases. REDEEMABLE IN GOLD removed from obligation over Federal Reserve Seal.

TEN DOLLAR NOTES (1934)
FEDERAL RESERVE NOTES

(Small Size)

SERIES OF 1934A,
SIGNATURES OF JULIAN-MORGENTHAU, GREEN SEAL

BANK	A.B.P.	V.FINE	UNC.	★UNC.	BANK	A.B.P.	V.FINE	UNC.	★UNC.
☐ Boston	12.00	15.00	50.00	310.00	☐ Chicago	12.00	15.50	50.00	310.00
☐ New York	12.00	15.00	50.00	310.00	☐ St. Louis	12.00	15.50	50.00	310.00
☐ Philadelphia	12.00	15.00	50.00	310.00	☐ Minneapolis	12.00	15.50	70.00	310.00
☐ Cleveland	12.00	15.00	50.00	310.00	☐ Kansas City	12.00	15.50	57.00	310.00
☐ Richmond	12.00	15.00	50.00	310.00	☐ Dallas	12.00	15.50	57.00	360.00
☐ Atlanta	12.00	15.00	50.00	330.00	☐ San Francisco*	12.00	15.50	50.00	360.00

* San Francisco, 1934A, with brown seal and overprinted HAWAII on face and back. Special issue for use in combat areas during World War II. Value in V. FINE $35, value in UNC. $275. ★UNC $2500.00

SERIES OF 1934B,
SIGNATURES OF JULIAN-VINSON, GREEN SEAL

BANK	A.B.P.	V.FINE	UNC.	★UNC.	BANK	A.B.P.	V.FINE	UNC.	★UNC.
☐ Boston	12.00	20.00	47.00	315.00	☐ Chicago	12.00	20.00	47.00	280.00
☐ New York	12.00	20.00	47.00	255.00	☐ St. Louis	12.00	20.00	52.00	305.00
☐ Philadelphia	12.00	20.00	47.00	315.00	☐ Minneapolis	12.00	20.00	55.00	315.00
☐ Cleveland	12.00	20.00	80.00	330.00	☐ Kansas City	12.00	20.00	55.00	315.00
☐ Richmond	12.00	20.00	65.00	330.00	☐ Dallas	12.00	20.00	55.00	355.00
☐ Atlanta	12.00	20.00	50.00	330.00	☐ San Francisco	12.00	20.00	52.00	355.00

SERIES OF 1934C,
SIGNATURES OF JULIAN-SNYDER, GREEN SEAL

BANK	A.B.P.	V.FINE	UNC.	★UNC.	BANK	A.B.P.	V.FINE	UNC.	★UNC.
☐ Boston	12.00	20.00	47.00	310.00	☐ Chicago	12.00	20.00	47.00	285.00
☐ New York	12.00	20.00	47.00	260.00	☐ St. Louis	12.00	20.00	47.00	335.00
☐ Philadelphia	12.00	20.00	47.00	360.00	☐ Minneapolis	12.00	20.00	82.00	410.00
☐ Cleveland	12.00	20.00	47.00	335.00	☐ Kansas City	12.00	20.00	47.00	335.00
☐ Richmond	12.00	20.00	47.00	335.00	☐ Dallas	12.00	20.00	47.00	410.00
☐ Atlanta	12.00	20.00	47.00	335.00	☐ San Francisco	12.00	20.00	47.00	410.00

SERIES OF 1934D,
SIGNATURES OF CLARK-SNYDER, GREEN SEAL

BANK	A.B.P.	V.FINE	UNC.	★UNC.	BANK	A.B.P.	V.FINE	UNC.	★UNC.
☐ Boston	12.00	20.00	47.00	310.00	☐ Chicago	12.00	20.00	67.00	210.00
☐ New York	12.00	20.00	47.00	210.00	☐ St. Louis	12.00	20.00	67.00	385.00
☐ Philadelphia	12.00	20.00	47.00	260.00	☐ Minneapolis	12.00	20.00	67.00	310.00
☐ Cleveland	12.00	20.00	47.00	335.00	☐ Kansas City	12.00	20.00	67.00	310.00
☐ Richmond	12.00	20.00	47.00	335.00	☐ Dallas	12.00	20.00	67.00	310.00
☐ Atlanta	12.00	20.00	47.00	335.00	☐ San Francisco	12.00	20.00	47.00	310.00

TEN DOLLAR NOTES (1950)
FEDERAL RESERVE NOTES
SERIES OF 1950, SIGNATURES OF CLARK-SNYDER, GREEN SEAL

BANK	A.B.P.	V.FINE	UNC.	★UNC.	BANK	A.B.P.	V.FINE	UNC.	★UNC.
☐ Boston	—	30.00	75.00	165.00	☐ Chicago	—	30.00	65.00	165.00
☐ New York	—	30.00	65.00	165.00	☐ St. Louis	—	30.00	75.00	165.00
☐ Philadelphia	—	30.00	75.00	165.00	☐ Minneapolis	—	30.00	95.00	165.00
☐ Cleveland	—	30.00	65.00	165.00	☐ Kansas City	—	35.00	85.00	165.00
☐ Richmond	—	30.00	65.00	165.00	☐ Dallas	—	30.00	65.00	165.00
☐ Atlanta	—	30.00	65.00	165.00	☐ San Francisco	—	30.00	65.00	665.00

(Small Size)

SERIES OF 1950A, SIGNATURES OF PRIEST-HUMPHERY, GREEN SEAL

BANK	A.B.P.	V.FINE	UNC.	★UNC.	BANK	A.B.P.	V.FINE	UNC.	★UNC.
☐ Boston	14.00	28.00	50.00	165.00	☐ Chicago	14.00	28.00	50.00	165.00
☐ New York	14.00	28.00	50.00	165.00	☐ St. Louis	14.00	28.00	50.00	165.00
☐ Philadelphia	14.00	28.00	50.00	205.00	☐ Minneapolis	15.00	30.00	80.00	365.00
☐ Cleveland	14.00	28.00	50.00	165.00	☐ Kansas City	15.00	30.00	55.00	165.00
☐ Richmond	14.00	28.00	50.00	165.00	☐ Dallas	15.00	30.00	55.00	165.00
☐ Atlanta	14.00	28.00	50.00	165.00	☐ San Francisco	14.00	28.00	50.00	165.00

SERIES OF 1950B, SIGNATURES OF PRIEST-ANDERSON, GREEN SEAL

BANK	A.B.P.	V.FINE	UNC.	★UNC.	BANK	A.B.P.	V.FINE	UNC.	★UNC.
☐ Boston	12.00	25.00	45.00	65.00	☐ Chicago	12.00	25.00	45.00	65.00
☐ New York	12.00	25.00	45.00	80.00	☐ St. Louis	12.00	25.00	45.00	65.00
☐ Philadelphia	12.00	25.00	45.00	65.00	☐ Minneapolis	12.00	28.00	50.00	255.00
☐ Cleveland	12.00	25.00	45.00	65.00	☐ Kansas City	12.00	28.00	50.00	65.00
☐ Richmond	12.00	25.00	45.00	65.00	☐ Dallas	12.00	28.00	50.00	380.00
☐ Atlanta	12.00	25.00	45.00	65.00	☐ San Francisco	12.00	25.00	45.00	65.00

SERIES OF 1950C, SIGNATURES OF SMITH-DILLON, GREEN SEAL

BANK	A.B.P.	V.FINE	UNC.	★UNC.	BANK	A.B.P.	V.FINE	UNC.	★UNC.
☐ Boston	12.00	25.00	45.00	160.00	☐ Chicago	12.00	25.00	45.00	140.00
☐ New York	12.00	25.00	45.00	140.00	☐ St. Louis	12.00	25.00	45.00	160.00
☐ Philadelphia	12.00	25.00	45.00	160.00	☐ Minneapolis	15.00	30.00	75.00	160.00
☐ Cleveland	12.00	25.00	45.00	260.00	☐ Kansas City	15.00	30.00	55.00	160.00
☐ Richmond	12.00	25.00	45.00	160.00	☐ Dallas	15.00	30.00	75.00	260.00
☐ Atlanta	12.00	25.00	45.00	210.00	☐ San Francisco	12.00	25.00	45.00	260.00

SERIES OF 1950D, SIGNATURES OF GRANAHAN-DILLON, GREEN SEAL

BANK	A.B.P.	V.FINE	UNC.	★UNC.	BANK	A.B.P.	V.FINE	UNC.	★UNC.
☐ Boston	12.00	25.00	50.00	95.00	☐ Chicago	12.00	25.00	45.00	160.00
☐ New York	12.00	25.00	45.00	120.00	☐ St. Louis	12.00	25.00	45.00	210.00
☐ Philadelphia	12.00	25.00	55.00	150.00	☐ Minneapolis	15.00	30.00	60.00	210.00
☐ Cleveland	12.00	25.00	45.00	150.00	☐ Kansas City	15.00	30.00	60.00	210.00
☐ Richmond	12.00	25.00	50.00	180.00	☐ Dallas	15.00	30.00	65.00	210.00
☐ Atlanta	12.00	25.00	50.00	210.00	☐ San Francisco	12.00	25.00	45.00	170.00

SERIES OF 1950E, SIGNATURES OF GRANAHAN-FOWLER, GREEN SEAL

BANK	A.B.P.	V.FINE	UNC.	★UNC.	BANK	A.B.P.	V.FINE	UNC.	★UNC.
					☐ Chicago	14.00	28.00	50.00	130.00
☐ New York	14.00	28.00	50.00	140.00					
					☐ San Francisco	14.00	28.00	50.00	175.00

TEN DOLLAR NOTES (1963)
FEDERAL RESERVE NOTES
(IN GOD WE TRUST IS ADDED ON BACK)
SERIES OF 1963, SIGNATURES OF GRANAHAN-DILLON, GREEN SEAL

BANK	A.B.P.	V.FINE	UNC.	★UNC.	BANK	A.B.P.	V.FINE	UNC.	★UNC.
☐ Boston	—	12.00	27.00	55.00	☐ Chicago	—	12.00	27.00	55.00
☐ New York	—	12.00	27.00	55.00	☐ St. Louis	—	12.00	27.00	55.00
☐ Philadelphia	—	12.00	27.00	55.00	☐ Minneapolis	—	12.00	27.00	55.00
☐ Cleveland	—	12.00	27.00	55.00	☐ Kansas City	—	12.00	27.00	55.00
☐ Richmond	—	12.00	27.00	55.00	☐ Dallas	—	12.00	27.00	55.00
☐ Atlanta	—	12.00	27.00	55.00	☐ San Francisco	—	12.00	27.00	55.00

SERIES OF 1963A, SIGNATURES OF GRANAHAN-FOWLER, GREEN SEAL

BANK	A.B.P.	V.FINE	UNC.	★UNC.	BANK	A.B.P.	V.FINE	UNC.	★UNC.
☐ Boston	—	12.00	27.00	70.00	☐ Chicago	—	12.00	27.00	60.00
☐ New York	—	12.00	27.00	60.00	☐ St. Louis	—	12.00	27.00	70.00
☐ Philadelphia	—	12.00	27.00	70.00	☐ Minneapolis	—	12.00	27.00	85.00
☐ Cleveland	—	12.00	27.00	70.00	☐ Kansas City	—	12.00	27.00	85.00
☐ Richmond	—	12.00	27.00	70.00	☐ Dallas	—	12.00	27.00	85.00
☐ Atlanta	—	12.00	27.00	70.00	☐ San Francisco	—	12.00	27.00	90.00

TEN DOLLAR NOTES (1969)
FEDERAL RESERVE NOTES
(WORDING IN GREEN TREASURY SEAL IS CHANGED FROM LATIN TO ENGLISH)

SERIES OF 1969, SIGNATURES OF ELSTON-KENNEDY, GREEN SEAL

BANK	A.B.P.	V.FINE	UNC.	★UNC.	BANK	A.B.P.	V.FINE	UNC.	★UNC.
☐ Boston	—	12.00	25.00	40.00	☐ Chicago	—	12.00	25.00	40.00
☐ New York	—	12.00	25.00	40.00	☐ St. Louis	—	12.00	25.00	40.00
☐ Philadelphia	—	12.00	25.00	40.00	☐ Minneapolis	—	12.00	25.00	40.00
☐ Cleveland	—	12.00	25.00	40.00	☐ Kansas City	—	12.00	25.00	40.00
☐ Richmond	—	12.00	25.00	40.00	☐ Dallas	—	12.00	25.00	40.00
☐ Atlanta	—	12.00	25.00	40.00	☐ San Francisco	—	12.00	25.00	40.00

SERIES OF 1969A, SIGNATURES OF KABIS-CONNALLY, GREEN SEAL

BANK	A.B.P.	V.FINE	UNC.	★UNC.	BANK	A.B.P.	V.FINE	UNC.	★UNC.
☐ Boston	—	12.00	20.00	25.00	☐ Chicago	—	12.00	20.00	25.00
☐ New York	—	12.00	20.00	25.00	☐ St. Louis	—	12.00	20.00	25.00
☐ Philadelphia	—	12.00	20.00	25.00	☐ Minneapolis	—	15.00	35.00	25.00
☐ Cleveland	—	12.00	20.00	25.00	☐ Kansas City	—	12.00	25.00	25.00
☐ Richmond	—	12.00	20.00	25.00	☐ Dallas	—	12.00	25.00	25.00
☐ Atlanta	—	12.00	20.00	25.00	☐ San Francisco	—	12.00	25.00	25.00

SERIES OF 1969B, SIGNATURES OF BANUELOS-CONNALLY, GREEN SEAL

BANK	A.B.P.	V.FINE	UNC.	★UNC.	BANK	A.B.P.	V.FINE	UNC.	★UNC.
☐ Boston	—	18.00	45.00	40.00	☐ Chicago	—	12.00	25.00	40.00
☐ New York	—	18.00	45.00	40.00	☐ St. Louis	—	12.00	25.00	40.00
☐ Philadelphia	—	18.00	45.00	40.00	☐ Minneapolis	—	18.00	45.00	40.00
☐ Cleveland	—	18.00	45.00	40.00	☐ Kansas City	—	18.00	45.00	40.00
☐ Richmond	—	18.00	45.00	40.00	☐ Dallas	—	18.00	45.00	40.00
☐ Atlanta	—	18.00	45.00	40.00	☐ San Francisco	—	18.00	45.00	40.00

SERIES OF 1969C, SIGNATURES OF BANUELOS-SHULTZ, GREEN SEAL

BANK	A.B.P.	V.FINE	UNC.	★UNC.	BANK	A.B.P.	V.FINE	UNC.	★UNC.
☐ Boston	—	—	24.00	30.00	☐ Chicago	—	—	24.00	30.00
☐ New York	—	—	24.00	30.00	☐ St. Louis	—	—	24.00	30.00
☐ Philadelphia	—	—.	24.00	30.00	☐ Minneapolis	—	—	26.00	30.00
☐ Cleveland	—	—	24.00	30.00	☐ Kansas City	—	—	24.00	30.00
☐ Richmond	—	—	24.00	30.00	☐ Dallas	—	—	24.00	30.00
☐ Atlanta	—	—	24.00	30.00	☐ San Francisco	—	—	24.00	30.00

TEN DOLLAR NOTES (1974)
FEDERAL RESERVE NOTES
SERIES OF 1974, SIGNATURES OF NEFF-SIMON, GREEN SEAL

BANK	A.B.P.	V.FINE	UNC.	★UNC.	BANK	A.B.P.	V.FINE	UNC.	★UNC.
☐ Boston	—	—	22.00	30.00	☐ Chicago	—	—	22.00	30.00
☐ New York	—	—	22.00	30.00	☐ St. Louis	—	—	22.00	30.00
☐ Philadelphia	—	—	22.00	30.00	☐ Minneapolis	—	—	24.00	30.00
☐ Cleveland	—	—	22.00	30.00	☐ Kansas City	—	—	22.00	30.00
☐ Richmond	—	—	24.00	30.00	☐ Dallas	—	—	22.00	30.00
☐ Atlanta	—	—	24.00	30.00	☐ San Francisco	—	—	22.00	30.00

TEN DOLLAR NOTES (1977)
FEDERAL RESERVE NOTES
SERIES OF 1977, SIGNATURES OF MORTON-BLUMENTHAL, GREEN SEAL

BANK	A.B.P.	V.FINE	UNC.	★UNC.	BANK	A.B.P.	V.FINE	UNC.	★UNC.
☐ Boston	—	—	20.00	30.00	☐ Chicago	—	—	20.00	30.00
☐ New York	—	—	20.00	30.00	☐ St. Louis	—	—	20.00	30.00
☐ Philadelphia	—	—	20.00	30.00	☐ Minneapolis	—	—	22.00	30.00
☐ Cleveland	—	—	20.00	30.00	☐ Kansas City	—	—	22.00	30.00
☐ Richmond	—	—	20.00	30.00	☐ Dallas	—	—	22.00	30.00
☐ Atlanta	—	—	20.00	30.00	☐ San Francisco	—	—	20.00	30.00

TEN DOLLAR NOTES (1981)
FEDERAL RESERVE NOTES
SERIES OF 1981, SIGNATURES OF BUCHANAN-REGAN, GREEN SEAL
★Notes not issued for all banks

BANK	A.B.P.	V.FINE	UNC.	★UNC.	BANK	A.B.P.	V.FINE	UNC.	★UNC.
☐ Boston	—	—	18.00	55.00	☐ Chicago	—	—	18.00	55.00
☐ New York	—	—	18.00	55.00	☐ St. Louis	—	—	18.00	55.00
☐ Philadelphia	—	—	18.00	55.00	☐ Minneapolis	—	—	19.00	55.00
☐ Cleveland	—	—	18.00	55.00	☐ Kansas City	—	—	19.00	55.00
☐ Richmond	—	—	18.00	55.00	☐ Dallas	—	—	19.00	55.00
☐ Atlanta	—	—	18.00	55.00	☐ San Francisco	—	—	18.00	55.00

SERIES OF 1981A, SIGNATURES OF ORTEGA-REGAN, GREEN SEAL
★Notes not issued for all banks

BANK	A.B.P.	V.FINE	UNC.	★UNC.	BANK	A.B.P.	V.FINE	UNC.	★UNC.
☐ Boston	—	—	17.00	40.00	☐Chicago	—	—	17.00	40.00
☐ New York	—	—	17.00	40.00	☐St. Louis	—	—	17.00	40.00
☐ Philadelphia	—	—	17.00	40.00	☐Minneapolis	—	—	19.00	40.00
☐ Cleveland	—	—	17.00	40.00	☐Kansas City	—	—	19.00	40.00
☐ Richmond	—	—	18.00	40.00	☐Dallas	—	—	19.00	40.00
☐ Atlanta	—	—	18.00	40.00	☐San Francisco—	—		17.00	40.00

TEN DOLLAR NOTES (1985)
FEDERAL RESERVE NOTES
SERIES OF 1985, SIGNATURES OF ORTEGA-BAKER, GREEN SEAL
★Notes not issued for all banks

BANK	A.B.P.	V.FINE	UNC.	★UNC.	BANK	A.B.P.	V.FINE	UNC.	★UNC.
☐ Boston	—	—	17.00	23.00	☐Chicago	—	—	17.00	23.00
☐ New York	—	—	17.00	23.00	☐St. Louis	—	—	17.00	23.00
☐ Philadelphia	—	—	17.00	23.00	☐Minneapolis	—	—	18.00	23.00
☐ Cleveland	—	—	17.00	23.00	☐Kansas City	—	—	18.00	23.00
☐ Richmond	—	—	18.00	23.00	☐Dallas	—	—	17.00	23.00
☐ Atlanta	—	—	17.00	23.00	☐San Francisco—	—		17.00	23.00

TEN DOLLAR NOTES (1988)
FEDERAL RESERVE NOTES
SERIES OF 1988A, SIGNATURES OF VILLALPANDO-BRADY, GREEN SEAL
★Notes not issued for all banks

BANK	A.B.P.	V.FINE	UNC.	★UNC.	BANK	A.B.P.	V.FINE	UNC.	★UNC.
☐ Boston	—	—	17.00	25.00	☐ Chicago	—	—	17.00	25.00
☐ New York	—	—	17.00	25.00	☐ St. Louis	—	—	17.00	25.00
☐ Philadelphia	—	—	17.00	25.00	☐ Minneapolis	—	—	18.00	25.00
☐ Cleveland	—	—	17.00	25.00	☐ Kansas City	—	—	18.00	25.00
☐ Richmond	—	—	17.00	25.00	☐ Dallas	—	—	18.00	25.00
☐ Atlanta	—	—	17.00	25.00	☐ San Francisco—	—		17.00	25.00

TEN DOLLAR NOTES (1990)
FEDERAL RESERVE NOTES
SERIES OF 1990, SIGNATURES OF VILLALPANDO-BRADY, GREEN SEAL

★Notes not issued for all banks

BANK	A.B.P.	V.FINE	UNC.	★UNC.	BANK	A.B.P.	V.FINE	UNC.	★UNC.
☐ Boston	—	—	12.00	22.00	☐ Chicago	—	—	12.00	22.00
☐ New York	—	—	12.00	22.00	☐ St. Louis	—	—	12.00	22.00
☐ Philadelphia	—	—	12.00	22.00	☐ Minneapolis	—	—	12.00	22.00
☐ Cleveland	—	—	12.00	22.00	☐ Kansas City	—	—	12.00	22.00
☐ Richmond	—	—	12.00	22.00	☐ Dallas	—	—	12.00	22.00
☐ Atlanta	—	—	12.00	22.00	☐ San Francisco	—	—	12.00	22.00

TEN DOLLAR NOTES (1993)
FEDERAL RESERVE NOTES
SERIES OF 1993, SIGNATURES OF WITHROW-BENTSEN, GREEN SEAL

★Notes not issued for all banks

BANK	A.B.P.	V.FINE	UNC.	★UNC.	BANK	A.B.P.	V.FINE	UNC.	★UNC.
☐ Boston	—	—	12.00	22.00	☐ Chicago	—	—	12.00	22.00
☐ New York	—	—	12.00	22.00	☐ St. Louis	—	—	12.00	22.00
☐ Philadelphia	—	—	12.00	22.00					
☐ Cleveland	—	—	12.00	22.00	☐ Kansas City	—	—	12.00	22.00
☐ Atlanta	—	—	12.00	22.00	☐ San Francisco	—	—	12.00	22.00

TEN DOLLAR NOTES (1995)
FEDERAL RESERVE NOTES
SERIES OF 1995, SIGNATURES OF WITHROW-RUBIN, GREEN SEAL

★Notes not issued for all banks

BANK	A.B.P.	V.FINE	UNC.	★UNC.	BANK	A.B.P.	V.FINE	UNC.	★UNC.
☐ Boston	—	15.00	25.00	25.00	☐ Chicago	—	—	16.00	25.00
					☐ St. Louis	—	—	16.00	25.00
☐ Cleveland	—	15.00	25.00	25.00	☐ Kansas City	—	—	16.00	25.00
					☐ Dallas	—	—	16.00	25.00
☐ Atlanta	—	—	16.00	25.00	☐ San Francisco	—	—	16.00	25.00

TEN DOLLAR NOTES (1915–1918)
FEDERAL RESERVE BANK NOTES
(Large Size)

Face Design: Portrait of President Jackson to left, bank and city in center, blue seal to the right.

Back Design: Similar to 1914 note.

BANK	SERIES	GOV'T SIGNATURES	BANK SIGNATURES	A.B.P.	GOOD	V.FINE	UNC.
☐New York	1918	Teehee-Burke	Hendricks-Strong				
				85.00	135.00	575.00	2600.00
☐Atlanta	1915	Teehee-Burke	Bell-Wellborn				
				220.00	435.00	1775.00	4300.00
☐Atlanta	1918	Elliott-Burke	Bell-Wellborn				
				85.00	135.00	575.00	2600.00
☐Chicago	1915	Teehee-Burke	McLallen-McDougal				
				85.00	135.00	575.00	2600.00
☐Chicago	1918	Teehee-Burke	McCloud-McDougal				
				85.00	135.00	575.00	2700.00
☐St. Louis	1918	Teehee-Burke	Attebery-Wells				
				85.00	135.00	575.00	2700.00
☐Kansas City	1915	Teehee-Burke	Anderson-Miller				
				85.00	135.00	575.00	2600.00

BANK	SERIES	GOV'T SIGNATURES	BANK SIGNATURES	A.B.P.	GOOD	V.FINE	UNC.
☐ Kansas City	1915	Teehee-Burke	Cross-Miller	85.00	145.00	550.00	2600.00
☐ Kansas City	1915	Teehee-Burke	Helm-Miller	220.00	385.00	1750.00	3700.00
☐ Dallas	1915	Teehee-Burke	Hoopes-Van Zandt	85.00	145.00	550.00	2700.00
☐ Dallas	1915	Teehee-Burke	Gilbert-Van Zandt	220.00	445.00	1775.00	4200.00
☐ Dallas	1918	Teehee-Burke	Talley-Van Zandt	120.00	245.00	1500.00	3300.00

TEN DOLLAR NOTES (1929)
FEDERAL RESERVE BANK NOTES

(Small Size)

Face Design: Portrait of Alexander Hamilton.

Back Design: Same as all Small Size $10 notes.
SIGNATURES OF JONES-WOODS, BROWN SEAL

BANK	SEAL	A.B.P.	GOOD	V.FINE	UNC.	★UNC.
☐ Boston	Brown	11.00	14.00	39.00	165.00	1700.00
☐ New York	Brown	11.00	14.00	31.00	125.00	1100.00
☐ Philadelphia	Brown	11.00	14.00	39.00	160.00	1350.00
☐ Cleveland	Brown	11.00	14.00	37.00	160.00	1350.00

BANK	SEAL	A.B.P.	GOOD	V.FINE	UNC.	★UNC.
☐Richmond	Brown	11.00	14.00	39.00	155.00	1700.00
☐Atlanta	Brown	11.00	14.00	39.00	135.00	1700.00
☐Chicago	Brown	11.00	14.00	39.00	145.00	1700.00
☐St. Louis	Brown	11.00	14.00	39.00	135.00	1200.00
☐Minneapolis	Brown	11.00	14.00	39.00	200.00	1600.00
☐Kansas City	Brown	11.00	14.00	25.00	155.00	850.00
☐Dallas	Brown	200.00	402.00	854.00	2010.00	3100.00
☐San Francisco	Brown	11.00	14.00	39.00	290.00	1350.00

TWENTY DOLLAR NOTES

TWENTY DOLLAR NOTES (1861) DEMAND NOTES
(Large Size)

Face Design: Liberty with sword and shield.

Back Design: Intricate design of numerals, "20." Demand
Notes have no Treasury Seal.

SERIES	PAYABLE AT	A.B.P.	GOOD	V.GOOD
☐1861	Boston (I)	RARE	RARE	RARE
☐1861	New York (I)	6000.00	9000.00	15,000.00
☐1861	Philadelphia (I)	6000.00	9000.00	15,000.00
☐1861	Cincinnati (I)	RARE	RARE	RARE
☐1861	St. Louis (I)	(Unknown in any collection)		
☐1861	Boston (II)	RARE	RARE	RARE
☐1861	New York (II)	6000.00	9000.00	15,000.00
☐1861	Philadelphia (II)	6000.00	9000.00	15,000.00
☐1861	Cincinnati (II)	RARE	RARE	RARE
☐1861	St. Louis (II)	(Unknown in any collection)		

Counterfeits exist. Use caution in buying.

TWENTY DOLLAR NOTES (1862–1863)
UNITED STATES NOTES
(ALSO KNOWN AS LEGAL TENDER NOTES)
(Large Size)

Face Design: Liberty with sword and shield.

Back Design: Second obligation. This note was also issued with first obligation on the back.

SERIES	SIGNATURES	SEAL	A.B.P.	GOOD	V.FINE	UNC.
☐1862	Chittenden-Spinner*	Red	400.00	600.00	2150.00	7200.00
☐1862	Chittenden-Spinner**	Red	400.00	600.00	2150.00	7200.00
☐1863	Chittenden-Spinner**	Red	400.00	600.00	2150.00	7200.00

* First Obligation: Similar to 1875–1907 $5 note.
** Second Obligation: Shown above.

TWENTY DOLLAR NOTES (1869)
UNITED STATES NOTES
(ALSO KNOWN AS LEGAL TENDER NOTES)
(Large Size)

SERIES	SIGNATURES	SEAL	A.B.P.	GOOD	V.FINE	UNC.
☐1869	Allison-Spinner	Red	350.00	500.00	2300.00	7500.00
Series Back Design: Revised						
☐1875	Allison-New	Red	215.00	350.00	1300.00	4200.00
☐1878	Allison-Gilfillan	Red	200.00	300.00	950.00	3000.00
☐1878	Watermark Paper		250.00	500.00	1850.00	4600.00
☐1880	Scofield-Gilfillan	Lg. Brown	95.00	175.00	1825.00	4050.00
☐1880	Bruce-Gilfillan	Lg. Brown	95.00	185.00	1625.00	3700.00
☐1880	Bruce-Wyman	Lg. Brown	95.00	175.00	850.00	2200.00
☐1880	Bruce-Wyman	Lg. Red	60.00	310.00	1725.00	4200.00
☐1880	Rosecrans-Jordan	Lg. Red	90.00	155.00	850.00	2200.00
☐1880	Rosecrans-Hyatt	Red Plain	90.00	155.00	875.00	2250.00
☐1880	Rosecrans-Hyatt	Red Spikes	90.00	155.00	775.00	2200.00
☐1880	Rosecrans-Huston	Lg. Red	90.00	155.00	775.00	2200.00
☐1880	Rosecrans-Huston	Lg. Brown	90.00	155.00	825.00	2300.00
☐1880	Rosecrans-Nebeker	Lg. Brown	90.00	155.00	1525.00	3600.00
☐1800	Rosecrans-Nebeker	Sm. Red	85.00	145.00	550.00	1500.00
☐1880	Tillman-Morgan	Sm. Red	85.00	145.00	550.00	1500.00
☐1880	Bruce-Roberts	Sm. Red	85.00	145.00	550.00	1500.00
☐1880	Lyons-Roberts	Sm. Red	85.00	145.00	650.00	1650.00
☐1880	Vernon-Treat	Sm. Red	85.00	145.00	700.00	1750.00
☐1880	Vernon-McClung	Sm. Red	85.00	145.00	650.00	1650.00
☐1880	Teehee-Burke	Sm. Red	85.00	140.00	625.00	1525.00
☐1880	Elliott-White	Sm. Red	75.00	90.00	550.00	1225.00

TWENTY DOLLAR NOTES (1863–1875)
NATIONAL BANK NOTES
FIRST CHARTER PERIOD (Large Size)

Face Design: Battle of Lexington left, name of bank in center. Columbia with flag right.

Back Design: Green border, black center picture of baptism of Pocahontas.

SERIES	SIGNATURES	SEAL	A.B.P.	GOOD	V.FINE	UNC.
☐ Original	Chittenden-Spinner	Red	225.00	375.00	1550.00	5100.00
☐ Original	Colby-Spinner	Red	225.00	375.00	1550.00	5000.00
☐ Original	Jeffries-Spinner	Red	225.00	625.00	2500.00	7300.00
☐ Original	Allison-Spinner	Red	225.00	375.00	1550.00	5050.00
☐ 1875	Allison-New	Red	225.00	375.00	1550.00	5050.00
☐ 1875	Allison-Wyman	Red	225.00	375.00	1550.00	5050.00
☐ 1875	Allison-Gilfillan	Red	225.00	375.00	1550.00	5050.00
☐ 1875	Scofield-Gilfillan	Red	225.00	375.00	1550.00	5050.00
☐ 1875	Bruce-Gilfillan	Red	225.00	375.00	1550.00	5050.00
☐ 1875	Bruce-Wyman	Red	225.00	375.00	1550.00	5550.00
☐ 1875	Rosecrans-Huston	Red	225.00	375.00	1550.00	5650.00
☐ 1875	Rosecrans-Nebeker	Red	225.00	475.00	1750.00	6050.00
☐ 1875	Tillman-Morgan	Red	225.00	475.00	1750.00	6050.00

TWENTY DOLLAR NOTES (1882)
NATIONAL BANK NOTES
SECOND CHARTER PERIOD (Large Size)

First Issue (Brown seal and brown backs.)
Face Design: Similar to First Charter Period note.
Back Design: Similar to 1882 $5 note. Border is brown, green Charter Number in center.

SERIES	SIGNATURES	SEAL	A.B.P.	GOOD	V.FINE	UNC.
☐1882	Bruce-Gilfillan	Brown	65.00	100.00	450.00	1250.00
☐1882	Bruce-Wyman	Brown	65.00	100.00	450.00	1250.00
☐1882	Bruce-Jordan	Brown	65.00	100.00	450.00	1250.00
☐1882	Rosecrans-Jordan	Brown	65.00	100.00	450.00	1250.00
☐1882	Rosecrans-Hyatt	Brown	65.00	100.00	450.00	1250.00
☐1882	Rosecrans-Huston	Brown	65.00	100.00	450.00	1250.00
☐1882	Rosecrans-Nebeker	Brown	65.00	100.00	450.00	1250.00
☐1882	Rosecrans-Morgan	Brown	135.00	290.00	820.00	2150.00
☐1882	Tillman-Morgan	Brown	65.00	100.00	450.00	1250.00
☐1882	Tillman-Roberts	Brown	65.00	100.00	450.00	1250.00
☐1882	Bruce-Roberts	Brown	65.00	100.00	450.00	1250.00
☐1882	Lyons-Roberts	Brown	65.00	100.00	450.00	1250.00
☐1882	Lyons-Treat	Brown	65.00	100.00	450.00	1250.00
☐1882	Vernon-Treat	Brown	65.00	100.00	450.00	1247.00

SECOND CHARTER PERIOD, Second Issue

Face Design: Similar to First Charter Period note.
Back Design: Similar to 1882 $5.00 Second Issue note.

SERIES	SIGNATURES	SEAL	A.B.P.	GOOD	V.FINE	UNC.
☐1882	Rosecrans-Huston	Blue	55.00	85.00	400.00	1050.00
☐1882	Rosecrans-Nebeker	Blue	55.00	85.00	400.00	1050.00
☐1882	Rosecrans-Morgan	Blue	120.00	300.00	900.00	1700.00
☐1882	Tillman-Morgan	Blue	55.00	85.00	400.00	1050.00
☐1882	Tillman-Roberts	Blue	55.00	85.00	400.00	1050.00
☐1882	Bruce-Roberts	Blue	55.00	85.00	400.00	1050.00
☐1882	Lyons-Roberts	Blue	55.00	85.00	400.00	1050.00
☐1882	Vernon-Treat	Blue	55.00	85.00	400.00	1050.00
☐1882	Napier-McClung	Blue	55.00	85.00	400.00	1050.00

SECOND CHARTER PERIOD, Third Issue. Large Size

Face Design: Similar to First Charter Period note with blue seal.
Back Design: Similar to 1882 Third Issue note, green back, value in block letters.

SERIES	SIGNATURES	SEAL	A.B.P.	GOOD	V.FINE	UNC.
☐1882	Tillman-Morgan	Blue	78.00	105.00	500.00	2100.00
☐1882	Lyons-Roberts	Blue	51.00	230.00	700.00	2425.00
☐1882	Lyons-Treat	Blue	88.00	130.00	500.00	2425 00
☐1882	Vernon-Treat	Blue	88.00	130.00	500.00	2100.00
☐1882	Napier-McClung	Blue	88.00	130.00	500.00	2100.00
☐1882	Teehee-Burke	Blue	88.00	130.00	600.00	2525.00

TWENTY DOLLAR NOTES (1902)
NATIONAL BANK NOTES
THIRD CHARTER PERIOD, First Issue (Large Size)

Face Design: Portrait of McCulloch left, name of bank center, Treasury Seal right.

SERIES	SIGNATURES	SEAL	A.B.P.	GOOD	V.FINE	UNC.
☐1902	Lyons-Roberts	Red	90.00	145.00	375.00	1300.00
☐1902	Lyons-Treat	Red	90.00	145.00	375.00	1300.00
☐1902	Vernon-Treat	Red	90.00	145.00	375.00	1300.00

Second Issue (Date "1902–1908" added on back, Treasury Seal and serial numbers blue)

SERIES	SIGNATURES	SEAL	A.B.P.	GOOD	V.FINE	UNC.
☐1902	Lyons-Roberts	Blue	25.00	35.00	90.00	425.00
☐1902	Lyons-Treat	Blue	25.00	35.00	90.00	425.00
☐1902	Vernon-Treat	Blue	25.00	35.00	90.00	425.00
☐1902	Vernon-McClung	Blue	25.00	35.00	90.00	425.00
☐1902	Napier-McClung	Blue	25.00	35.00	90.00	425.00
☐1902	Napier-Thompson	Blue	25.00	39.00	100.00	640.00
☐1902	Napier-Burke	Blue	25.00	35.00	90.00	425.00
☐1902	Parker-Burke	Blue	25.00	35.00	90.00	425.00

Third Issue (Date "1902–1908" removed from back, seal and serial numbers blue)

SERIES	SIGNATURES	SEAL	A.B.P.	GOOD	V.FINE	UNC.
☐1902	Lyons-Roberts	Blue	25.00	34.00	87.00	380.00
☐1902	Lyons-Treat	Blue	25.00	34.00	87.00	380.00
☐1902	Vernon-Treat	Blue	25.00	34.00	87.00	380.00
☐1902	Vernon-McClung	Blue	25.00	34.00	87.00	380.00

SERIES	SIGNATURES	SEAL	A.B.P.	GOOD	V.FINE	UNC.
☐1902	Napier-McClung	Blue	25.00	35.00	87.00	385.00
☐1902	Napier-Thompson	Blue	25.00	53.00	92.00	385.00
☐1902	Napier-Burke	Blue	25.00	35.00	87.00	385.00
☐1902	Parker-Burke	Blue	25.00	35.00	87.00	385.00
☐1902	Teehee-Burke	Blue	25.00	35.00	87.00	385.00
☐1902	Elliott-Burke	Blue	25.00	35.00	87.00	385.00
☐1902	Elliott-White	Blue	25.00	35.00	87.00	385.00
☐1902	Speelman-White	Blue	25.00	35.00	87.00	385.00
☐1902	Woods-White	Blue	25.00	35.00	87.00	385.00
☐1902	Woods-Tate	Blue	25.00	45.00	167.00	525.00
☐1902	Jones-Woods	Blue	32.00	603.00	1107.00	5225.00

TWENTY DOLLAR NOTES (1929)
NATIONAL BANK NOTES

(Small Size)

Face Design, Type I: Portrait of President Jackson in center, name of bank to left, brown seal right. Charter number in black.

Face Design, Type II.

Back Design: The White House, similar to all $20 Small Notes.

SERIES	SIGNATURES	SEAL	A.B.P.	GOOD	V.FINE	UNC.
☐1929, Type I	Jones-Woods	Brown	20.00	25.00	42.00	140.00
☐1929, Type II	Jones-Woods	Brown	20.00	25.00	44.00	155.00

TWENTY DOLLAR NOTES (1880)
SILVER CERTIFICATES

(Large Size)

Face Design: Portrait of Stephen Decatur right. TWENTY SILVER DOLLARS in center.

Back Design: SILVER in large block letters.

SERIES	SIGNATURES	SEAL	A.B.P.	GOOD	V.FINE	UNC.
☐1880	Scofield-Gilfillan	Brown	650.00	950.00	4700.00	20000.00
☐1880	Bruce-Gilfillan	Brown	650.00	950.00	4700.00	20000.00
☐1880	Bruce-Wyman	Brown	650.00	950.00	4700.00	20000.00
☐1880	Bruce-Wyman	Sm. Red	850.00	1650.00	5900.00	22500.00

This note was also issued in the Series of 1878. They are very rare.

TWENTY DOLLAR NOTES (1886)
SILVER CERTIFICATES

(Large Size)

Face Design: Portrait of Daniel Manning center, Agriculture left, Industry right.

Back Design: Double-diamond design center.

SERIES	SIGNATURES	SEAL	A.B.P.	GOOD	V.FINE	UNC.
☐1886	Rosecrans-Hyatt	Lg. Red	750.00	1200.00	4600.00	22000.00
☐1886	Rosecrans-Huston	Lg. Brown	750.00	1200.00	4600.00	22000.00
☐1886	Rosecrans-Nebeker	Lg. Brown	750.00	1200.00	4600.00	22000.00
☐1886	Rosecrans-Nebeker	Sm. Red	750.00	1200.00	5350.00	22000.00

TWENTY DOLLAR NOTES (1891)
SILVER CERTIFICATES
(NOT ISSUED IN SMALL SIZE NOTES)
(Large Size)

Face Design: Same as 1886 note.

Back Design: Revised.

SERIES	SIGNATURES	SEAL	A.B.P.	GOOD	V.FINE	UNC.
☐1891	Rosecrans-Nebeker	Red	140.00	190.00	1575.00	4550.00
☐1891	Tillman-Morgan	Red	140.00	190.00	1575.00	4550.00
☐1891	Bruce-Roberts	Red	140.00	190.00	1575.00	4550.00
☐1891	Lyons-Roberts	Red	140.00	190.00	1575.00	4550.00
☐1891	Parker-Burke	Blue	140.00	190.00	1575.00	4550.00
☐1891	Teehee-Burke	Blue	140.00	190.00	1575.00	4550.00

TWENTY DOLLAR NOTES (1882) GOLD CERTIFICATES
(Large Size)

Face Design: Portrait of President Garfield right, TWENTY DOLLARS IN GOLD COIN center.

Back Design: Large "20" left, eagle and arrows center, bright orange color.

SERIES	SIGNATURES	SEAL	A.B.P.	GOOD	V.FINE	UNC.
☐1882*	Bruce-Gilfillan	Brown	3200.00	5000.00	18,000.00	26,500.00
☐1882	Bruce-Gilfillan	Brown	2500.00	4000.00	11500.00	18,500.00
☐1882	Bruce-Wyman	Brown	1200.00	1800.00	10000.00	16000.00
☐1882	Rosecrans-Huston	Brown	1500.00	2450.00	10500.00	17000.00
☐1882	Lyons-Roberts	Red	105.00	165.00	1100.00	4500.00

*This note has a countersigned signature.

TWENTY DOLLAR NOTES (1905) GOLD CERTIFICATES
(Large Size)

Face Design: Portrait of President Washington center, "XX"
left, Treasury Seal right.

Back Design: Eagle and shield center, printed in bright
orange color.

SERIES	SIGNATURES	SEAL	A.B.P.	GOOD	V.FINE	UNC.
☐1905	Lyons-Roberts	Red	210.00	300.00	1930.00	8700.00
☐1905	Lyons-Treat	Red	210.00	300.00	1930.00	8700.00
☐1906	Vernon-Treat	Gold	65.00	100.00	350.00	1100.00
☐1906	Vernon-McClung	Gold	65.00	100.00	350.00	1100.00
☐1906	Napier-McClung	Gold	65.00	100.00	350.00	1100.00
☐1906	Napier-Thompson	Gold	80.00	125.00	600.00	1750.00
☐1906	Parker-Burke	Gold	65.00	100.00	350.00	1100.00
☐1906	Tehee-Burke	Gold	65.00	100.00	350.00	1100.00
☐1922	Speelman-White	Gold	65.00	100.00	350.00	1075.00

TWENTY DOLLAR NOTES (1928) GOLD CERTIFICATES
(Small Size)

Face Design: Portrait of President Jackson center, gold
seal left, gold serial numbers.

Back Design: The White House, printed green, similar to all
Small Size $20 Notes.

SERIES	SIGNATURES	SEAL	A.B.P.	V.FINE	UNC.
☐1928	Woods-Mellon	Gold	35.00	100.00	500.00

TWENTY DOLLAR NOTES (1890) TREASURY NOTES
(Large Size)

Face Design: Portrait of John Marshall, Supreme Court
Chief Justice, left, "20" center.

Back Design

SERIES	SIGNATURES	SEAL	A.B.P.	GOOD	V.FINE	UNC.
☐1890	Rosecrans-Huston	Brown	700.00	1000.00	5300.00	14,100.00
☐1890	Rosecrans-Nebeker	Brown	700.00	1000.00	5300.00	14,100.00
☐1890	Rosecrans-Nebeker	Red	700.00	1000.00	5300.00	14,100.00

(Large Size)

**Back
Design**

Face Design: Same as previous note.

SERIES	SIGNATURES	SEAL	A.B.P.	GOOD	V.FINE	UNC.
☐1891	Tillman-Morgan	Red	650.00	1000.00	5100.00	13,000.00
☐1891	Bruce-Roberts	Red	650.00	1000.00	5100.00	13,000.00

TWENTY DOLLAR NOTES (1914)
FEDERAL RESERVE NOTES

(Large Size)
Face Design: Portrait of President Cleveland center,
Federal Reserve Seal left, Treasury Seal right.

Back Design: Scenes of transportation. Locomotive left, steamship right.

(Small Size)

SERIES OF 1914, SIGNATURES OF BURKE-McADOO, RED TREASURY SEAL

BANK	A.B.P.	V.FINE	UNC.	BANK	A.B.P.	V.FINE	UNC.
☐ Boston	40.00	400.00	1500.00	☐ Chicago	40.00	400.00	1600.00
☐ New York	40.00	400.00	1500.00	☐ St. Louis	40.00	400.00	1600.00
☐ Philadelphia	40.00	400.00	1500.00	☐ Minneapolis	40.00	550.00	1800.00
☐ Cleveland	40.00	400.00	1500.00	☐ Kansas City	40.00	500.00	1750.00
☐ Richmond	40.00	550.00	1800.00	☐ Dallas	40.00	300.00	1500.00
☐ Atlanta	40.00	750.00	2000.00	☐ San Francisco	40.00	550.00	1800.00

SERIES OF 1914, BLUE TREASURY SEAL AND BLUE SERIAL NUMBERS

(Small Size)

This note was issued with signatures of Burke-McAdoo, Burke-Glass, Burke-Huston, and White-Mellon.

TWENTY DOLLAR NOTES (1914)
FEDERAL RESERVE NOTES
1914, BLUE TREASURY SEAL AND BLUE NUMBERS

DATE	CITY	SIGNATURES	SEAL	A.B.P.	GOOD	V.FINE	UNC.
1914	Boston	Burke-McAdoo	Blue	30.00	45.00	125.00	360.00
1914	Boston	Burke-Glass	Blue	34.00	50.00	175.00	410.00
1914	Boston	Burke-Huston	Blue	30.00	40.00	90.00	260.00
1914	Boston	White-Mellon	Blue	30.00	40.00	90.00	260.00
1914	New York	Burke-McAdoo	Blue	30.00	40.00	90.00	260.00
1914	New York	Burke-Glass	Blue	30.00	40.00	90.00	260.00
1914	New York	Burke-Huston	Blue	30.00	40.00	90.00	260.00
1914	New York	White-Mellon	Blue	30.00	40.00	90.00	260.00
1914	Phila.	Burke-McAdoo	Blue	30.00	42.00	105.00	310.00
1914	Phila.	Burke-Glass	Blue	31.00	45.00	165.00	435.00
1914	Phila.	Burke-Huston	Blue	30.00	40.00	90.00	260.00
1914	Phila.	White-Mellon	Blue	30.00	40.00	90.00	260.00
1914	Cleveland	Burke-McAdoo	Blue ˙	30.00	40.00	120.00	360.00

DATE	CITY	SIGNATURES	SEAL	A.B.P.	GOOD	V.FINE	UNC.
1914	Cleveland	Burke-Glass	Blue	30.00	45.00	165.00	435.00
1914	Cleveland	Burke-Huston	Blue	30.00	40.00	95.00	310.00
1914	Cleveland	White-Mellon	Blue	30.00	40.00	90.00	260.00
1914	Richmond	Burke-McAdoo	Blue	30.00	50.00	160.00	480.00
1914	Richmond	Burke-Glass	Blue	30.00	50.00	155.00	460.00
1914	Richmond	Burke-Huston	Blue	30.00	47.00	125.00	380.00
1914	Richmond	White-Mellon	Blue	30.00	45.00	120.00	350.00
1914	Atlanta	Burke-McAdoo	Blue	30.00	40.00	90.00	260.00
1914	Atlanta	Burke-Glass	Blue	84.00	165.00	1025.00	1560.00
1914	Atlanta	Burke-Huston	Blue	30.00	40.00	115.00	310.00
1914	Atlanta	White-Mellon	Blue	30.00	50.00	170.00	340.00
1914	Chicago	Burke-McAdoo	Blue	30.00	40.00	90.00	260.00
1914	Chicago	Burke-Glass	Blue	30.00	40.00	90.00	260.00
1914	Chicago	Burke-Huston	Blue	30.00	40.00	90.00	260.00
1914	Chicago	White-Mellon	Blue	30.00	40.00	90.00	260.00
1914	St. Louis	Burke-McAdoo	Blue	30.00	40.00	90.00	260.00
1914	St. Louis	Burke-Glass	Blue	30.00	50.00	165.00	435.00
1914	St. Louis	Burke-Huston	Blue	30.00	40.00	90.00	260.00
1914	St. Louis	White-Mellon	Blue	30.00	45.00	120.00	360.00
1914	Minneapolis	Burke-McAdoo	Blue	30.00	40.00	95.00	310.00
1914	Minneapolis	Burke-Glass	Blue	39.00	65.00	525.00	1175.00
1914	Minneapolis	Burke-Huston	Blue	30.00	40.00	95.00	310.00
1914	Minneapolis	White-Mellon	Blue	30.00	40.00	90.00	260.00
1914	Kansas City	Burke-McAdoo	Blue	30.00	40.00	125.00	370.00
1914	Kansas City	Burke-Glass	Blue	84.00	165.00	1025.00	1625.00
1914	Kansas City	Burke-Huston	Blue	30.00	40.00	95.00	310.00
1914	Kansas City	White-Mellon	Blue	34.00	50.00	170.00	435.00
1914	Dallas	Burke-McAdoo	Blue	30.00	40.00	95.00	310.00
1914	Dallas	Burke-Glass	Blue	30.00	50.00	175.00	510.00
1914	Dallas	Burke-Huston	Blue	30.00	40.00	100.00	320.00
1914	Dallas	White-Mellon	Blue	30.00	40.00	100.00	335.00
1914	San Fran.	Burke-McAdoo	Blue	30.00	40.00	105.00	335.00
1914	San Fran.	Burke-Glass	Blue	30.00	40.00	125.00	360.00
1914	San Fran.	Burke-Huston	Blue	30.00	40.00	120.00	345.00
1914	San Fran.	White-Mellon	Blue	30.00	40.00	90.00	360.00

TWENTY DOLLAR NOTES (1928)
FEDERAL RESERVE NOTES
(Small Size)

Face Design: Portrait of President Jackson center, black Federal Reserve Seal with numeral for district in center. City of issuing bank in Seal circle. Green Treasury Seal right.

Back Design: Picture of the White House, similar to all Small Size $20 Notes.
(Small Size)

SERIES OF 1928, SIGNATURES OF TATE-MELLON, GREEN SEAL

BANK	A.B.P.	V.FINE	UNC.	★UNC.	BANK	A.B.P.	V.FINE	UNC.	★UNC.
☐ Boston	31.00	54.00	145.00	1250.00	☐ Chicago	31.00	44.00	145.00	645.00
☐ New York	31.00	44.00	145.00	625.00	☐ St. Louis	31.00	54.00	145.00	1250.00
☐ Philadelphia	31.00	54.00	150.00	625.00	☐ Minneapolis	31.00	54.00	145.00	1250.00
☐ Cleveland	31.00	74.00	145.00	625.00	☐ Kansas City	31.00	64.00	190.00	625.00
☐ Richmond	31.00	74.00	150.00	2450.00	☐ Dallas	31.00	64.00	165.00	4550.00
☐ Atlanta	31.00	64.00	140.00	625.00	☐ San Francisco	31.00	54.00	145.00	650.00

(Small Size)

SERIES OF 1928A,
SIGNATURES OF WOODS-MELLON, GREEN SEAL

CITY	A.B.P.	V.FINE	UNC.	★UNC.	CITY	A.B.P.	V.FINE	UNC.	★UNC.
☐ Boston	33.00	62.00	165.00	1250.00	☐ Chicago	33.00	62.00	160.00	1250.00
☐ New York	33.00	62.00	165.00	1250.00	☐ St. Louis	33.00	72.00	180.00	1250.00
☐ Philadelphia	33.00	67.00	165.00	1250.00	☐ Minneapolis		NOT ISSUED		
☐ Cleveland	33.00	72.00	180.00	1250.00	☐ Kansas City	45.00	82.00	180.00	1250.00
☐ Richmond	25.00	52.00	165.00	1250.00	☐ Dallas	25.00	62.00	165.00	1250.00
☐ Atlanta	33.00	62.00	165.00	1250.00	☐ San Francisco		NOT ISSUED		

TWENTY DOLLAR NOTES (1928)
FEDERAL RESERVE NOTES

(Small Size)

SERIES OF 1928B,
SIGNATURES OF WOODS-MELLON, GREEN SEAL

The face and back design are similar to previous note. Numeral in Federal Reserve Seal is now changed to a letter.

BANK	A.B.P.	V.FINE	UNC.	★UNC.	BANK	A.B.P.	V.FINE	UNC.	★UNC.
☐ Boston	23.00	42.00	100.00	460.00	☐ Chicago	21.00	37.00	100.00	460.00
☐ New York	23.00	42.00	100.00	460.00	☐ St. Louis	21.00	52.00	135.00	460.00
☐ Philadelphia	23.00	42.00	100.00	460.00	☐ Minneapolis	21.00	52.00	135.00	460.00
☐ Cleveland	23.00	32.00	105.00	460.00	☐ Kansas City	21.00	37.00	125.00	460.00
☐ Richmond	23.00	37.00	105.00	460.00	☐ Dallas	21.00	67.00	215.00	460.00
☐ Atlanta	23.00	22.00	140.00	460.00	☐ San Francisco	21.00	37.00	140.00	460.00

SERIES OF 1928C, SIGNATURES OF WOODS-MILLS, GREEN SEAL

Only two banks issued this note.

BANK	A.B.P.	V.FINE	UNC.	★UNC.	BANK	A.B.P.	V.FINE	UNC.	★UNC.
☐ Chicago	76.00	275.00	1100.00	NONE	☐ San Francisco	75.00	324.00	1300.00	NONE

TWENTY DOLLAR NOTES (1934)
FEDERAL RESERVE NOTES

(Small Size)

SIGNATURES OF JULIAN-MORGENTHAU, GREEN SEAL

Face and back design are similar to previous note. "Redeemable in Gold" removed from obligation over Federal Reserve Seal.

BANK	GOOD	V.FINE	UNC.	★UNC.	BANK	GOOD	V.FINE	UNC.	★UNC.
☐ Boston	22.00	27.00	80.00	260.00	☐ St. Louis	22.00	27.00	80.00	260.00
☐ New York	22.00	27.00	80.00	260.00	☐ Minneapolis	22.00	27.00	115.00	260.00
☐ Philadelphia	22.00	27.00	80.00	260.00	☐ Kansas City	22.00	27.00	100.00	260.00
☐ Cleveland	22.00	27.00	80.00	260.00	☐ Dallas	22.00	27.00	105.00	260.00
☐ Richmond	22.00	27.00	85.00	260.00	☐ San Francisco	22.00	27.00	85.00	260.00
☐ Atlanta	22.00	27.00	85.00	260.00	☐ San Francisco*				
☐ Chicago	22.00	27.00	80.00	260.00	(HAWAII)	36.00	145.00	1200.00	2100.00

* The San Francisco Federal Reserve Note with brown seal and brown serial numbers, and overprinted HAWAII on face and back, was a special issue for the armed forces in the Pacific area during World War II.

TWENTY DOLLAR NOTES (1934A)
FEDERAL RESERVE NOTES

(Small Size)

SERIES OF 1934A, SIGNATURES OF JULIAN-MORGENTHAU

BANK	A.B.P.	V.FINE	UNC.	★UNC.	BANK	A.B.P.	V.FINE	UNC.	★UNC.
☐ Boston	22.00	30.00	55.00	350.00	☐ St. Louis	22.00	35.00	55.00	360.00
☐ New York	22.00	30.00	65.00	350.00	☐ Minneapolis	31.00	50.00	100.00	360.00
☐ Philadelphia	22.00	30.00	65.00	350.00	☐ Kansas City	22.00	37.00	65.00	360.00
☐ Cleveland	22.00	30.00	60.00	350.00	☐ Dallas	22.00	37.00	65.00	360.00
☐ Richmond	22.00	30.00	80.00	350.00	☐ San Francisco	22.00	32.00	65.00	360.00
☐ Atlanta	22.00	30.00	60.00	350.00	☐ San Francisco*				
☐ Chicago	22.00	30.00	75.00	350.00	(HAWAII)	28.00	53.00	985.00	2600.00

* The San Francisco Federal Reserve Note with brown seal and brown serial numbers, and overprinted HAWAII on face and back, was a special issue for the armed forces in the Pacific area during World War II.

(Small Size)

SERIES OF 1934B,
SIGNATURES OF JULIAN-VINSON, GREEN SEAL

BANK	A.B.P.	V.FINE	UNC.	★UNC.	BANK	A.B.P.	V.FINE	UNC.	★UNC.
☐ Boston	21.00	30.00	70.00	640.00	☐ Chicago	21.00	30.00	80.00	650.00
☐ New York	21.00	30.00	85.00	640.00	☐ St. Louis	21.00	30.00	75.00	650.00
☐ Philadelphia	21.00	30.00	75.00	640.00	☐ Minneapolis	21.00	30.00	80.00	650.00
☐ Cleveland	21.00	30.00	75.00	640.00	☐ Kansas City	21.00	30.00	80.00	650.00
☐ Richmond	21.00	30.00	85.00	640.00	☐ Dallas	21.00	30.00	80.00	650.00
☐ Atlanta	21.00	30.00	80.00	640.00	☐ San Francisco	21.00	30.00	75.00	650.00

SERIES OF 1934C,
SIGNATURES OF JULIAN-SNYDER, GREEN SEAL

Back Design: This has been modified with this series, balcony added to the White House.

BANK	A.B.P.	V.FINE	UNC.	★UNC.	BANK	A.B.P.	V.FINE	UNC.	★UNC.
☐ Boston	22.00	29.00	68.00	445.00	☐ Chicago	22.00	30.00	68.00	445.00
☐ New York	22.00	29.00	68.00	445.00	☐ St. Louis	22.00	30.00	68.00	445.00
☐ Philadelphia	22.00	29.00	68.00	445.00	☐ Minneapolis	22.00	30.00	68.00	445.00
☐ Cleveland	22.00	29.00	68.00	445.00	☐ Kansas City	22.00	30.00	68.00	445.00
☐ Richmond	22.00	29.00	68.00	445.00	☐ Dallas	22.00	30.00	68.00	445.00
☐ Atlanta	22.00	29.00	68.00	445.00	☐ San Francisco	22.00	30.00	68.00	445.00

SERIES OF 1934D,
SIGNATURES OF CLARK-SNYDER, GREEN SEAL

BANK	A.B.P.	V.FINE	UNC.	★UNC.	BANK	A.B.P.	V.FINE	UNC.	★UNC.
☐ Boston	22.00	28.00	53.00	410.00	☐ Chicago	22.00	30.00	58.00	410.00
☐ New York	22.00	28.00	58.00	410.00	☐ St. Louis	22.00	30.00	73.00	410.00
☐ Philadelphia	22.00	28.00	53.00	410.00	☐ Minneapolis	22.00	30.00	78.00	410.00
☐ Cleveland	22.00	28.00	53.00	410.00	☐ Kansas City	22.00	30.00	53.00	410.00
☐ Richmond	22.00	28.00	63.00	410.00	☐ Dallas	22.00	30.00	53.00	410.00
☐ Atlanta	22.00	28.00	63.00	410.00	☐ San Francisco	22.00	30.00	63.00	410.00

TWENTY DOLLAR NOTES (1950)
FEDERAL RESERVE NOTES

(Small Size)

SERIES OF 1950,
SIGNATURES OF CLARK-SNYDER, GREEN SEAL

The black Federal Seal and green Treasury Seal are slightly smaller.

BANK	A.B.P.	V.FINE	UNC.	★UNC.	BANK	A.B.P.	V.FINE	UNC.	★UNC.
☐ Boston	22.00	30.00	62.00	320.00	☐ Chicago	22.00	30.00	62.00	320.00
☐ New York	22.00	30.00	62.00	320.00	☐ St. Louis	22.00	30.00	62.00	320.00
☐ Philadelphia	22.00	30.00	62.00	320.00	☐ Minneapolis	22.00	30.00	62.00	320.00
☐ Cleveland	22.00	30.00	62.00	320.00	☐ Kansas City	22.00	30.00	62.00	320.00

BANK	A.B.P.	V.FINE	UNC.	★UNC.	BANK	A.B.P.	V.FINE	UNC.	★UNC.
☐ Richmond	22.00	30.00	62.00	310.00	☐ Dallas	26.00	30.00	62.00	310.00
☐ Atlanta	22.00	30.00	62.00	310.00	☐ San Francisco	26.00	30.00	62.00	310.00

SERIES OF 1950A, SIGNATURES OF PRIEST-HUMPHERY, GREEN SEAL

BANK	A.B.P.	V.FINE	UNC.	★UNC.	BANK	A.B.P.	V.FINE	UNC.	★UNC.
☐ Boston	21.00	25.00	57.00	285.00	☐ Chicago	21.00	25.00	57.00	285.00
☐ New York	21.00	25.00	57.00	285.00	☐ St. Louis	21.00	25.00	57.00	285.00
☐ Philadelphia	21.00	25.00	57.00	285.00	☐ Minneapolis	21.00	27.00	62.00	285.00
☐ Cleveland	21.00	25.00	62.00	285.00	☐ Kansas City	21.00	25.00	57.00	285.00
☐ Richmond	21.00	25.00	62.00	285.00	☐ Dallas	21.00	25.00	57.00	285.00
☐ Atlanta	21.00	25.00	62.00	285.00	☐ San Francisco	21.00	25.00	57.00	285.00

SERIES OF 1950B, SIGNATURES OF PRIEST-ANDERSON, GREEN SEAL

BANK	A.B.P.	V.FINE	UNC.	★UNC.	BANK	A.B.P.	V.FINE	UNC.	★UNC.
☐ Boston	21.00	25.00	57.00	155.00	☐ Chicago	21.00	25.00	57.00	155.00
☐ New York	21.00	25.00	57.00	155.00	☐ St. Louis	21.00	25.00	57.00	155.00
☐ Philadelphia	21.00	25.00	57.00	155.00	☐ Minneapolis	21.00	25.00	57.00	155.00
☐ Cleveland	21.00	25.00	57.00	155.00	☐ Kansas City	21.00	25.00	57.00	155.00
☐ Richmond	21.00	25.00	57.00	155.00	☐ Dallas	21.00	25.00	57.00	155.00
☐ Atlanta	21.00	25.00	57.00	155.00	☐ San Francisco	21.00	25.00	57.00	155.00

SERIES OF 1950C, SIGNATURES OF SMITH-DILLON, GREEN SEAL

BANK	A.B.P.	V.FINE	UNC.	★UNC.	BANK	A.B.P.	V.FINE	UNC.	★UNC.
☐ Boston	21.00	24.00	50.00	205.00	☐ Chicago	21.00	24.00	50.00	205.00
☐ New York	21.00	24.00	50.00	205.00	☐ St. Louis	21.00	24.00	50.00	205.00
☐ Philadelphia	21.00	24.00	50.00	205.00	☐ Minneapolis	21.00	24.00	50.00	205.00
☐ Cleveland	21.00	24.00	50.00	205.00	☐ Kansas City	21.00	24.00	50.00	205.00
☐ Richmond	21.00	24.00	50.00	205.00	☐ Dallas	21.00	24.00	50.00	205.00
☐ Atlanta	21.00	24.00	50.00	205.00	☐ San Francisco	21.00	24.00	50.00	205.00

SERIES OF 1950D, SIGNATURES OF GRANAHAN-DILLON, GREEN SEAL

BANK	A.B.P.	V.FINE	UNC.	★UNC.	BANK	A.B.P.	V.FINE	UNC.	★UNC.
☐ Boston	21.00	24.00	50.00	350.00	☐ Chicago	21.00	24.00	50.00	350.00
☐ New York	21.00	24.00	50.00	350.00	☐ St. Louis	21.00	24.00	50.00	350.00
☐ Philadelphia	21.00	24.00	50.00	350.00	☐ Minneapolis	21.00	24.00	50.00	350.00
☐ Cleveland	21.00	24.00	50.00	350.00	☐ Kansas City	21.00	24.00	50.00	350.00
☐ Richmond	21.00	24.00	50.00	350.00	☐ Dallas	21.00	24.00	50.00	350.00
☐ Atlanta	21.00	24.00	50.00	350.00	☐ San Francisco	21.00	24.00	50.00	350.00

SERIES OF 1950E, SIGNATURES OF GRANAHAN-FOWLER, GREEN SEAL

BANK	A.B.P.	V.FINE	UNC.	★UNC.	BANK	A.B.P.	V.FINE	UNC.	★UNC.
☐ Boston	21.00	25.00	50.00	180.00	☐ Chicago	21.00	25.00	50.00	180.00
☐ New York	21.00	25.00	50.00	180.00	☐ St. Louis	21.00	25.00	50.00	180.00
☐ Philadelphia	21.00	25.00	50.00	180.00	☐ Minneapolis	21.00	25.00	50.00	180.00
☐ Cleveland	21.00	25.00	50.00	180.00	☐ Kansas City	21.00	25.00	50.00	180.00
☐ Richmond	21.00	25.00	50.00	180.00	☐ Dallas	21.00	25.00	50.00	180.00
☐ Atlanta	21.00	25.00	50.00	180.00	☐ San Francisco	21.00	25.00	50.00	180.00

TWENTY DOLLAR NOTES (1963)
FEDERAL RESERVE NOTES
SERIES OF 1963, SIGNATURES OF GRANAHAN-FOWLER, GREEN SEAL

BANK	A.B.P.	V.FINE	UNC.	★UNC.	BANK	A.B.P.	V.FINE	UNC.	★UNC.
☐ Boston	21.00	25.00	50.00	67.00	☐ Chicago	21.00	25.00	50.00	67.00
☐ New York	21.00	25.00	50.00	67.00	☐ St. Louis	21.00	25.00	50.00	67.00
☐ Philadelphia	21.00	25.00	50.00	67.00	☐ Minneapolis	21.00	25.00	50.00	67.00
☐ Cleveland	21.00	25.00	55.00	67.00	☐ Kansas City	21.00	25.00	50.00	67.00
☐ Richmond	21.00	25.00	55.00	67.00	☐ Dallas	21.00	25.00	50.00	67.00
☐ Atlanta	21.00	25.00	55.00	67.00	☐ San Francisco	21.00	25.00	50.00	67.00

SERIES OF 1963A, SIGNATURES OF GRANAHAN-FOWLER, GREEN SEAL

BANK	A.B.P.	V.FINE	UNC.	★UNC.	BANK	A.B.P.	V.FINE	UNC.	★UNC.
☐ Boston	21.00	24.00	50.00	67.00	☐ Chicago	21.00	24.00	50.00	67.00
☐ New York	21.00	24.00	50.00	67.00	☐ St. Louis	21.00	24.00	50.00	67.00
☐ Philadelphia	21.00	24.00	50.00	67.00	☐ Minneapolis	21.00	24.00	50.00	67.00
☐ Cleveland	21.00	24.00	50.00	67.00	☐ Kansas City	21.00	24.00	50.00	67.00
☐ Richmond	21.00	24.00	50.00	67.00	☐ Dallas	21.00	24.00	50.00	67.00
☐ Atlanta	21.00	24.00	50.00	67.00	☐ San Francisco	21.00	24.00	50.00	67.00

TWENTY DOLLAR NOTES (1969)
FEDERAL RESERVE NOTES
SERIES OF 1969, SIGNATURES OF ELSTON-KENNEDY, GREEN SEAL

BANK	A.B.P.	V.FINE	UNC.	★UNC.	BANK	A.B.P.	V.FINE	UNC.	★UNC.
☐ Boston	—	23.00	45.00	67.00	☐ Chicago	—	23.00	45.00	67.00
☐ New York	—	23.00	45.00	67.00	☐ St. Louis	—	23.00	45.00	67.00
☐ Philadelphia	—	23.00	45.00	67.00	☐ Minneapolis	—	23.00	50.00	67.00
☐ Cleveland	—	23.00	45.00	67.00	☐ Kansas City	—	23.00	50.00	67.00
☐ Richmond	—	23.00	45.00	67.00	☐ Dallas	—	23.00	50.00	67.00
☐ Atlanta	—	23.00	45.00	67.00	☐ San Francisco	—	23.00	45.00	67.00

SERIES OF 1969A, SIGNATURES OF KABIS-CONNALLY, GREEN SEAL

BANK	A.B.P.	V.FINE	UNC.	★UNC.	BANK	A.B.P.	V.FINE	UNC.	★UNC.
☐ Boston	—	23.00	40.00	52.00	☐ Chicago	—	23.00	40.00	52.00
☐ New York	—	23.00	40.00	52.00	☐ St. Louis	—	23.00	40.00	52.00
☐ Philadelphia	—	23.00	40.00	52.00	☐ Minneapolis	—	23.00	40.00	52.00
☐ Cleveland	—	23.00	40.00	52.00	☐ Kansas City	—	23.00	40.00	52.00
☐ Richmond	—	23.00	40.00	52.00	☐ Dallas	—	23.00	40.00	52.00
☐ Atlanta	—	23.00	40.00	52.00	☐ San Francisco	—	23.00	40.00	52.00

SERIES OF 1969B, SIGNATURES OF BANUELOS-CONNALLY, GREEN SEAL

BANK	A.B.P.	V.FINE	UNC.	★UNC.	BANK	A.B.P.	V.FINE	UNC.	★UNC.
☐ Boston	—	23.00	40.00	77.00	☐ Chicago	—	23.00	40.00	77.00
☐ New York	—	23.00	40.00	77.00	☐ St. Louis	—	23.00	40.00	77.00
☐ Philadelphia	—	23.00	40.00	77.00	☐ Minneapolis	—	23.00	40.00	77.00
☐ Cleveland	—	23.00	40.00	77.00	☐ Kansas City	—	23.00	40.00	77.00
☐ Richmond	—	23.00	40.00	77.00	☐ Dallas	—	23.00	40.00	77.00
☐ Atlanta	—	23.00	40.00	77.00	☐ San Francisco	—	23.00	40.00	77.00

SERIES of 1969C, SIGNATURES OF BANUELOS-SHULTZ, GREEN SEAL

BANK	A.B.P.	V.FINE	UNC.	★UNC.	BANK	A.B.P.	V.FINE	UNC.	★UNC.
☐ Boston	—	23.00	40.00	50.00	☐ Chicago	—	23.00	40.00	50.00
☐ New York	—	23.00	40.00	50.00	☐ St. Louis	—	23.00	40.00	50.00
☐ Philadelphia	—	23.00	40.00	50.00	☐ Minneapolis	—	23.00	40.00	50.00
☐ Cleveland	—	23.00	40.00	50.00	☐ Kansas City	—	23.00	40.00	50.00
☐ Richmond	—	23.00	40.00	50.00	☐ Dallas	—	23.00	40.00	50.00
☐ Atlanta	—	23.00	40.00	50.00	☐ San Francisco	—	23.00	40.00	50.00

TWENTY DOLLAR NOTES (1974)
FEDERAL RESERVE NOTES
SERIES OF 1974, SIGNATURES OF NEFF-SIMON, GREEN SEAL

BANK	A.B.P.	V.FINE	UNC.	★UNC.	BANK	A.B.P.	V.FINE	UNC.	★UNC.
☐ Boston	—	23.00	40.00	50.00	☐ Chicago	—	23.00	40.00	50.00
☐ New York	—	23.00	40.00	50.00	☐ St. Louis	—	23.00	40.00	50.00
☐ Philadelphia	—	26.00	45.00	50.00	☐ Minneapolis	—	26.00	45.00	50.00
☐ Cleveland	—	26.00	45.00	50.00	☐ Kansas City	—	26.00	45.00	50.00
☐ Richmond	—	26.00	45.00	50.00	☐ Dallas	—	26.00	45.00	50.00
☐ Atlanta	—	23.00	40.00	50.00	☐ San Francisco	—	23.00	40.00	50.00

TWENTY DOLLAR NOTES (1977)
FEDERAL RESERVE NOTES
SERIES OF 1977, SIGNATURES OF MORTON-BLUMENTHAL, GREEN SEAL

BANK	A.B.P.	V.FINE	UNC.	★UNC.	BANK	A.B.P.	V.FINE	UNC.	★UNC.
☐ Boston	—	22.00	40.00	50.00	☐ Chicago	—	22.00	40.00	50.00
☐ New York	—	22.00	40.00	50.00	☐ St. Louis	—	22.00	40.00	50.00
☐ Philadelphia	—	22.00	40.00	50.00	☐ Minneapolis	—	25.00	45.00	50.00
☐ Cleveland	—	22.00	40.00	50.00	☐ Kansas City	—	25.00	45.00	50.00
☐ Richmond	—	25.00	45.00	50.00	☐ Dallas	—	25.00	45.00	50.00
☐ Atlanta	—	25.00	45.00	50.00	☐ San Francisco	—	22.00	40.00	50.00

TWENTY DOLLAR NOTES (1981)
FEDERAL RESERVE NOTES
SERIES OF 1981, SIGNATURES OF BUCHANAN-REGAN, GREEN SEAL

BANK	A.B.P.	V.FINE	UNC.	★UNC.	BANK	A.B.P.	V.FINE	UNC.	★UNC.
☐ Boston	—	19.00	38.00	45.00	☐ Chicago	—	19.00	38.00	45.00
☐ New York	—	19.00	38.00	45.00	☐ St. Louis	—	19.00	38.00	45.00
☐ Philadelphia	—	19.00	38.00	45.00	☐ Minneapolis	—	22.00	40.00	45.00
☐ Cleveland	—	19.00	38.00	45.00	☐ Kansas City	—	22.00	40.00	45.00
☐ Richmond	—	19.00	38.00	45.00	☐ Dallas	—	22.00	40.00	45.00
☐ Atlanta	—	19.00	38.00	45.00	☐ San Francisco	—	19.00	38.00	45.00

SERIES OF 1981A, SIGNATURES OF ORTEGA-REGAN, GREEN SEAL
★Notes not issued for all banks

BANK	A.B.P.	V.FINE	UNC.	★UNC.	BANK	A.B.P.	V.FINE	UNC.	★UNC.
☐ Boston	—	19.00	35.00	45.00	☐ Chicago	—	19.00	38.00	45.00
☐ New York	—	19.00	35.00	45.00	☐ St. Louis	—	19.00	38.00	45.00
☐ Philadelphia	—	19.00	35.00	45.00	☐ Minneapolis	—	22.00	40.00	45.00
☐ Cleveland	—	19.00	35.00	45.00	☐ Kansas City	—	22.00	40.00	45.00
☐ Richmond	—	19.00	35.00	45.00	☐ Dallas	—	22.00	40.00	45.00
☐ Atlanta	—	19.00	35.00	45.00	☐ San Francisco	—	19.00	38.00	45.00

TWENTY DOLLAR NOTES (1985)
FEDERAL RESERVE NOTES
SERIES OF 1985, SIGNATURES OF ORTEGA-BAKER, GREEN SEAL
★Notes not issued for all banks

BANK	A.B.P.	V.FINE	UNC.	★UNC.	BANK	A.B.P.	V.FINE	UNC.	★UNC.
☐ Boston	—	19.00	35.00	40.00	☐ Chicago	—	19.00	35.00	40.00
☐ New York	—	19.00	35.00	40.00	☐ St. Louis	—	19.00	35.00	40.00
☐ Philadelphia	—	19.00	35.00	40.00	☐ Minneapolis	—	19.00	38.00	40.00
☐ Cleveland	—	19.00	35.00	40.00	☐ Kansas City	—	19.00	38.00	40.00
☐ Richmond	—	19.00	35.00	40.00	☐ Dallas	—	19.00	38.00	40.00
☐ Atlanta	—	19.00	35.00	40.00	☐ San Francisco	—	19.00	35.00	40.00

TWENTY DOLLAR NOTES (1988)
FEDERAL RESERVE NOTES
SERIES OF 1988A, SIGNATURES OF VILLALPANDO-BRADY, GREEN SEAL

★Notes not issued for all banks

BANK	A.B.P.	V.FINE	UNC.	★UNC.	BANK	A.B.P.	V.FINE	UNC.	★UNC.
☐ Boston	—	21.00	25.00	42.00	☐ Chicago	—	21.00	25.00	42.00
☐ New York	—	21.00	25.00	42.00	☐ St. Louis	—	21.00	25.00	42.00
☐ Philadelphia	—	21.00	25.00	42.00	☐ Minneapolis	—	21.00	25.00	42.00
☐ Cleveland	—	21.00	25.00	42.00	☐ Kansas City	—	21.00	25.00	42.00
☐ Richmond	—	21.00	25.00	42.00	☐ Dallas	—	21.00	25.00	42.00
☐ Atlanta	—	21.00	25.00	42.00	☐ San Francisco	—	21.00	25.00	42.00

TWENTY DOLLAR NOTES (1990)
FEDERAL RESERVE NOTES
SERIES OF 1990, SIGNATURES OF VILLALPANDO-BRADY, GREEN SEAL

★Notes not issued for all banks

BANK	A.B.P.	V.FINE	UNC.	★UNC.	BANK	A.B.P.	V.FINE	UNC.	★UNC.
☐ Boston	—	21.00	25.00	42.00	☐ Chicago	—	21.00	25.00	42.00
☐ New York	—	21.00	25.00	42.00	☐ St. Louis	—	21.00	25.00	42.00
☐ Philadelphia	—	21.00	25.00	42.00	☐ Minneapolis	—	21.00	25.00	42.00
☐ Cleveland	—	21.00	25.00	42.00	☐ Kansas City	—	21.00	25.00	42.00
☐ Richmond	—	21.00	25.00	42.00	☐ Dallas	—	21.00	25.00	42.00
☐ Atlanta	—	21.00	25.00	42.00	☐ San Francisco	—	21.00	25.00	42.00

TWENTY DOLLAR NOTES (1993)
FEDERAL RESERVE NOTES
SERIES OF 1993, SIGNATURES OF WITHROW-BENTSEN, GREEN SEAL

★Notes are not issued for all banks

BANK	A.B.P.	V.FINE	UNC.	★UNC.	BANK	A.B.P.	V.FINE	UNC.	★UNC.
☐ Boston	—	21.00	25.00	42.00	☐ Chicago	—	21.00	25.00	42.00
☐ New York	—	21.00	25.00	42.00	☐ St. Louis	—	21.00	25.00	42.00
☐ Philadelphia	—	21.00	25.00	42.00	☐ Minneapolis	—	21.00	25.00	42.00
☐ Cleveland	—	21.00	25.00	42.00	☐ Kansas City	—	21.00	25.00	42.00
☐ Richmond	—	21.00	25.00	42.00	☐ Dallas	—	21.00	25.00	42.00
☐ Atlanta	—	21.00	25.00	42.00	☐ San Francisco	—	21.00	25.00	42.00

TWENTY DOLLAR NOTES (1995)
FEDERAL RESERVE NOTES
SERIES OF 1995, SIGNATURES OF WITHROW-RUBIN, GREEN SEAL
★Notes not issued for all banks

BANK	A.B.P.	V.FINE	UNC.	★UNC.	BANK	A.B.P.	V.FINE	UNC.	★UNC.
☐ Boston	—	22.00	34.00	42.00	☐ Chicago	—	22.00	34.00	42.00
☐ New York	—	22.00	34.00	42.00	☐ St. Louis	—	22.00	34.00	42.00
☐ Philadelphia	—	22.00	34.00	42.00	☐ Minneapolis	—	22.00	36.00	42.00
☐ Cleveland	—	22.00	36.00	42.00	☐ Kansas City	—	22.00	36.00	42.00
☐ Richmond	—	22.00	34.00	42.00	☐ Dallas	—	22.00	34.00	42.00
☐ Atlanta	—	22.00	34.00	42.00	☐ San Francisco	—	22.00	34.00	42.00

TWENTY DOLLAR NOTES (1915–1918)
FEDERAL RESERVE BANK NOTES
(ALL HAVE BLUE SEALS)

(Large Size)

Face Design:
Portrait of
President
Cleveland left,
name of bank
and city center,
blue seal right.

Back Design:
Locomotive
and steamship,
similar to
1914 note.

BANK SERIES	GOV'T SIGNATURES	BANK SIGNATURES	A.B.P.	GOOD	V.FINE	UNC.
☐Atlanta 1915	Teehee-Burke	Bell-Wellborn	340.00	600.00	1225.00	7100.00
1915	Teehee-Burke	Pike-McCord	540.00	800.00	1225.00	8600.00
☐Atlanta 1918	Elliott-Burke	Bell-Wellborn	180.00	300.00	1000.00	3800.00
☐Chicago 1915	Teehee-Burke	McLallen-McDougal	180.00	300.00	1000.00	3800.00
☐St. Louis 1918	Teehee-Burke	Attebery-Wells	180.00	300.00	1000.00	3800.00

BANK	SERIES	GOV'T SIGNATURES	BANK SIGNATURES	A.B.P.	GOOD	V.FINE	UNC.
☐Kansas City	1915	Teehee-Burke	Anderson-Miller				
				180.00	250.00	1050.00	3800.00
☐Kansas City	1915	Teehee-Burke	Cross-Miller				
				180.00	250.00	1025.00	3800.00
☐Dallas	1915	Teehee-Burke	Hoopes-Van Zandt				
				180.00	250.00	1025.00	3800.00
☐Dallas	1915	Teehee-Burke	Gilbert-Van Zandt				
				300.00	500.00	3575.00	6900.00
☐Dallas	1915	Teehee-Burke	Talley-Van Zandt				
				300.00	500.00	3675.00	7100.00

TWENTY DOLLAR NOTES (1929)
FEDERAL RESERVE BANK NOTES
(Small Size)

Face Design:
Portrait of
President
Jackson center,
name of bank
and city left,
blue seal right.

Back Design: The White House.

BANK	A.B.P.	V.FINE	UNC.	★UNC.	BANK	A.B.P.	V.FINE	UNC.	★UNC.
☐ Boston	23.00	130.00	230.00	301.00	☐ Chicago	20.00	90.00	435.00	301.00
☐ New York	23.00	90.00	165.00	301.00	☐ St. Louis	20.00	90.00	195.00	301.00
☐ Philadelphia	23.00	65.00	185.00	301.00	☐ Minneapolis	20.00	90.00	190.00	301.00
☐ Cleveland	23.00	90.00	210.00	301.00	☐ Kansas City	20.00	90.00	195.00	301.00
☐ Richmond	23.00	90.00	210.00	301.00	☐ Dallas	20.00	225.00	605.00	301.00
☐ Atlanta	23.00	90.00	210.00	301.00	☐ San Francisco	26.00	90.00	210.00	301.00

FIFTY DOLLAR NOTES

ORDER OF ISSUE

FIFTY DOLLAR NOTES (1862–1863)
UNITED STATES NOTES
(ALSO KNOWN AS LEGAL TENDER NOTES)
(Large Size)

Face Design: Portrait of Hamilton to left.

Back Design

SERIES	SIGNATURES	SEAL	A.B.P.	GOOD	V.FINE	UNC.
☐1862	Chittenden-Spinner*	Red	2100.00	3500.00	11,200.00	100,000.00
☐1862	Chittenden-Spinner**	Red	2100.00	3500.00	11,200.00	100,000.00
☐1863	Chittenden-Spinner**	Red	2100.00	3500.00	11,200.00	100,000.00

*First Obligation: Similar to 1862 $5 note.
**Second Obligation: Shown above.

FIFTY DOLLAR NOTES (1869) UNITED STATES NOTES (ALSO KNOWN AS LEGAL TENDER NOTES)
(Large Size)

Face Design: Portrait of Henry Clay to right.

Back Design

SERIES	SIGNATURES	SEAL	A.B.P.	GOOD	V.FINE	UNC.
☐1869	Allison-Spinner	Red	3100.00	4500.00	24,000.00	52,000.00

Only twenty-four pieces of this note remain unredeemed.

FIFTY DOLLAR NOTES (1874–1880)
UNITED STATES NOTES
(Large Size)

Face Design: Franklin to left.

Back Design

SERIES	SIGNATURES	SEAL	A.B.P.	GOOD	V.FINE	UNC.
☐ 1874 Allison-Spinner	Sm. Red	700.00	1500.00	6000.00	26,000.00
☐ 1875 Allison-Wyman	Sm. Red	1000.00	16,000.00	75,000.00	RARE
☐ 1878 Allison-Gilfillan	Sm. Red	1000.00	1600.00	6000.00	35,000.00
☐ 1880 Bruce-Gilfillan	Lg. Brown	700.00	1250.00	4700.00	12,000.00
☐ 1880 Bruce-Wyman	Lg. Brown	700.00	1250.00	4700.00	12,000.00
☐ 1880 Rosecrans-Jordan	Lg. Red	700.00	1250.00	5600.00	16,000.00
☐ 1880 Rosecrans-Hyatt	Red Plain	VERY RARE			
☐ 1880 Rosecrans-Hyatt	Red Spike	1550.00	3000.00	6400.00	22,500.00
☐ 1880 Rosecrans-Huston	Lg. Red	2000.00	3500.00	11,000.00	20,000.00
☐ 1880 Rosecrans-Huston	Lg. Brown	650.00	1150.00	5400.00	13,000.00
☐ 1880 Tillman-Morgan	Sm. Red	1050.00	1600.00	5900.00	14,500.00
☐ 1880 Bruce-Roberts	Sm. Red	1050.00	1600.00	5900.00	14,500.00
☐ 1880 Lyons-Roberts	Sm. Red	600.00	950.00	3900.00	11,000.00

FIFTY DOLLAR NOTES (1875) NATIONAL BANK NOTES
FIRST CHARTER PERIOD (Large Size)

Face Design: Washington crossing Delaware left, Washington at Valley Forge, right.

Back Design: Embarkation of the Pilgrims.

SERIES	SIGNATURES	SEAL	A.B.P.	GOOD	V.FINE	UNC.
☐ Original	Chittenden-Spinner	Red w/r	1000.00	1500.00	4750.00	20,000.00
☐ Original	Colby-Spinner	Red w/r	1000.00	1500.00	4750.00	20,000.00
☐ Original	Allison-Spinner	Red w/r	1000.00	1500.00	4750.00	20,000.00
☐ 1875	Allison-New	Red w/s	1000.00	1500.00	4750.00	20,000.00
☐ 1875	Allison-Wyman	Red w/s	1000.00	1500.00	4750.00	20,000.00
☐ 1875	Allison-Gilfillan	Red w/s	1000.00	1500.00	4750.00	20,000.00
☐ 1875	Scofield-Gilfillan	Red w/s	1000.00	1500.00	4750.00	20,000.00
☐ 1875	Bruce-Gilfillan	Red w/s	1000.00	1500.00	4750.00	20,000.00
☐ 1875	Bruce-Wyman	Red w/s	1000.00	1500.00	4750.00	20,000.00
☐ 1875	Rosecrans-Huston	Red w/s	1000.00	1500.00	4750.00	20,000.00
☐ 1875	Rosecrans-Nebeker	Red w/s	1000.00	1500.00	4750.00	20,000.00
☐ 1875	Tillman-Morgan	Red w/s	1000.00	1500.00	4750.00	20,000.00

FIFTY DOLLAR NOTES (1882) NATIONAL BANK NOTES
SECOND CHARTER PERIOD (Large Size)

First Issue (Brown seal and brown back)
Back Design
Face Design: Similar to First Charter Period note.

SERIES	SIGNATURES	SEAL	A.B.P.	GOOD	V.FINE	UNC.
☐1882	Bruce-Gilfillan	Brown	325.00	525.00	1775.00	6800.00
☐1882	Bruce-Wyman	Brown	325.00	525.00	1775.00	6800.00
☐1882	Bruce-Jordan	Brown	325.00	525.00	1775.00	6800.00
☐1882	Rosecrans-Jordan	Brown	325.00	525.00	1775.00	6800.00
☐1882	Rosecrans-Hyatt	Brown	325.00	525.00	1775.00	6800.00
☐1882	Rosecrans-Huston	Brown	325.00	525.00	1775.00	6800.00
☐1882	Rosecrans-Nebeker	Brown	325.00	525.00	1775.00	6800.00
☐1882	Rosecrans-Morgan	Brown	400.00	750.00	2325.00	7600.00
☐1882	Tillman-Morgan	Brown	325.00	525.00	1775.00	6800.00
☐1882	Tillman-Roberts	Brown	325.00	525.00	1775.00	6800.00
☐1882	Bruce-Roberts	Brown	325.00	525.00	1775.00	6800.00
☐1882	Lyons-Roberts	Brown	325.00	525.00	1775.00	6800.00
☐1882	Vernon-Treat	Brown	450.00	850.00	2525.00	7600.00

FIFTY DOLLAR NOTES (1882) NATIONAL BANK NOTES
SECOND CHARTER PERIOD (Large Size)

Second Issue (Blue seal, green back with date "1882–1908")
Face Design: Washington crossing Delaware left,
Washington at Valley Forge right.

Back Design

SERIES	SIGNATURES	SEAL	A.B.P.	GOOD	V.FINE	UNC.
☐1882	Rosecrans-Huston	Blue	300.00	475.00	1125.00	4600.00
☐1882	Rosecrans-Nebeker	Blue	300.00	475.00	1125.00	4600.00
☐1882	Tillman-Morgan	Blue	300.00	475.00	1125.00	4600.00
☐1882	Tillman-Roberts	Blue	300.00	475.00	1125.00	4600.00
☐1882	Bruce-Roberts	Blue	300.00	475.00	1125.00	4600.00
☐1882	Lyons-Roberts	Blue	300.00	475.00	1125.00	4600.00
☐1882	Vernon-Treat	Blue	300.00	475.00	1125.00	4600.00
☐1882	Napier-McClung	Blue	300.00	475.00	1125.00	4600.00

Third Issue (as above, "FIFTY DOLLARS" replaces
1882–1908—excessively rare!)

☐1882	Lyons-Roberts		20,000.00	25,000.00	45,000.00	95,000.00

FIFTY DOLLAR NOTES (1902) NATIONAL BANK NOTES
THIRD CHARTER PERIOD (Large Size)

First Issues (Red seal and numbers)
Face Design: Portrait of Sherman left. Name of bank center. Treasury Seal and numbers.

SERIES	SIGNATURES	SEAL	A.B.P.	GOOD	V.FINE	UNC.
☐1902 Lyons-Roberts	Red	320.00	500.00	1525.00	6800.00
☐1902 Lyons-Treat	Red	320.00	500.00	1525.00	6800.00
☐1902 Vernon-Treat	Red	320.00	500.00	1525.00	6800.00

Second Issue (Treasury Seal)
   Numbers remain blue, date "1902–1908" added on back.

☐1902 Lyons-Roberts	Blue	110.00	175.00	625.00	2150.00
☐1902 Lyons-Treat	Blue	110.00	175.00	625.00	2150.00
☐1902 Vernon-Treat	Blue	110.00	175.00	625.00	2150.00
☐1902 Vernon-McClung	Blue	110.00	175.00	625.00	2150.00
☐1902 Napier-McClung	Blue	100.00	175.00	625.00	2150.00
☐1902 Napier-Thompson	Blue	110.00	175.00	625.00	2150.00
☐1902 Napier-Burke	Blue	110.00	175.00	625.00	2150.00
☐1902 Parker-Burke	Blue	110.00	175.00	625.00	2150.00
☐1902 Teehee-Burke	Blue	110.00	175.00	625.00	2150.00

Third Issue (Treasury Seal)
   Numbers remain blue, date "1902–1908" removed from back.

☐1902 Lyons-Roberts	Blue	105.00	150.00	550.00	1950.00
☐1902 Lyons-Treat	Blue	105.00	150.00	550.00	1950.00
☐1902 Vernon-Treat	Blue	105.00	150.00	550.00	1950.00
☐1902 Vernon-McClung	Blue	105.00	150.00	550.00	1950.00
☐1902 Napier-McClung	Blue	105.00	150.00	550.00	1950.00
☐1902 Napier-Thompson	Blue	105.00	150.00	550.00	1950.00
☐1902 Napier-Burke	Blue	105.00	150.00	550.00	1950.00
☐1902 Parker-Burke	Blue	105.00	150.00	550.00	1950.00
☐1902 Teehee-Burke	Blue	105.00	150.00	550.00	1950.00
☐1902 Elliott-Burke	Blue	105.00	150.00	550.00	1950.00
☐1902 Elliott-White	Blue	105.00	150.00	550.00	1950.00

SERIES	SIGNATURES	SEAL	A.B.P.	GOOD	V.FINE	UNC.
☐1902	Speelman-White	Blue	105.00	150.00	525.00	1950.00
☐1902	Woods-White	Blue	105.00	150.00	525.00	1950.00

FIFTY DOLLAR NOTES (1929) NATIONAL BANK NOTES
(Small Size)

Face Design: Portrait of President Grant center. Bank left, brown seal right. Brown serial numbers, black Charter Numbers.

Back Design: The Capitol.

SERIES	SIGNATURES	SEAL	A.B.P.	V.FINE	UNC.
☐1929, Type I*	Jones-Wood	Brown	60.00	100.00	275.00
☐1929, Type II*	Jones-Wood	Brown	75.00	125.00	325.00

*See Page 78. Type I—Charter Number in black. Type II—Similar. Charter Number added in brown.

FIFTY DOLLAR NOTES (1878–1880)
SILVER CERTIFICATES
(Large Size)

Face Design: Portrait of Edward Everett.

Back Design

SERIES	SIGNATURES	SEAL	A.B.P.	GOOD	V.FINE	UNC.
☐ 1878	Varied	Red				VERY RARE
☐ 1880	Scofield-Gilfillan	Brown	1250.00	2550.00	25,000.00	50,000.00
☐ 1880	Bruce-Gilfillan	Brown	1250.00	2550.00	25,000.00	50,000.00
☐ 1880	Bruce-Wyman	Brown	1250.00	2550.00	25,000.00	50,000.00
☐ 1880	Rosecrans-Huston	Brown	1250.00	2550.00	25,000.00	50,000.00
☐ 1880	Rosecrans-Nebeker	Red	1250.00	2550.00	12,500.00	45,000.00

FIFTY DOLLAR NOTES (1891) SILVER CERTIFICATES
(Large Size)

Face Design: Portrait of Edward Everett.

Back Design

SERIES	SIGNATURES	SEAL	A.B.P.	GOOD	V.FINE	UNC.
☐1891	Rosecrans-Nebeker	Red	450.00	1000.00	3500.00	8000.00
☐1891	Tillman-Morgan	Red	450.00	1000.00	3500.00	8000.00
☐1891	Bruce-Roberts	Red	450.00	1000.00	3500.00	8000.00
☐1891	Lyons-Roberts	Red	450.00	1000.00	3500.00	8000.00
☐1891	Vernon-Treat	Red	450.00	1000.00	3500.00	8000.00
☐1891	Parker-Burke	Blue	450.00	1000.00	3500.00	8000.00

FIFTY DOLLAR NOTES (1882) GOLD CERTIFICATES
(Large Size)

Face Design: Portrait of Silas Wright to left.

Back Design: Bright yellow color.

SERIES	SIGNATURES	SEAL	A.B.P.	GOOD	V.FINE	UNC.
☐1882	Bruce-Gilfillan	Brown	525.00	875.00	4050.00	18,900.00
☐1882	Bruce-Wyman	Brown	525.00	875.00	4050.00	18,900.00
☐1882	Rosecrans-Hyatt	Red	525.00	875.00	4050.00	18,900.00
☐1882	Rosecrans-Huston	Brown	525.00	875.00	4050.00	18,900.00
☐1882	Lyons-Roberts	Red	425.00	800.00	2400.00	9400.00
☐1882	Lyons-Treat	Red	450.00	900.00	2600.00	10400.00
☐1882	Vernon-Treat	Red	395.00	700.00	2600.00	9400.00
☐1882	Vernon-McClung	Red	425.00	900.00	2600.00	9900.00
☐1882	Napier-McClung	Red	350.00	550.00	2000.00	7000.00

FIFTY DOLLAR NOTES (1913) GOLD CERTIFICATES
(Large Size)

Face Design: Portrait of President Grant.

Back Design: Bright yellow color.

SERIES	SIGNATURES	SEAL	A.B.P.	GOOD	V.FINE	UNC.
☐1913 Parker-Burke		Gold	150.00	275.00	1550.00	4000.00
☐1913 Teehee-Burke		Gold	150.00	250.00	900.00	3000.00
☐1922 Speelman-White		Gold	175.00	275.00	650.00	2900.00

FIFTY DOLLAR NOTES (1928) GOLD CERTIFICATES
(Small Size)

Back Design: Same as 1929 note.

SERIES	SIGNATURES	SEAL	A.B.P.	GOOD	V.FINE	UNC.
☐1928	Woods-Mellon	Gold	65.00	90.00	300.00	1800.00

FIFTY DOLLAR NOTES (1891) TREASURY OR COIN NOTES
(Large Size)

Face Design: Portrait of William H. Seward. Only twenty-five pieces remain unredeemed.
Back Design: Green.

SERIES	SIGNATURES	SEAL	A.B.P.	GOOD	V.FINE	UNC.
☐1891	Rosecrans-Nebeker	Red	5500.00	8000.00	26,000.00	RARE

FIFTY DOLLAR NOTES (1914)
FEDERAL RESERVE NOTES

(Large Size)

SERIES OF 1914,
SIGNATURES OF BURKE-McADOO, RED SEAL AND
RED SERIAL NUMBERS

BANK	A.B.P.	V.FINE	UNC.	CITY	A.B.P.	V.FINE	UNC.
☐ Boston	400.00	1075.00	2850.00	☐ Chicago	400.00	925.00	3000.00
☐ New York	400.00	925.00	2850.00	☐ St. Louis	400.00	850.00	2900.00
☐ Philadelphia	400.00	925.00	2850.00	☐ Minneapolis	400.00	875.00	2950.00
☐ Cleveland	400.00	925.00	3000.00	☐ Kansas City	400.00	905.00	3000.00
☐ Richmond	400.00	925.00	2950.00	☐ Dallas	400.00	875.00	2950.00
☐ Atlanta	400.00	925.00	3000.00	☐ San Francisco	400.00	875.00	2950.00

FIFTY DOLLAR NOTES (1914)
FEDERAL RESERVE NOTES
1914, BLUE TREASURY SEAL AND BLUE NUMBERS

DATE	BANK	SIGNATURES	SEAL	A.B.P.	GOOD	V.FINE	UNC.
1914	Boston	Burke-McAdoo	Blue	65.00	90.00	440.00	1625.00
1914	Boston	Burke-Glass	Blue	65.00	90.00	440.00	1625.00
1914	Boston	Burke-Huston	Blue	160.00	315.00	2065.00	3725.00
1914	Boston	White-Mellon	Blue	65.00	75.00	265.00	1275.00
1914	New York	Burke-McAdoo	Blue	65.00	90.00	565.00	1925.00
1914	New York	Burke-Glass	Blue	65.00	80.00	365.00	1475.00
1914	New York	Burke-Huston	Blue	65.00	75.00	265.00	1275.00
1914	New York	White-Mellon	Blue	65.00	75.00	310.00	1275.00

DATE	BANK	SIGNATURES	SEAL	A.B.P.	GOOD	V.FINE	UNC.
1914	Philadelphia	Burke-McAdoo	Blue	65.00	95.00	515.00	1875.00
1914	Philadelphia	Burke-Glass	Blue	65.00	115.00	865.00	2275.00
1914	Philadelphia	Burke-Huston	Blue	65.00	75.00	315.00	1375.00
1914	Philadelphia	White-Mellon	Blue	65.00	75.00	265.00	1275.00
1914	Cleveland	Burke-McAdoo	Blue	65.00	75.00	315.00	1375.00
1914	Cleveland	Burke-Glass	Blue	65.00	115.00	565.00	1975.00
1914	Cleveland	Burke-Huston	Blue	65.00	90.00	415.00	1575.00
1914	Cleveland	White-Mellon	Blue	65.00	75.00	365.00	1275.00
1914	Richmond	Burke-McAdoo	Blue	65.00	115.00	565.00	1975.00
1914	Richmond	Burke-Glass	Blue	65.00	140.00	865.00	2275.00
1914	Richmond	Burke-Huston	Blue	65.00	90.00	365.00	1475.00
1914	Richmond	White-Mellon	Blue	65.00	115.00	515.00	1875.00
1914	Atlanta	Burke-McAdoo	Blue	65.00	115.00	565.00	1975.00
1914	Atlanta	Burke-Glass	Blue	110.00	215.00	1565.00	2775.00
1914	Atlanta	Burke-Huston	Blue	65.00	75.00	265.00	1275.00
1914	Atlanta	White-Mellon	Blue	65.00	115.00	565.00	1975.00
1914	Chicago	Burke-McAdoo	Blue	65.00	75.00	290.00	1325.00
1914	Chicago	Burke-Glass	Blue	65.00	75.00	290.00	1325.00
1914	Chicago	Burke-Huston	Blue	65.00	90.00	415.00	1575.00
1914	Chicago	White-Mellon	Blue	65.00	90.00	415.00	1575.00
1914	St. Louis	Burke-McAdoo	Blue	65.00	115.00	515.00	1875.00
1914	St. Louis	Burke-Glass	Blue	65.00	90.00	415.00	1575.00
1914	St. Louis	Burke-Huston	Blue	65.00	75.00	305.00	1375.00
1914	St. Louis	White-Mellon	Blue	135.00	315.00	2065.00	3775.00
1914	Minneapolis	Burke-McAdoo	Blue	65.00	115.00	540.00	1925.00
1914	Minneapolis	Burke-Glass	Blue	135.00	315.00	2065.00	3775.00
1914	Minneapolis	Burke-Huston	Blue	110.00	265.00	1915.00	3275.00
1914	Minneapolis	White-Mellon	Blue	135.00	315.00	2065.00	3775.00
1914	Kansas City	Burke-McAdoo	Blue	65.00	95.00	465.00	1775.00
1914	Kansas City	White-Mellon	Blue		ONLY 1 KNOWN—RARE		
1914	Dallas	Burke-McAdoo	Blue	65.00	115.00	540.00	1925.00
1914	Dallas	Burke-Glass	Blue	135.00	315.00	2065.00	3775.00
1914	Dallas	Burke-Huston	Blue	135.00	315.00	2065.00	3775.00
1914	Dallas	White Mellon	Blue	135.00	315.00	2065.00	3775.00
1914	San Francisco	Burke-McAdoo	Blue	65.00	80.00	365.00	1475.00
1914	San Francisco	Burke-Glass	Blue	135.00	315.00	2065.00	3775.00
1914	San Francisco	Burke-Huston	Blue	65.00	80.00	365.00	1475.00
1914	San Francisco	White-Mellon	Blue	65.00	110.00	515.00	1875.00

FIFTY DOLLAR NOTES (1928)
FEDERAL RESERVE NOTES

(Small Size)

Face Design: Portrait of President Grant center. Black Federal Reserve Seal with number to left. Green Treasury Seal to right.
Back Design: Same as 1929 note.

FIFTY DOLLAR NOTES (1928)
FEDERAL RESERVE NOTES
SERIES OF 1928, SIGNATURES OF WOODS-MELLON, GREEN SEAL

BANK	A.B.P.	V.FINE	UNC.	★UNC.	BANK	A.B.P.	V.FINE	UNC.	★UNC.
☐ Boston	75.00	125.00	545.00	—	☐ Chicago	70.00	120.00	445.00	—
☐ New York	75.00	125.00	445.00	—	☐ St. Louis	70.00	120.00	445.00	—
☐ Philadelphia	75.00	125.00	445.00	—	☐ Minneapolis	70.00	120.00	720.00	—
☐ Cleveland	70.00	120.00	445.00	—	☐ Kansas City	75.00	125.00	545.00	—
☐ Richmond	70.00	120.00	545.00	—	☐ Dallas	75.00	125.00	545.00	—
☐ Atlanta	70.00	120.00	445.00	—	☐ San Francisco	75.00	125.00	445.00	—

SERIES OF 1928A, SIGNATURES OF WOODS-MELLON, GREEN SEAL

BANK	A.B.P.	V.FINE	UNC.	★UNC.	BANK	A.B.P.	V.FINE	UNC.	★UNC.
☐ Boston	60.00	100.00	470.00	—	☐ Chicago	60.00	100.00	420.00	—
☐ New York	60.00	100.00	420.00	—	☐ St. Louis	60.00	100.00	470.00	—
☐ Philadelphia	60.00	100.00	470.00	—	☐ Minneapolis	68.00	110.00	545.00	—
☐ Cleveland	60.00	100.00	470.00	—	☐ Kansas City	68.00	110.00	470.00	—
☐ Richmond	60.00	100.00	470.00	—	☐ Dallas	68.00	110.00	470.00	—
☐ Atlanta	60.00	100.00	470.00	—	☐ San Francisco	60.00	100.00	470.00	—

FIFTY DOLLAR NOTES (1934)
FEDERAL RESERVE NOTES
SERIES OF 1934, SIGNATURES OF JULIAN-MORGENTHAU, GREEN SEAL

BANK	A.B.P.	V.FINE	UNC.	★UNC.	BANK	A.B.P.	V.FINE	UNC.	★UNC.
☐ Boston	55.00	75.00	260.00	600.00	☐ Chicago	55.00	75.00	285.00	600.00
☐ New York	55.00	75.00	260.00	600.00	☐ St. Louis	55.00	75.00	285.00	600.00
☐ Philadelphia	55.00	75.00	260.00	600.00	☐ Minneapolis	55.00	75.00	285.00	600.00
☐ Cleveland	55.00	75.00	260.00	600.00	☐ Kansas City	55.00	75.00	285.00	600.00
☐ Richmond	55.00	75.00	260.00	600.00	☐ Dallas	55.00	75.00	285.00	600.00
☐ Atlanta	55.00	75.00	260.00	600.00	☐ San Francisco	55.00	75.00	285.00	600.00

SERIES OF 1934A, SIGNATURES OF JULIAN-MORGENTHAU, GREEN SEAL

BANK	A.B.P.	V.FINE	UNC.	★UNC.	BANK	A.B.P.	V.FINE	UNC.	★UNC.
☐ Boston	55.00	90.00	205.00	545.00	☐ Chicago	—	90.00	205.00	545.00
☐ New York	55.00	90.00	205.00	545.00	☐ St. Louis	—	90.00	205.00	545.00
☐ Philadelphia	55.00	90.00	205.00	545.00	☐ Minneapolis	—	100.00	215.00	545.00
☐ Cleveland	55.00	90.00	205.00	545.00	☐ Kansas City	—	100.00	215.00	545.00
☐ Richmond	55.00	90.00	205.00	545.00	☐ Dallas	—	100.00	215.00	545.00
☐ Atlanta	55.00	90.00	205.00	545.00	☐ San Francisco	—	90.00	205.00	545.00

SERIES OF 1934B, SIGNATURES OF JULIAN-VINSON, GREEN SEAL

BANK	A.B.P.	V.FINE	UNC.	★UNC.	BANK	A.P.B.	V.FINE	UNC.	★UNC.
☐ Boston	55.00	85.00	180.00	545.00	☐ Chicago	—	85.00	180.00	545.00
☐ New York	55.00	85.00	180.00	545.00	☐ St. Louis	—	85.00,	180.00	545.00
☐ Philadelphia	55.00	85.00	180.00	545.00	☐ Minneapolis	65.00	105.00	205.00	545.00
☐ Cleveland	55.00	85.00	180.00	545.00	☐ Kansas City	65.00	105.00	205.00	545.00
☐ Richmond	55.00	85.00	180.00	545.00	☐ Dallas	65.00	105.00	205.00	545.00
☐ Atlanta	55.00	85.00	180.00	545.00	☐ San Francisco	—	85.00	180.00	545.00

SERIES OF 1934C, SIGNATURES OF JULIAN-SNYDER, GREEN SEAL

BANK	A.B.P.	V.FINE	UNC.	★UNC.	BANK	A.B.P.	V.FINE	UNC.	★UNC.
☐ Boston	55.00	90.00	180.00	545.00	☐ Chicago	55.00	90.00	180.00	545.00
☐ New York	55.00	90.00	180.00	545.00	☐ St. Louis	55.00	90.00	180.00	545.00
☐ Philadelphia	55.00	90.00	180.00	545.00	☐ Minneapolis	55.00	90.00	180.00	545.00
☐ Cleveland	55.00	85.00	170.00	545.00	☐ Kansas City	55.00	85.00	170.00	545.00
☐ Richmond	55.00	85.00	170.00	545.00	☐ Dallas	55.00	85.00	170.00	545.00
☐ Atlanta	55.00	85.00	170.00	545.00	☐ San Francisco	55.00	85.00	170.00	545.00

SERIES OF 1934D, SIGNATURES OF CLARK-SNYDER, GREEN SEAL

BANK	A.B.P.	V.FINE	UNC.	★UNC.	BANK	A.B.P.	V.FINE	UNC.	★UNC.
☐ Boston	65.00	105.00	205.00	545.00	☐ Chicago	—	75.00	155.00	545.00
☐ New York	—	75.00	155.00	545.00					
☐ Philadelphia	—	75.00	155.00	545.00					
☐ Richmond	65.00	105.00	205.00	545.00	☐ Dallas	65 .00	105.00	205.00	545.00
☐ Atlanta	65.00	105.00	205.00	545.00					

FIFTY DOLLAR NOTES (1950)
FEDERAL RESERVE NOTES
SERIES OF 1950, SIGNATURES OF CLARK-SNYDER, GREEN SEAL

BANK	A.B.P.	V.FINE	UNC.	★UNC.	BANK	A.P.B.	V.FINE	UNC.	★UNC.
☐ Boston	55.00	90.00	180.00	510.00	☐ Chicago	55.00	90.00	180.00	510.00
☐ New York	55.00	90.00	180.00	510.00	☐ St. Louis	55.00	90.00	180.00	510.00
☐ Philadelphia	55.00	90.00	180.00	510.00	☐ Minneapolis	55.00	90.00	180.00	510.00
☐ Cleveland	—	85.00	170.00	510.00	☐ Kansas City	55.00	90.00	180.00	510.00
☐ Richmond	—	85.00	170.00	510.00	☐ Dallas	55.00	90.00	180.00	510.00
☐ Atlanta	—	85.00	170.00	510.00	☐ San Francisco	55.00	90.00	180.00	510.00

SERIES OF 1950A, SIGNATURES OF PRIEST-HUMPHERY, GREEN SEAL

BANK	A.B.P.	V.FINE	UNC.	★UNC.	BANK	A.B.P.	V.FINE	UNC.	★UNC.
☐ Boston	55.00	75.00	185.00	500.00	☐ Chicago	55.00	75.00	185.00	500.00
☐ New York	55.00	75.00	185.00	500.00	☐ St. Louis	55.00	75.00	185.00	500.00
☐ Philadelphia	55.00	75.00	185.00	500.00	☐ Minneapolis	55.00	75.00	185.00	500.00
☐ Cleveland	55.00	75.00	185.00	500.00	☐ Kansas City	55.00	75.00	185.00	500.00
☐ Richmond	55.00	75.00	185.00	500.00	☐ Dallas	55.00	75.00	185.00	500.00
☐ Atlanta	55.00	75.00	185.00	500.00	☐ San Francisco	55.00	75.00	185.00	500.00

SERIES OF 1950B, SIGNATURES OF PRIEST-ANDERSON, GREEN SEAL

BANK	A.B.P.	V.FINE	UNC.	★UNC.	BANK	A.B.P.	V.FINE	UNC.	★UNC.
☐ Boston	52.00	70.00	175.00	500.00	☐ Chicago	52.00	70.00	175.00	500.00
☐ New York	52.00	70.00	175.00	500.00	☐ St. Louis	52.00	70.00	175.00	500.00
☐ Philadelphia	52.00	70.00	175.00	500.00	☐ Minneapolis	52.00	70.00	175.00	500.00
☐ Cleveland	52.00	70.00	175.00	500.00	☐ Kansas City	52.00	70.00	175.00	500.00
☐ Richmond	52.00	70.00	175.00	500.00	☐ Dallas	52.00	70.00	175.00	500.00
☐ Atlanta	52.00	70.00	175.00	500.00	☐ San Francisco	52.00	70.00	175.00	500.00

SERIES OF 1950C, SIGNATURES OF SMITH-DILLON, GREEN SEAL

BANK	A.B.P.	V.FINE	UNC.	★UNC.	BANK	A.B.P.	V.FINE	UNC.	★UNC.
☐ Boston	52.00	70.00	150.00	455.00	☐ Chicago	52.00	70.00	150.00	455.00
☐ New York	52.00	70.00	150.00	455.00	☐ St. Louis	52.00	70.00	150.00	455.00
☐ Philadelphia	52.00	70.00	150.00	455.00	☐ Minneapolis	52.00	70.00	150.00	455.00
☐ Cleveland	52.00	70.00	150.00	455.00	☐ Kansas City	52.00	70.00	150.00	455.00
☐ Richmond	52.00	70.00	150.00	455.00	☐ Dallas	52.00	70.00	150.00	455.00
☐ Atlanta	52.00	70.00	150.00	455.00	☐ San Francisco	52.00	70.00	150.00	455.0C

SERIES OF 1950D, SIGNATURES OF GRANAHAN-DILLON, GREEN SEAL

BANK	A.B.P.	V.FINE	UNC.	★UNC.	BANK	A.B.P.	V.FINE	UNC.	★UNC.
☐ Boston	65.00	105.00	180.00	515.00	☐ Chicago	58.00	95.00	165.00	515.00
☐ New York	65.00	105.00	180.00	515.00	☐ St. Louis	58.00	95.00	165.00	515.00
☐ Philadelphia	65.00	105.00	180.00	515.00	☐ Minneapolis	58.00	95.00	165.00	515.00
☐ Cleveland	58.00	95.00	165.00	515.00	☐ Kansas City	58.00	95.00	165.00	515.00
☐ Richmond	58.00	95.00	165.00	515.00	☐ Dallas	65.00	105.00	180.00	515.00
☐ Atlanta	58.00	95.00	165.00	515.00	☐ San Francisco	65.00	105.00	180.00	515.00

SERIES OF 1950E, SIGNATURES OF GRANAHAN-FOWLER, GREEN SEAL

BANK	A.B.P.	V.FINE	UNC.	★UNC.	BANK	A.B.P.	V.FINE	UNC.	★UNC.
					☐ Chicago		75.00	125.00	200.00	—
☐ New York		75.00	125.00	200.00	—					
					☐ San Francisco	80.00	125.00	210.00	—

FIFTY DOLLAR NOTES (1963)
FEDERAL RESERVE NOTES
SERIES OF 1963,
(THERE WERE NOT ANY NOTES PRINTED FOR THIS SERIES.)

SERIES OF 1963A, SIGNATURES OF GRANAHAN-FOWLER, GREEN SEAL

BANK	A.B.P.	V.FINE	UNC.	BANK	A.B.P.	V.FINE	UNC.
☐Boston	—	65.00	240.00	☐Chicago	—	65.00	240.00
☐New York	—	65.00	240.00	☐St. Louis	—	90.00	240.00
☐Philadelphia	—	65.00	240.00	☐Minneapolis	—	90.00	240.00
☐Cleveland	—	65.00	240.00	☐Kansas City	—	90.00	240.00
☐Richmond	—	65.00	240.00	☐Dallas	—	65.00	240.00
☐Atlanta	—	65.00	240.00	☐San Francisco	—	65.00	240.00

FIFTY DOLLAR NOTES (1969)
FEDERAL RESERVE NOTES
(WORDING IN GREEN TREASURY SEAL IS CHANGED
FROM LATIN TO ENGLISH)

SERIES OF 1969, SIGNATURES OF ELSTON-KENNEDY, GREEN SEAL

BANK	A.B.P.	V.FINE	UNC.	BANK	A.B.P.	V.FINE	UNC.
☐ Boston	—	75.00	210.00	☐Chicago	—	75.00	210.00
☐ New York	—	75.00	210.00	☐St. Louis	—	90.00	235.00
☐ Philadelphia	—	75.00	210.00	☐Minneapolis	—	90.00	235.00
☐ Cleveland	—	75.00	210.00	☐Kansas City	—	90.00	235.00
☐ Richmond	—	75.00	210.00	☐Dallas	—	75.00	210.00
☐ Atlanta	—	90.00	235.00	☐San Francisco—	75.00	210.00

SERIES OF 1969A, SIGNATURES OF KABIS-CONNALLY, GREEN SEAL

BANK	A.B.P.	V.FINE	UNC.	BANK	A.B.P.	V.FINE	UNC.
☐ Boston	—	60.00	195.00	☐Chicago	—	60.00	195.00
☐ New York	—	60.00	195.00	☐St. Louis	—	65.00	205.00
☐ Philadelphia	—	60.00	195.00	☐Minneapolis	—	65.00	205.00
☐ Cleveland	—	60.00	195.00	☐Kansas City	—	65.00	205.00
☐ Richmond	—	60.00	195.00	☐Dallas	—	60.00	195.00
☐ Atlanta	—	60.00	195.00	☐San Francisco—	60.00	195.00

SERIES OF 1969B, SIGNATURES OF BANUELOS-CONNALLY, GREEN SEAL

BANK	A.B.P.	V.FINE	UNC.	BANK	A.B.P.	V.FINE	UNC.
☐ Boston	—	65.00	195.00	☐Chicago	—	65.00	195.00
☐ New York	—	65.00	195.00				
☐ Richmond	—	65.00	195.00	☐Dallas	—	65.00	195.00
☐ Atlanta	—	75.00	210.00				

SERIES OF 1969C, SIGNATURES OF BANUELOS-SHULTZ, GREEN SEAL

BANK	A.B.P.	V.FINE	UNC.	BANK	A.B.P.	V.FINE	UNC.
☐ Boston	—	75.00	190.00	☐ Chicago	—	65.00	175.00
☐ New York	—	75.00	190.00	☐ St. Louis	—	65.00	175.00
☐ Philadelphia	—	75.00	190.00	☐ Minneapolis	—	65.00	190.00
☐ Cleveland	—	65.00	175.00	☐ Kansas City	—	65.00	175.00
☐ Richmond	—	65.00	175.00	☐ Dallas	—	65.00	175.00
☐ Atlanta	—	65.00	175.00	☐ San Francisco	—	65.00	175.00

FIFTY DOLLAR NOTES (1974)
FEDERAL RESERVE NOTES
SERIES OF 1974, SIGNATURES OF NEFF-SIMON, GREEN SEAL

BANK	A.B.P.	V.FINE	UNC.	BANK	A.B.P.	V.FINE	UNC.
☐ Boston	—	70.00	167.00	☐ Chicago	—	70.00	167.00
☐ New York	—	70.00	167.00	☐ St. Louis	—	70.00	167.00
☐ Philadelphia	—	70.00	167.00	☐ Minneapolis	—	75.00	182.00
☐ Cleveland	—	70.00	167.00	☐ Kansas City	—	75.00	182.00
☐ Richmond	—	70.00	167.00	☐ Dallas	—	70.00	167.00
☐ Atlanta	—	70.00	167.00	☐ San Francisco	—	70.00	167.00

FIFTY DOLLAR NOTES (1977)
FEDERAL RESERVE NOTES
SERIES OF 1977, SIGNATURES OF MORTON-BLUMENTHAL, GREEN SEAL

BANK	A.B.P.	V.FINE	UNC.	BANK	A.B.P.	V.FINE	UNC.
☐ Boston	—	60.00	142.00	☐ Chicago	—	60.00	142.00
☐ New York	—	60.00	142.00	☐ St. Louis	—	60.00	142.00
☐ Philadelphia	—	60.00	142.00	☐ Minneapolis	—	60.00	142.00
☐ Cleveland	—	60.00	142.00	☐ Kansas City	—	60.00	142.00
☐ Richmond	—	60.00	142.00	☐ Dallas	—	60.00	142.00
☐ Atlanta	—	60.00	142.00	☐ San Francisco	—	60.00	142.00

FIFTY DOLLAR NOTES (1981)
FEDERAL RESERVE NOTES
SERIES OF 1981, SIGNATURES OF BUCHANAN-REGAN, GREEN SEAL

BANK	A.B.P.	V.FINE	UNC.	BANK	A.B.P.	V.FINE	UNC.
☐ Boston	—	54.00	132.00	☐ Chicago	—	54.00	132.00
☐ New York	—	54.00	132.00	☐ St. Louis	—	54.00	132.00
☐ Philadelphia	—	54.00	132.00	☐ Minneapolis	—	56.00	132.00
☐ Cleveland	—	54.00	132.00	☐ Kansas City	—	56.00	132.00
☐ Richmond	—	54.00	132.00	☐ Dallas	—	56.00	132.00
☐ Atlanta	—	54.00	132.00	☐ San Francisco	—	54.00	132.00

SERIES OF 1981A, SIGNATURES OF ORTEGA-REGAN, GREEN SEAL

BANK	A.B.P.	V.FINE	UNC.	BANK	A.B.P.	V.FINE	UNC.
☐ Boston	—	54.00	127.00	☐ Chicago	—	54.00	127.00
☐ New York	—	54.00	127.00	☐ St. Louis	—	54.00	127.00
☐ Philadelphia	—	54.00	127.00	☐ Minneapolis	—	56.00	132.00
☐ Cleveland	—	54.00	127.00	☐ Kansas City	—	56.00	132.00
☐ Richmond	—	54.00	127.00	☐ Dallas	—	56.00	132.00
☐ Atlanta	—	54.00	127.00	☐ San Francisco—		54.00	127.00

FIFTY DOLLAR NOTES (1985)
FEDERAL RESERVE NOTES
SERIES OF 1985, SIGNATURES OF ORTEGA-BAKER, GREEN SEAL

BANK	A.B.P.	V.FINE	UNC.	BANK	A.B.P.	V.FINE	UNC.
☐ Boston	—	55.00	90.00	☐ Chicago	—	55.00	95.00
☐ New York	—	55.00	90.00	☐ St. Louis	—	55.00	90.00
☐ Philadelphia	—	55.00	90.00	☐ Minneapolis	—	55.00	95.00
☐ Cleveland	—	55.00	90.00	☐ Kansas City	—	55.00	95.00
☐ Richmond	—	55.00	90.00	☐ Dallas	—	55.00	90.00
☐ Atlanta	—	55.00	90.00	☐ San Francisco—		55.00	90.00

FIFTY DOLLAR NOTES (1988)
FEDERAL RESERVE NOTES
SERIES OF 1988, SIGNATURES OF ORTEGA-BRADY, GREEN SEAL

BANK	A.B.P.	V.FINE	UNC.	BANK	A.B.P.	V.FINE	UNC.
☐ Boston	—	55.00	85.00	☐ Chicago	—	55.00	85.00
☐ New York	—	55.00	85.00	☐ St. Louis	—	55.00	80.00
☐ Philadelphia	—	55.00	80.00	☐ Minneapolis	—	55.00	85.00
☐ Cleveland	—	55.00	85.00	☐ Kansas City	—	55.00	85.00
☐ Richmond	—	55.00	85.00	☐ Dallas	—	55.00	85.00
☐ Atlanta	—	55.00	85.00	☐ San Francisco—		55.00	80.00

FIFTY DOLLAR NOTES (1990)
FEDERAL RESERVE NOTES
SERIES OF 1990, SIGNATURES OF VILLALPANDO-BRADY, GREEN SEAL

BANK	A.B.P.	V.FINE	UNC.	BANK	A.B.P.	V.FINE	UNC.
☐ Boston	—	55.00	80.00	☐ Chicago	—	55.00	80.00
☐ New York	—	55.00	80.00	☐ St. Louis	—	55.00	80.00
☐ Philadelphia	—	55.00	90.00	☐ Minneapolis	—	55.00	80.00
☐ Cleveland	—	55.00	80.00	☐ Kansas City	—	55.00	80.00
☐ Richmond	—	55.00	80.00	☐ Dallas	—	55.00	80.00
☐ Atlanta	—	55.00	80.00	☐ San Francisco—		55.00	80.00

FIFTY DOLLAR NOTES (1993)
FEDERAL RESERVE NOTES
SERIES OF 1993, SIGNATURES OF WITHROW-BENTSEN, GREEN SEAL

BANK	A.B.P.	V.FINE	UNC.	BANK	A.B.P.	V.FINE	UNC.
☐ Boston	—	55.00	80.00	☐ Chicago	—	55.00	80.00
☐ New York	—	55.00	80.00	☐ St. Louis	—	55.00	80.00
☐ Philadelphia	—	55.00	80.00	☐ Minneapolis	—	55.00	80.00
☐ Cleveland	—	55.00	80.00	☐ Kansas City	—	55.00	80.00
☐ Richmond	—	55.00	80.00	☐ Dallas	—	55.00	80.00
☐ Atlanta	—	55.00	80.00	☐ San Francisco	—	55.00	80.00

FIFTY DOLLAR NOTES (1995)
FEDERAL RESERVE NOTES
SERIES OF 1995, SIGNATURES OF WITHROW-BENTSEN, GREEN SEAL

BANK	A.B.P.	V.FINE	UNC.	BANK	A.B.P.	V.FINE	UNC.
☐ Boston	—	55.00	70.00	☐ Chicago	—	55.00	70.00
☐ New York	—	55.00	70.00	☐ St. Louis	—	55.00	70.00
☐ Philadelphia	—	55.00	70.00	☐ Minneapolis	—	55.00	70.00
☐ Cleveland	—	55.00	70.00	☐ Kansas City	—	55.00	70.00
☐ Richmond	—	55.00	70.00	☐ Dallas	—	55.00	70.00
☐ Atlanta	—	55.00	70.00	☐ San Francisco	—	55.00	70.00

FIFTY DOLLAR NOTES (1918)

FEDERAL RESERVE BANK NOTES

(Large Size)

Face Design: Portrait of President Grant to left, Federal Reserve Bank in center, blue seal right.

Back Design: Female figure of Panama between merchant ship and battleship. Plates were made for all twelve Federal Reserve Districts. Only St. Louis bank issued. Less than thirty notes are known today.

BANK	SERIES	GOV'T SIGNATURES	BANK SIGNATURES	A.B.P.	VF	UNC.
☐ St. Louis	1918	Teehee-Burke	Attebery-Wells	850.00	5000.00	19,000.00

FIFTY DOLLAR NOTES (1929)
FEDERAL RESERVE BANK NOTES

(Small Size)

Face Design:
Portrait of
Grant center,
name of bank
left, brown
serial numbers,
black letter for
Federal Reserve
District.

Back Design:
Same as 1929 $50 note.

BANK	SERIES	SIGNATURES	SEAL	A.B.P.	V.FINE	UNC.
☐New York	1929	Jones-Woods	Brown	76.00	160.00	350.00
☐Cleveland	1929	Jones-Woods	Brown	80.00	170.00	350.00
☐Chicago	1929	Jones-Woods	Brown	76.00	160.00	360.00
☐Minneapolis	1929	Jones-Woods	Brown	70.00	160.00	450.00
☐Kansas City	1929	Jones-Woods	Brown	70.00	140.00	350.00
☐Dallas	1929	Jones-Woods	Brown	80.00	190.00	400.00
☐San Francisco	1929	Jones-Woods	Brown	135.00	265.00	525.00

ONE HUNDRED DOLLAR NOTES

ORDER OF ISSUE

ONE HUNDRED DOLLAR NOTES (1862–1863)
UNITED STATES NOTES
(ALSO KNOWN AS LEGAL TENDER NOTES)
(Large Size)

Face Design: Eagle with spread wings left, three discs with "100," red seal numbers.

Back Design: Green, two variations of the wording in obligation.

SERIES	SIGNATURES	SEAL	A.B.P.	GOOD	V.FINE	UNC.
☐1862	Chittenden-Spinner*	Red	3200.00	4900.00	19,200.00	75,000.00
☐1862	Chittenden-Spinner**	Red	3200.00	4900.00	19,200.00	75,000.00
☐1863	Chittenden-Spinner**	Red	3200.00	4900.00	19,200.00	75,000.00

*First Obligation: Similar to 1875–1907 $5 note.
**Second Obligation: Shown above.

ONE HUNDRED DOLLAR NOTES (1869–1880)
UNITED STATES NOTES
(Large Size)

Face Design: Portrait of President Lincoln.

Back Design: First Issue

Back Design: Second Issue.

SERIES	SIGNATURES	SEAL	A.B.P.	GOOD	V.FINE	UNC.
☐1869	Allison-Spinner	Red	2700.00	4500.00	24,000.00	62,000.00

The following notes have a modified back design.

(Small Size)
Second Issue

SERIES	SIGNATURES	SEAL	A.B.P.	GOOD	V.FINE	UNC.
☐1875	Allison-New	Sm. Red	2000.00	3750.00	20,500.00	47,500.00
☐1875	Allison-Wyman	Sm. Red	3100.00	5850.00	28,500.00	77,500.00
☐1878	Allison-Gilfillan	Sm. Red	1700.00	3050.00	17,000.00	46,500.00
☐1880	Bruce-Gilfillan	Lg. Brown	1200.00	2350.00	13,500.00	39,500.00
☐1880	Bruce-Wyman	Lg. Brown	1200.00	2450.00	13,500.00	39,500.00
☐1880	Rosecrans-Jordan	Lg. Red	1200.00	2250.00	13,500.00	38,500.00
☐1880	Rosecrans-Hyatt	Red Plain	1700.00	3250.00	13,000.00	40,500.00
☐1880	Rosecrans-Hyatt	Red Spike	1200.00	2250.00	13,500.00	38,500.00
☐1880	Rosecrans-Huston	Lg. Red	1200.00	2250.00	11,000.00	40,500.00
☐1880	Rosecrans-Huston	Lg. Brown	1200.00	2750.00	11,000.00	38,500.00
☐1880	Tillman-Morgan	Sm. Red	1000.00	1650.00	8500.00	23,500.00
☐1880	Bruce-Roberts	Sm. Red	1000.00	1650.00	7500.00	21,500.00
☐1880	Lyons-Roberts	Sm. Red	1000.00	1650.00	7500.00	21,500.00

ONE HUNDRED DOLLAR NOTES (1966) U.S. NOTES
(ALSO KNOWN AS LEGAL TENDER NOTES)
(Small Size)

Face Design: Portrait of Franklin, red seal, red serial numbers.

Back Design: Independence Hall.

SERIES	SIGNATURES	SEAL	A.B.P.	V.FINE	UNC.	*UNC
☐1966*	Granahan-Fowler	Red	120.00	160.00	390.00	1300.00
☐1966A	Elston-Kennedy	Red	125.00	225.00	655.00	—

*This is the first note to be issued with the new Treasury Seal with wording in English instead of Latin.

ONE HUNDRED DOLLAR NOTES (1875)
NATIONAL BANK NOTES

FIRST CHARTER PERIOD (Large Size)

Face Design: Perry leaving the Saint Lawrence, left.

Back Design: Border green, center black, signing of the Declaration of Independence.

SERIES	SIGNATURES	SEAL	A.B.P.	GOOD	V.FINE	UNC.
☐Original	Chittenden-Spinner	Red	1300.00	2100.00	6200.00	35,500.00
☐Original	Colby-Spinner	Red	1300.00	2100.00	6200.00	35,500.00
☐Original	Allison-Spinner	Red	1300.00	2100.00	6200.00	35,500.00
☐1875	Allison-New	Red	1200.00	2000.00	6100.00	37,000.00
☐1875	Allison-Wyman	Red	1200.00	2000.00	6100.00	37,000.00
☐1875	Allison-Gilfillan	Red	1200.00	2000.00	6100.00	37,000.00
☐1875	Scofield-Gilfillan	Red	1200.00	2000.00	6100.00	37,000.00
☐1875	Bruce-Gilfillan	Red	1200.00	2000.00	6100.00	37,000.00
☐1875	Bruce-Wyman	Red	1200.00	2000.00	6100.00	37,000.00
☐1875	Rosecrans-Huston	Red	1200.00	2000.00	6100.00	37,000.00
☐1875	Tillman-Morgan	Red	1200.00	2000.00	6100.00	37,000.00

ONE HUNDRED DOLLAR NOTES (1882)
NATIONAL BANK NOTES
SECOND CHARTER PERIOD (Large Size)
First Issue (Brown seal and brown backs.)

SERIES	SIGNATURES	SEAL	A.B.P.	GOOD	V.FINE	UNC.
☐1882	Bruce-Gilfillan	Brown	385.00	625.00	2075.00	8400.00
☐1882	Bruce-Wyman	Brown	385.00	625.00	2075.00	8400.00
☐1882	Bruce-Jordan	Brown	385.00	625.00	2075.00	8400.00
☐1882	Rosecrans-Jordan	Brown	385.00	625.00	2075.00	8400.00
☐1882	Rosecrans-Hyatt	Brown	385.00	625.00	2075.00	8400.00
☐1882	Rosecrans-Huston	Brown	385.00	625.00	2075.00	8400.00
☐1882	Rosecrans-Nebeker	Brown	385.00	625.00	2075.00	8400.00
☐1882	Rosecrans-Morgan	Brown	385.00	1050.00	2575.00	9100.00
☐1882	Tillman-Morgan	Brown	385.00	625.00	2075.00	8400.00
☐1882	Tillman-Roberts	Brown	385.00	625.00	2075.00	8400.00
☐1882	Bruce-Roberts	Brown	385.00	625.00	2075.00	8400.00
☐1882	Lyons-Roberts	Brown	385.00	625.00	2075.00	8400.00

SECOND CHARTER PERIOD (Large Size)
Second Issue (Blue seal, green back with date "1882–1908")

Back Design: Green with date "1882–1908" center.

SERIES	SIGNATURES	SEAL	A.B.P.	GOOD	V.FINE	UNC.
☐1882	Rosecrans-Huston	Blue	275.00	528.00	1600.00	5000.00
☐1882	Rosecrans-Nebeker	Blue	275.00	528.00	1600.00	5000.00
☐1882	Tillman-Morgan	Blue	275.00	528.00	1600.00	5000.00
☐1882	Tillman-Roberts	Blue	275.00	528.00	1600.00	5000.00
☐1882	Bruce-Roberts	Blue	275.00	528.00	1600.00	5000.00
☐1882	Lyons-Roberts	Blue	275.00	528.00	1600.00	5000.00
☐1882	Vernon-Treat	Blue	275.00	528.00	1600.00	5000.00
☐1882	Napier-McClung	Blue	275.00	528.00	1600.00	5000.00

This note was also issued with (value) ONE HUNDRED DOLLARS
on the back. Very rare. — 40,100.00 5,000.00 95,000.00 —

ONE HUNDRED DOLLAR NOTES (1902)
NATIONAL BANK NOTES
THIRD CHARTER PERIOD (Large Size)

Face Design: Portrait of John J. Knox left.

Back Design: Male figures with shield and flags.
First Issue (Red seal)

SERIES	SIGNATURES	SEAL	A.B.P.	GOOD	V.FINE	UNC.
☐1902	Lyons-Roberts	Red	430.00	675.00	2025.00	10,200.00
☐1902	Lyons-Treat	Red	340.00	525.00	1825.00	8700.00
☐1902	Vernon-Treat	Red	340.00	525.00	1825.00	8700.00

Second Issue*
Design is similar to previous note. Seal and serial numbers are now blue; back of note has date "1902–1908" added.

SERIES	SIGNATURES	SEAL	A.B.P.	GOOD	V.FINE	UNC.
		Blue	160.00	225.00	650.00	2700.00

Third Issue*
Design continues as previous notes. Seal and serial numbers remain blue, date "1902–1908" removed from back.

SERIES	SIGNATURES	SEAL	A.B.P.	GOOD	V.FINE	UNC.
		Blue	145.00	210.00	550.00	2500.00

* The notes of the **Second and Third Issue** appeared with various signatures: Lyons-Roberts, Lyons-Treat, Vernon-Treat, Vernon-McClung, Napier-McClung, Parker-Burke, Teehee-Burke, Elliott-Burke, Elliott-White, Speelman-White, Woods-White.

ONE HUNDRED DOLLAR NOTES (1929)
NATIONAL BANK NOTES
(Small Size)

Face Design: Portrait of Franklin center. Name of bank and city left. Brown seal right.

SERIES SIGNATURES	SEAL	A.B.P.	V.FINE	UNC.
☐1929 Type I Jones-Woods	Brown	125.00	165.00	360.00
☐1929 Type II Jones-Woods	Brown	140.00	215.00	400.00

ONE HUNDRED DOLLAR NOTES (1878)
SILVER CERTIFICATES

SERIES	SIGNATURES	SEAL	A.B.P.	GOOD	V.FINE	UNC.
☐1878	Scofield-Gilfillan-White	Red				UNIQUE
☐1878	Scofield-Gilfillan-Hopper	Red		NO SPECIMENS KNOWN		
☐1878	Scofield-Gilfillan-Hillhouse	Red		NO SPECIMENS KNOWN		
☐1878	Scofield-Gilfillan-Anthony	Red				UNIQUE
☐1878	Scofield-Gilfillan-Wyman (printed signature of Wyman)	Red		NO SPECIMENS KNOWN		
☐1878	Scofield-Gilfillan	Red				VERY RARE
☐1880	Scofield-Gilfillan	Brown		EXTREMELY RARE		
☐1880	Bruce-Gilfillan	Brown	1750.00	3150.00	14,500.00	36,000.00
☐1880	Bruce-Wyman	Brown	1750.00	3150.00	20,500.00	36,000.00
☐1880	Rosecrans-Huston	Brown	1750.00	3150.00	15,000.00	37,500.00
☐1880	Rosecrans-Nebeker	Brown	1750.00	3150.00	15,000.00	38,500.00

ONE HUNDRED DOLLAR NOTES (1891)
SILVER CERTIFICATES

(Large Size)

Face Design: Portrait of President Monroe.

SERIES	SIGNATURES	SEAL	A.B.P.	GOOD	V.FINE	UNC.
☐1891	Rosecrans-Nebeker	Red	1500.00	3000.00	10,500.00	18,000.00
☐1891	Tillman-Morgan	Red	1500.00	3000.00	10,500.00	18,000.00

This note was also issued in the Series of 1878 and 1880.
They are very rare.

ONE HUNDRED DOLLAR NOTES (1882–1922)
GOLD CERTIFICATES

(Large Size)

Face Design: Portrait of Thomas H. Benton.

SERIES	SIGNATURES	SEAL	A.B.P.	GOOD	V.FINE	UNC.
☐1882	Bruce-Gilfillan	Brown	530.00	875.00	8200.00	22,200.00
☐1882	Bruce-Wyman	Brown	530.00	875.00	8200.00	22,200.00
☐1882	Rosecrans-Hyatt	Lg. Red	530.00	875.00	8700.00	32,200.00
☐1882	Rosecrans-Huston	Lg. Brown	530.00	875.00	8200.00	20,200.00
☐1882	Lyons-Roberts	Sm. Red	185.00	250.00	1800.00	5200.00
☐1882	Lyons-Treat	Sm. Red	185.00	250.00	2600.00	5700.00
☐1882	Vernon-Treat	Sm. Red	185.00	250.00	2000.00	5200.00
☐1882	Vernon-McClung	Sm. Red	185.00	250.00	1600.00	5200.00
☐1882	Napier-McClung	Sm. Red	185.00	275.00	2000.00	5200.00
☐1882	Napier-Thompson	Sm. Red	200.00	375.00	1700.00	10,200.00
☐1882	Napier-Burke	Sm. Red	185.00	240.00	950.00	5200.00
☐1882	Parker-Burke	Sm. Red	185.00	240.00	950.00	5200.00
☐1882	Teehee-Burke	Sm. Red	185.00	240.00	950.00	3950.00
☐1922	Speelman-White	Sm. Red	185.00	250.00	850.00	3850.00

ONE HUNDRED DOLLAR NOTES (1928)
GOLD CERTIFICATES

(Small Size)

Face Design: Portrait of Franklin center. Yellow seal to left. Yellow numbers.

SERIES	SIGNATURES	SEAL	A.B.P.	GOOD	V.FINE	UNC.
☐1928	Woods-Mellon	Gold	135.00	210.00	825.00	3100.00

ONE HUNDRED DOLLAR NOTES (1890–1891)
TREASURY OR COIN NOTES

(Large Size)

Face Design: Portrait of Commodore Farragut to right.

Back Design: Large "100," called "Watermelon Note."

Back Design: ONE HUNDRED in scalloped medallion.

SERIES	SIGNATURES	SEAL	A.B.P.	GOOD	V.FINE	UNC.
☐1890	Rosecrans-Huston	Brown	6200.00	10,100.00	53,000.00	125,000.00+
☐1890	Rosecrans-Nebeker	Red	6200.00	10,100.00	53,000.00	125,000.00+

ONE HUNDRED DOLLAR NOTES (1914)
FEDERAL RESERVE NOTES
(Large Size)

Face Design: Portrait of Franklin in center.
Back Design: Group of five allegorical figures.

SERIES OF 1914,
SIGNATURES OF BURKE-McADOO, RED SEAL
AND RED SERIAL NUMBERS

BANK	A.B.P.	GOOD	V.FINE	UNC.	BANK	A.B.P.	GOOD	V.FINE	UNC.
☐ Boston	200.00	400.00	1100.00	3800.00	☐ Chicago	200.00	400.00	1100.00	3800.00
☐ New York	200.00	400.00	1100.00	3800.00	☐ St. Louis	200.00	400.00	1100.00	3800.00
☐ Philadelphia	200.00	400.00	1100.00	3800.00	☐ Minneapolis	200.00	400.00	1100.00	3800.00
☐ Cleveland	200.00	400.00	1100.00	3800.00	☐ Kansas City	200.00	400.00	1100.00	3800.00
☐ Richmond	200.00	400.00	1100.00	3800.00	☐ Dallas	200.00	400.00	1100.00	3800.00
☐ Atlanta	200.00	400.00	1100.00	3800.00	☐ San Francisco	200.00	400.00	1100.00	3800.00

SERIES OF 1914, DESIGN CONTINUES AS PREVIOUS NOTE, BLUE
SEAL AND BLUE SERIAL NUMBERS

This note was issued with various signatures for each bank (Burke-McAdoo, Burke-Glass, Burke-Huston, White-Mellon).

BANK	A.B.P.	V.FINE	UNC.	BANK	A.B.P.	V.FINE	UNC.
☐ Boston	160.00	500.00	1500.00	☐ Chicago	190.00	500.00	1500.00
☐ New York	160.00	500.00	1500.00	☐ St. Louis	190.00	500.00	1500.00
☐ Philadelphia	160.00	500.00	1500.00	☐ Minneapolis	190.00	500.00	1500.00
☐ Cleveland	160.00	500.00	1500.00	☐ Kansas City	190.00	500.00	1500.00
☐ Richmond	160.00	500.00	1500.00	☐ Dallas	190.00	500.00	1500.00
☐ Atlanta	160.00	500.00	1500.00	☐ San Francisco	190.00	500.00	1500.00

ONE HUNDRED DOLLAR NOTES (1928)
FEDERAL RESERVE NOTES
(Small Size)

Face Design: Portrait of Franklin, black Federal Reserve Seal left with number, green Treasury Seal right.

SERIES OF 1928,
SIGNATURES OF WOODS-MELLON, GREEN SEAL

BANK	A.B.P.	V.FINE	UNC.	BANK	A.B.P.	V.FINE	UNC.
☐Boston	110.00	210.00	525.00	☐ Chicago	110.00	200.00	480.00
☐New York	110.00	170.00	480.00	☐ St. Louis	110.00	175.00	480.00
☐Philadelphia	110.00	170.00	525.00	☐ Minneapolis	110.00	175.00	480.00
☐Cleveland	110.00	210.00	480.00	☐ Kansas City	110.00	180.00	480.00
☐Richmond	110.00	210.00	525.00	☐ Dallas	150.00	200.00	455.00
☐Atlanta	110.00	210.00	525.00	☐ San Francisco	110.00	180.00	455.00

SERIES OF 1928A,
SIGNATURES OF WOODS-MELLON, GREEN SEAL

The number is in black and the Federal Reserve Seal is changed to a letter.
(Small Size)

BANK	A.B.P.	V.FINE	UNC.	BANK	A.B.P.	V.FINE	UNC.
☐Boston	110.00	210.00	380.00	☐ Chicago	110.00	160.00	305.00
☐New York	110.00	180.00	305.00	☐ St. Louis	110.00	160.00	355.00
☐Philadelphia	110.00	210.00	360.00	☐ Minneapolis	110.00	180.00	400.00
☐Cleveland	110.00	175.00	345.00	☐ Kansas City	110.00	200.00	455.00
☐Richmond	110.00	220.00	480.00	☐ Dallas	110.00	160.00	380.00
☐Atlanta	150.00	200.00	405.00	☐ San Francisco	110.00	160.00	355.00

ONE HUNDRED DOLLAR NOTES (1934)
FEDERAL RESERVE NOTES
SERIES OF 1934, SIGNATURES OF JULIAN-MORGENTHAU, GREEN SEAL

BANK	A.B.P.	V.FINE	UNC.	BANK	A.B.P.	V.FINE	UNC.
☐ Boston	110.00	140.00	260.00	☐ Chicago	110.00	140.00	260.00
☐ New York	110.00	140.00	260.00	☐ St. Louis	110.00	140.00	260.00

☐ Philadelphia	110.00	140.00	260.00	☐ Minneapolis	110.00	140.00	260.00
☐ Cleveland	110.00	140.00	260.00	☐ Kansas City	110.00	140.00	260.00
☐ Richmond	110.00	140.00	260.00	☐ Dallas	110.00	140.00	260.00
☐ Atlanta	110.00	140.00	260.00	☐ San Francisco	110.00	140.00	260.00

SERIES OF 1934A, SIGNATURES OF JULIAN-MORGENTHAU, GREEN SEAL

BANK	A.B.P.	V.FINE	UNC.	BANK	A.B.P.	V.FINE	UNC.
☐ Boston	105.00	130.00	250.00	☐ Chicago	105.00	130.00	250.00
☐ New York	105.00	130.00	250.00	☐ St. Louis	—	130.00	250.00
☐ Philadelphia	—	130.00	250.00	☐ Minneapolis	105.00	130.00	250.00
☐ Cleveland	105.00	130.00	250.00	☐ Kansas City	—	130.00	250.00
☐ Richmond	105.00	130.00	250.00	☐ Dallas	105.00	130.00	250.00
☐ Atlanta	105.00	130.00	250.00	☐ San Francisco	105.00	130.00	250.00

SERIES OF 1934B, SIGNATURES OF JULIAN-VINSON, GREEN SEAL

BANK	A.B.P.	V.FINE	UNC.	BANK	A.B.P.	V.FINE	UNC.
☐ Boston	115.00	185.00	380.00	☐ Chicago	120.00	200.00	355.00
☐ New York	115.00	185.00	380.00	☐ St. Louis	120.00	200.00	355.00
☐ Philadelphia	120.00	200.00	355.00	☐ Minneapolis	120.00	200.00	355.00
☐ Cleveland	120.00	200.00	355.00	☐ Kansas City	115.00	185.00	380.00
☐ Richmond	120.00	200.00	355.00	☐ Dallas	115.00	185.00	380.00
☐ Atlanta	120.00	200.00	355.00	☐ San Francisco	115.00	185.00	380.00

SERIES OF 1934C, SIGNATURES OF JULIAN-SNYDER, GREEN SEAL

BANK	A.B.P.	V.FINE	UNC.	BANK	A.B.P.	V.FINE	UNC.
☐ Boston	115.00	185.00	375.00	☐ Chicago	115.00	220.00	250.00
☐ New York	115.00	185.00	240.00	☐ St. Louis	115.00	200.00	250.00
☐ Philadelphia	115.00	185.00	375.00	☐ Minneapolis	115.00	200.00	250.00
☐ Cleveland	115.00	200.00	240.00	☐ Kansas City	115.00	200.00	250.00
☐ Richmond	115.00	200.00	240.00	☐ Dallas	115.00	200.00	250.00
☐ Atlanta	115.00	200.00	240.00	☐ San Francisco	115.00	200.00	250.00

SERIES OF 1934D, SIGNATURES OF JULIAN-SNYDER, GREEN SEAL

BANK	A.B.P.	V.FINE	UNC.	BANK	A.B.P.	V.FINE	UNC.
☐ New York	—	1000.00	1500.00	☐ St. Louis	—	200.00	335.00
☐ Philadelphia	—	200.00	300.00	☐ Dallas	—	200.00	350.00
☐ Atlanta	—	200.00	300.00				
☐ Chicago	—	200.00	350.00				

ONE HUNDRED DOLLAR NOTES (1950)
FEDERAL RESERVE NOTES
SERIES OF 1950, SIGNATURES OF CLARK-SNYDER, GREEN SEAL

BANK	A.B.P.	V.FINE	UNC.	UNC.★	BANK	A.B.P.	V.FINE	UNC.	UNC.★
☐ Boston	110.00	130.00	225.00	815.00	☐ Chicago	110.00	130.00	225.00	815.00
☐ New York	110.00	130.00	225.00	815.00	☐ St. Louis	110.00	130.00	225.00	815.00
☐ Philadelphia	—	115.00	210.00	815.00	☐ Minneapolis	—	115.00	210.00	815.00
☐ Cleveland	110.00	130.00	225.00	815.00	☐ Kansas City	110.00	130.00	225.00	815.00
☐ Richmond	110.00	130.00	225.00	815.00	☐ Dallas	110.00	130.00	225.00	815.00
☐ Atlanta	110.00	130.00	225.00	815.00	☐ San Francisco	—	115.00	210.00	815.00

SERIES OF 1950A, SIGNATURES OF PRIEST-HUMPHERY, GREEN SEAL

BANK	A.B.P.	V.FINE	UNC.	UNC.★	BANK	A.B.P.	V.FINE	UNC.	UNC.★
☐ Boston	—	130.00	220.00	745.00	☐ Chicago	—	130.00	220.00	745.00
☐ New York	—	130.00	220.00	745.00	☐ St. Louis	—	120.00	210.00	745.00
☐ Philadelphia	—	120.00	210.00	745.00	☐ Minneapolis	—	130.00	220.00	745.00
☐ Cleveland	—	120.00	210.00	745.00	☐ Kansas City	—	130.00	220.00	745.00
☐ Richmond	—	120.00	210.00	745.00	☐ Dallas	—	120.00	210.00	745.00
☐ Atlanta	—	130.00	220.00	745.00	☐ San Francisco	—	120.00	210.00	745.00

SERIES OF 1950B, SIGNATURES OF PRIEST-ANDERSON, GREEN SEAL

BANK	A.B.P.	V.FINE	UNC.	UNC.★	BANK	A.B.P.	V.FINE	UNC.	UNC.★
☐ Boston	110.00	130.00	235.00	710.00	☐ Chicago	100.00	110.00	235.00	710.00
☐ New York	110.00	130.00	235.00	710.00	☐ St. Louis	100.00	130.00	235.00	710.00
☐ Philadelphia	100.00	110.00	235.00	710.00	☐ Minneapolis	100.00	130.00	235.00	710.00
☐ Cleveland	110.00	130.00	235.00	710.00	☐ Kansas City	100.00	130.00	235.00	710.00
☐ Richmond	110.00	130.00	235.00	710.00	☐ Dallas	100.00	130.00	235.00	710.00
☐ Atlanta	100.00	110.00	235.00	710.00	☐ San Francisco	100.00	130.00	235.00	710.00

SERIES OF 1950C, SIGNATURES OF SMITH-DILLON, GREEN SEAL

BANK	A.B.P.	V.FINE	UNC.	UNC.★	BANK	A.B.P.	V.FINE	UNC.	UNC.★
☐ Boston	105.00	125.00	235.00	585.00	☐ Chicago	105.00	115.00	235.00	585.00
☐ New York	105.00	125.00	235.00	585.00	☐ St. Louis	105.00	125.00	235.00	585.00
☐ Philadelphia	105.00	125.00	235.00	585.00	☐ Minneapolis	105.00	125.00	235.00	585.00
☐ Cleveland	105.00	115.00	235.00	585.00	☐ Kansas City	105.00	125.00	235.00	585.00
☐ Richmond	105.00	115.00	235.00	585.00	☐ Dallas	105.00	125.00	235.00	585.00
☐ Atlanta	105.00	115.00	235.00	585.00	☐ San Francisco	105.00	125.00	235.00	585.00

SERIES OF 1950D, SIGNATURES OF GRANAHAN-DILLON, GREEN SEAL

BANK	A.B.P.	V.FINE	UNC.	UNC.★	BANK	A.B.P.	V.FINE	UNC.	UNC.★
☐ Boston	105.00	145.00	280.00	910.00	☐ Chicago	105.00	145.00	280.00	910.00
☐ New York	105.00	145.00	280.00	910.00	☐ St. Louis	105.00	145.00	280.00	910.00
☐ Philadelphia	105.00	125.00	255.00	910.00	☐ Minneapolis	105.00	145.00	280.00	910.00
☐ Cleveland	105.00	125.00	255.00	910.00	☐ Kansas City	105.00	125.00	255.00	910.00
☐ Richmond	105.00	125.00	255.00	910.00	☐ Dallas	105.00	125.00	255.00	910.00
☐ Atlanta	105.00	125.00	255.00	910.00	☐ San Francisco	105.00	125.00	255.00	910.00

SERIES OF 1950E, SIGNATURES OF GRANAHAN-FOWLER, GREEN SEAL

BANK	A.B.P.	V.FINE	UNC.	BANK	A.B.P.	V.FINE	UNC.
				☐ Chicago	130.00	220.00	850.00
☐ New York	130.00	220.00	850.00				
				☐ San Francisco	130.00	220.00	850.00

ONE HUNDRED DOLLAR NOTES (1963)
FEDERAL RESERVE NOTES
SERIES OF 1963, (THERE WERE NOT ANY NOTES PRINTED FOR THIS SERIES.)

SERIES OF 1963A, SIGNATURES OF GRANAHAN-FOWLER, GREEN SEAL

BANK	A.B.P.	V.FINE	UNC.	UNC.★	BANK	A.B.P.	V.FINE	UNC.	UNC.★
☐ Boston	105.00	125.00	225.00	335.00	☐ Chicago	105.00	125.00	225.00	335.00
☐ New York	105.00	125.00	225.00	335.00	☐ St. Louis	105.00	125.00	225.00	335.00
☐ Philadelphia	—	115.00	215.00	335.00	☐ Minneapolis	105.00	125.00	225.00	335.00
☐ Cleveland	—	115.00	215.00	335.00	☐ Kansas City	105.00	125.00	225.00	335.00
☐ Richmond	—	115.00	215.00	335.00	☐ Dallas	105.00	125.00	225.00	335.00
☐ Atlanta	—	115.00	215.00	335.00	☐ San Francisco	105.00	125.00	225.00	335.00

ONE HUNDRED DOLLAR NOTES (1969)
FEDERAL RESERVE NOTES
SERIES OF 1969, SIGNATURES OF ELSTON-KENNEDY, GREEN SEAL

BANK	A.B.P.	V.FINE	UNC.	UNC.★	BANK	A.B.P.	V.FINE	UNC.	UNC.★
☐ Boston	—	110.00	190.00	395.00	☐ Chicago	—	110.00	190.00	395.00
☐ New York	—	110.00	190.00	395.00	☐ St. Louis	—	110.00	190.00	395.00
☐ Philadelphia	—	110.00	190.00	395.00	☐ Minneapolis	—	110.00	190.00	395.00
☐ Cleveland	—	110.00	190.00	395.00	☐ Kansas City	—	110.00	190.00	395.00
☐ Richmond	—	110.00	190.00	395.00	☐ Dallas	—	110.00	190.00	395.00
☐ Atlanta	—	110.00	190.00	395.00	☐ San Francisco	—	110.00	190.00	395.00

SERIES OF 1969A, SIGNATURES OF KABIS-CONNALLY, GREEN SEAL

BANK	A.B.P.	V.FINE	UNC.	UNC.★	BANK	A.B.P.	V.FINE	UNC.	UNC.★
☐ Boston	—	110.00	160.00	335.00	☐ Chicago	—	110.00	160.00	335.00
☐ New York	—	110.00	160.00	335.00	☐ St. Louis	—	110.00	160.00	335.00
☐ Philadelphia	—	110.00	150.00	335.00	☐ Minneapolis	—	110.00	160.00	335.00
☐ Cleveland	—	110.00	150.00	335.00	☐ Kansas City	—	110.00	150.00	335.00
☐ Richmond	—	110.00	150.00	335.00	☐ Dallas	—	110.00	150.00	335.00
☐ Atlanta	—	110.00	150.00	335.00	☐ San Francisco	—	110.00	150.00	335.00

SERIES OF 1969B, (THERE WERE NOT ANY NOTES PRINTED FOR THIS SERIES.)

SERIES OF 1969C, SIGNATURES OF BANUELOS-SHULTZ, GREEN SEAL

BANK	A.B.P.	V.FINE	UNC.	UNC.★	BANK	A.B.P.	V.FINE	UNC.	UNC.★
☐ Boston	—	110.00	160.00	235.00	☐ Chicago	—	110.00	150.00	235.00
☐ New York	—	110.00	160.00	235.00	☐ St. Louis	—	110.00	150.00	235.00
☐ Philadelphia	—	110.00	160.00	235.00	☐ Minneapolis	—	110.00	150.00	235.00
☐ Cleveland	—	110.00	150.00	235.00	☐ Kansas City	—	110.00	150.00	235.00
☐ Richmond	—	110.00	150.00	235.00	☐ Dallas	—	110.00	150.00	235.00
☐ Atlanta	—	110.00	150.00	235.00	☐ San Francisco	—	110.00	150.00	235.00

ONE HUNDRED DOLLAR NOTES (1974)
FEDERAL RESERVE NOTES
SERIES OF 1974, SIGNATURES OF NEFF-SIMON, GREEN SEAL

BANK	A.B.P.	V.FINE	UNC.	UNC.★	BANK	A.B.P.	V.FINE	UNC.	UNC.★
☐ Boston	—	110.00	195.00	215.00	☐ Chicago	—	110.00	195.00	215.00
☐ New York	—	110.00	195.00	215.00	☐ St. Louis	—	110.00	195.00	215.00
☐ Philadelphia	—	110.00	195.00	215.00	☐ Minneapolis	—	110.00	195.00	215.00
☐ Cleveland	—	110.00	195.00	215.00	☐ Kansas City	—	110.00	195.00	215.00
☐ Richmond	—	110.00	195.00	215.00	☐ Dallas	—	110.00	195.00	215.00
☐ Atlanta	—	110.00	195.00	215.00	☐ San Francisco	—	110.00	195.00	215.00

ONE HUNDRED DOLLAR NOTES (1977)
FEDERAL RESERVE NOTES
SERIES OF 1977, SIGNATURES OF MORTON-BLUMENTHAL, GREEN SEAL

BANK	A.B.P.	V.FINE	UNC.	UNC.★	BANK	A.B.P.	V.FINE	UNC.	UNC.★
☐ Boston	—	110.00	140.00	215.00	☐ Chicago	—	110.00	130.00	215.00
☐ New York	—	110.00	130.00	215.00	☐ St. Louis	—	110.00	130.00	215.00
☐ Philadelphia	—	110.00	140.00	215.00	☐ Minneapolis	—	110.00	130.00	215.00
☐ Cleveland	—	110.00	140.00	215.00	☐ Kansas City	—	110.00	130.00	215.00
☐ Richmond	—	110.00	140.00	215.00	☐ Dallas	—	110.00	130.00	215.00
☐ Atlanta	—	110.00	140.00	215.00	☐ San Francisco	—	110.00	130.00	215.00

ONE HUNDRED DOLLAR NOTES (1981)
FEDERAL RESERVE NOTES
SERIES OF 1981, SIGNATURES OF BUCHANAN-REGAN, GREEN SEAL

BANK	A.B.P.	V.FINE	UNC.	BANK	A.B.P.	V.FINE	UNC.
☐ Boston	—	110.00	180.00	☐ Chicago	—	110.00	180.00
☐ New York	—	110.00	180.00	☐ St. Louis	—	110.00	180.00
☐ Philadelphia	—	110.00	180.00	☐ Minneapolis	—	110.00	180.00
☐ Cleveland	—	110.00	180.00	☐ Kansas City	—	110.00	180.00
☐ Richmond	—	110.00	180.00	☐ Dallas	—	110.00	180.00
☐ Atlanta	—	110.00	180.00	☐ San Francisco	—	110.00	180.00

SERIES OF 1981A, SIGNATURES OF ORTEGA-REGAN, GREEN SEAL

BANK	A.B.P.	V.FINE	UNC.	BANK	A.B.P.	V.FINE	UNC.
☐ Boston	—	110.00	215.00	☐ Chicago	—	110.00	205.00
☐ New York	—	110.00	215.00	☐ St. Louis	—	110.00	205.00
☐ Philadelphia	—	110.00	215.00	☐ Minneapolis	—	110.00	205.00
☐ Cleveland	—	110.00	205.00	☐ Kansas City	—	110.00	215.00
☐ Richmond	—	110.00	205.00	☐ Dallas	—	110.00	215.00
☐ Atlanta	—	110.00	205.00	☐ San Francisco	—	110.00	215.00

ONE HUNDRED DOLLAR NOTES (1985)
FEDERAL RESERVE NOTES
SERIES OF 1985, SIGNATURES OF ORTEGA-REGAN, GREEN SEAL

BANK	A.B.P.	V.FINE	UNC.	BANK	A.B.P.	V.FINE	UNC.
☐ Boston	—	110.00	190.00	☐ Chicago	—	110.00	190.00
☐ New York	—	110.00	190.00	☐ St. Louis	—	110.00	190.00
☐ Philadelphia	—	110.00	190.00	☐ Minneapolis	—	110.00	190.00
☐ Cleveland	—	110.00	190.00	☐ Kansas City	—	110.00	190.00
☐ Richmond	—	110.00	190.00	☐ Dallas	—	110.00	190.00
☐ Atlanta	—	110.00	190.00	☐ San Francisco	—	110.00	190.00

ONE HUNDRED DOLLAR NOTES (1988)
FEDERAL RESERVE NOTES
SERIES OF 1988, SIGNATURES OF ORTEGA-BRADY, GREEN SEAL

BANK	A.B.P.	V.FINE	UNC.	BANK	A.B.P.	V.FINE	UNC.
☐ Boston	—	110.00	150.00	☐ Chicago	—	110.00	150.00
☐ New York	—	110.00	150.00	☐ St. Louis	—	110.00	150.00
☐ Philadelphia	—	110.00	150.00	☐ Minneapolis	—	110.00	150.00
☐ Cleveland	—	110.00	150.00	☐ Kansas City	—	110.00	150.00
☐ Richmond	—	110.00	150.00	☐ Dallas	—	110.00	150.00
☐ Atlanta	—	110.00	150.00	☐ San Francisco	—	110.00	150.00

ONE HUNDRED DOLLAR NOTES (1990)
FEDERAL RESERVE NOTES
SERIES OF 1990, SIGNATURES OF VILLALPANDO-BRADY, GREEN SEAL

BANK	A.B.P.	V.FINE	UNC.	BANK	A.B.P.	V.FINE	UNC.
☐ Boston	—	—	125.00	☐ Chicago	—	—	125.00
☐ New York	—	—	125.00	☐ St. Louis	—	—	125.00
☐ Philadelphia	—	—	125.00	☐ Minneapolis	—	—	125.00
☐ Cleveland	—	—	125.00	☐ Kansas City	—	—	125.00
☐ Richmond	—	—	125.00	☐ Dallas	—	—	125.00
☐ Atlanta	—	—	125.00	☐ San Francisco	—	—	125.00

ONE HUNDRED DOLLAR NOTES (1993)
FEDERAL RESERVE NOTES
SERIES OF 1993, SIGNATURES OF WITHROW-BENTSEN, GREEN SEAL

BANK	A.B.P.	V.FINE	UNC.	BANK	A.B.P.	V.FINE	UNC.
☐ Boston	—	—	125.00	☐ Chicago	—	—	125.00
☐ New York	—	—	125.00	☐ St. Louis	—	—	125.00
☐ Philadelphia	—	—	125.00	☐ Minneapolis	—	—	125.00
☐ Cleveland	—	—	125.00	☐ Kansas City	—	—	125.00
☐ Richmond	—	—	125.00	☐ Dallas	—	—	125.00
☐ Atlanta	—	—	125.00	☐ San Francisco	—	—	125.00

ONE HUNDRED DOLLAR NOTES (1996)
FEDERAL RESERVE NOTES
SERIES OF 1996, SIGNATURES OF WITHROW-RUBIN, GREEN SEAL

BANK	A.B.P.	V.FINE	UNC.	BANK	A.B.P.	V.FINE	UNC.
☐ Boston	—	—	118.00	☐ Chicago	—	—	118.00
☐ New York	—	—	118.00	☐ St. Louis	—	—	118.00
☐ Philadelphia	—	—	118.00	☐ Minneapolis	—	—	118.00
☐ Cleveland	—	—	118.00	☐ Kansas City	—	—	118.00
☐ Richmond	—	—	118.00	☐ Dallas	—	—	118.00
☐ Atlanta	—	—	118.00	☐ San Francisco	—	—	118.00

ONE HUNDRED DOLLAR NOTES (1929)
FEDERAL RESERVE BANK NOTES
(ISSUED ONLY IN SERIES OF 1929)
(Small Size)

Face Design: Portrait of Franklin, brown seal and numbers.

Back Design

BANK & CITY	SIGNATURES	SEAL	A.B.P.	V.FINE	UNC.
☐New York	Jones-Woods	Brown	105.00	160.00	425.00
☐Cleveland	Jones-Woods	Brown	105.00	160.00	425.00
☐Richmond	Jones-Woods	Brown	105.00	170.00	775.00
☐Chicago	Jones-Woods	Brown	105.00	160.00	425.00
☐Minneapolis	Jones-Woods	Brown	105.00	175.00	425.00
☐Kansas City	Jones-Woods	Brown	105.00	135.00	550.00
☐Dallas	Jones-Woods	Brown	105.00	185.00	1575.00

FIVE HUNDRED, ONE THOUSAND, FIVE THOUSAND, AND TEN THOUSAND DOLLAR NOTES

(Production of notes in denominations above one hundred dollars was discontinued in 1969.)

FEDERAL RESERVE
FIVE HUNDRED DOLLAR NOTES

	A.B.P.	V.FINE	UNC.	BANK
☐ 1928	650.00	800.00	1550.00	ALL BANKS
☐ 1934	625.00	750.00	1225.00	ALL BANKS
☐ 1934A	625.00	725.00	1200.00	ALL BANKS EXCEPT BOSTON/ATLANTA
☐ 1934B	—	RARE	RARE	ATLANTA ONLY
☐ 1934C	—	RARE	RARE	BOSTON ONLY
Gold Certs.				
☐ 1928	800.00	3525.00	19,000.00	

ONE THOUSAND DOLLAR NOTES

	A.B.P.	V.FINE	UNC.
☐ 1928	1200.00	1575.00	2750.00
☐ 1934	1200.00	1500.00	2150.00
☐ 1934A	1200.00	1425.00	2100.00
Gold:			
☐ 1928	1300.00	3600.00	19,500.00
☐ 1934	RARE	RARE	RARE

FIVE THOUSAND DOLLAR NOTES

	A.B.P.	V.FINE	UNC.	BANK
☐ 1928	—	26,000.00	45,000.00	
☐ 1934	—	24,500.00	38,000.00	
☐ 1934A	—	RARE	RARE	ST. LOUIS ONLY
☐ 1934B	—	RARE	RARE	NEW YORK
☐ Gold Certs.		VERY RARE		

TEN THOUSAND DOLLAR NOTES

	A.B.P.	V.FINE	UNC.	BANK
☐ 1928	—	37,500.00	106,000.00	
☐ 1934	—	37,000.00	67,500.00	
☐ 1934A	—	RARE	RARE	CHICAGO ONLY
☐ Gold Certs.		VERY RARE		

SPECIAL REPORT: UNCUT SHEETS

As very few notes exist in the form of full uncut sheets, this is a limited area for the collector. Also, the prices are high, well out of range for most hobbyists.

Uncut sheets available on the market are of Small Size Notes exclusively. In most instances it is not known precisely how they reached public hands. Some were undoubtedly presented as souvenir gifts to Treasury Department officials. In any event, uncut sheets have never been illegal to own, since the notes they comprise are precisely the same as those released into general circulation.

The sheets differ in the number of notes, from a low of six in National Currency sheets to a high of eighteen for some sheets of United States (Legal Tender) Notes and Silver Certificates. Others have twelve notes. These differences are due entirely to the printing method being used at their time of manufacture. Any given note was always printed in sheets of the same size, with the same number of specimens per sheet. If you have an uncut sheet with twelve notes, it means that all notes from the series were printed twelve to a sheet.

The condition standards for uncut sheets are the same as those for single notes. Obviously, an uncut sheet did not circulate as money, but some specimens became worn or damaged as a result of careless storage, accident, or other causes. These impaired sheets do turn up in the market, but there is not much demand for them. Almost every buyer of uncut sheets wants Uncirculated condition. Quite often an uncut sheet will be framed when you buy it. This should be considered a plus, as the frame has probably kept the sheet in immaculate condition. Just to be entirely safe, however, it is wise to examine the reverse side of the sheet for possible staining or other problems.

The following prices were current for uncut sheets in Uncirculated grade at publication time. Gem Uncirculated sheets in absolutely pristine condition command higher prices than those shown.

SILVER CERTIFICATES

DENOMINATION	SERIES	NO. OF NOTES PER SHEET	CURRENT PRICE RANGE IN UNC. CONDITION
$1	1928	12	1950.00–2500.00
$1	1934	12	2400.00–3000.00
$5	1934	12	1400.00–2000.00
$10	1934	12	3900.00–5000.00
$1	1935	12	700.00–900.00
$5	1953	18	1200.00–1600.00
$10	1953	18	3900.00–4800.00

UNITED STATES NOTES (LEGAL TENDER NOTES)

DENOMINATION	SERIES	NO. OF NOTES PER SHEET	CURRENT PRICE RANGE IN UNC. CONDITION
$1	1928	12	9000.00–10,500.00
$2	1928	12	900.00–1150.00
$5	1928	12	1450.00–2250.00
$2	1953	18	800.00–1000.00
$5	1953	18	1500.00–2100.00

NATIONAL CURRENCY

DENOMINATION	SERIES	NO. OF NOTES PER SHEET	CURRENT PRICE RANGE IN UNC. CONDITION
$5	1929	6	750.00–2500.00
$10	1929	6	775.00–2600.00
$20	1929	6	825.00–3000.00
$50	1929	6	4000.00–8000.00
$100	1929	6	5000.00–10,000.00
EMERGENCY NOTES:			
Hawaii $1	1935A		4500.00–7000.00
No. Africa $1	1935A		5000.00–9000.00

MULES
(MIXED PLATE NUMBERS)

All U.S. currency has plate numbers on the face and back. These plate numbers are in the lower right corner somewhat close to the fine scroll design. They refer to the number of the engraved plate used to print the sheet of notes. Each plate can be used for about 100,000 impressions. It is then destroyed and a new plate with the next number in sequence is put into use.

During the term of Treasury officials Julian and Morgenthau, the plate numbers were changed from almost a microscopic to a larger size, far easier to read. Due to this improvement the series designation then in use was an advance on United States Notes, Silver Certificates, and Federal Reserve Notes. The signatures remained Julian-Morgenthau. National Currency and Gold Certificates were not affected, as these were discontinued earlier.

During the changeover period in printing, plates were sometimes mixed up, producing a note with a large number on one side and a small number on the other side. Notes of this variety are called "mules," or "mule notes." This is from a term applied to coins struck with the obverse or reverse die of one year and the opposite side from a die of another year.

Many collectors are eager to add one or more of these mule notes to their collection. Some of the most common mule notes are:

$2 UNITED STATES NOTES	$1 SILVER CERTIFICATES
1928-C, 1928-D	1935, 1935-A
$5 UNITED STATES NOTES	**$5 SILVER CERTIFICATES**
1928-B, 1928-C, 1928-D, 1928-E	1934, 1934-A, 1934-B, 1934-C
	$10 SILVER CERTIFICATES
	1934, 1934A

Mules were also issued in the Federal Reserve Note Series. However, these are not as popular with collectors as the United States Notes and Silver Certificates because of the higher denominations and the twelve districts involved.

The schedule below shows some of the most common mule notes and their values in new condition. The combination of the prefix and suffix letters of the serial numbers on notes is known as "Blocks." For instance: A—A Block, B—A Block.

			UNC.
$2 UNITED STATES NOTE	1928-D	B—A	575.00
		C—A	100.00
		*—A	110.00
$5 UNITED STATES NOTE	1928-B	E—A	150.00
		*—A	575.00
	1928-C	E—A	130.00
		*—A	145.00
$1 SILVER CERTIFICATE	1935	N—A	
		Thru	190.00
		P—A	
	1935-A	M—A	
		Thru	100.00
		V—A	
		C—B	100.00
$5 SILVER CERTIFICATE	1934-A	D—A	
		Thru	100.00
		G—A	
		*—A	185.00
$10 SILVER CERTIFICATE	1934	A—A	110.00
		*—A	150.00
	1934-A	A—A	235.00

Front   **SIZES DIFFERENT**   **Back**

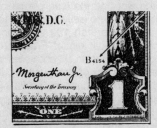

INTRODUCTION TO UNITED STATES FRACTIONAL CURRENCY

Events following the outbreak of the Civil War resulted in a shortage of circulating coinage. Trade was hampered as many merchants, especially in large cities, were unable to make change and only customers presenting the exact amount for a purchase could buy—but they were generally as short on coins as the shop proprietors. Various attempts were made to solve this problem by issuing credit slips (which most customers didn't care for), tokens (which they also didn't care for), and using postage stamps as money. Finally, in 1862, the government stepped in, recognizing that the economy was being seriously hurt, and issued a series of small paper notes as equivalents of coinage denominations. They carried designs adapted from the current postage stamps of the day and were known as Postage Currency or Postal Currency. The more popular title is now Fractional Currency. There were five separate issues of Fractional Currency, three of which occurred during the Civil War and two thereafter, the final one as late as 1874. That a need existed for coin substitutes as late as the 1870s demonstrates the drain placed upon coinage during the war and the long period of recovery. A total of six denominations were issued, from 3¢ to 50¢, comprising 23 designs and more than 100 varieties. Because of its small size and lack of visual impact, Fractional Currency was long shunned by collectors. In recent years it has enjoyed an unprecedented surge of popularity, which, if continued, promises to drive prices beyond present levels. All told, more than $360,000,000 worth of Fractional Currency was circulated. It would be extremely plentiful today but for the fact that most notes were redeemed, leaving only about

$2,000,000 outstanding. This is what collectors have to work with, and a good deal of these are badly preserved.

FIRST ISSUE—Postage Currency August 21st, 1862
5-10-25-50
SECOND ISSUE—Fractional Currency October 10th, 1863
5-10-25-50
THIRD ISSUE—Fractional Currency December 5th, 1864
3-5-10-15-25-50
FOURTH ISSUE—Fractional Currency July 14th, 1869
10-15-25-50
FIFTH ISSUE—Fractional Currency February 26th, 1874
10-25-50

THE FRACTIONAL CURRENCY SHIELD

Fractional currency shields were sold by the Treasury Department in 1866. Specimen notes printed only on one side were used. Very Good–condition shields are valued at $3000 to $3500. Choice condition shields in contemporary frames can sell for $4200. Shields with pink, green, or other backgrounds are more valuable.

FRACTIONAL CURRENCY NOTES

The following notes may be collected by issue or by denomination. We list them here by denomination for convenience. Also, since most of these notes were hastily cut from large sheets, the margin size can vary. Specimens are narrow margined while proofs have wide margins. Prices listed are for Nice "well centered" Uncirculated notes.

THREE-CENT NOTES

THIRD ISSUE

Face Design:	SPECIMEN	FACE		REVERSE
Portrait of President	Light Port.	140.00		60.00
Washington.	Dark Port.	90.00		60.00
	PROOF			
	Light Port	6000.00		225.00
	Dark Port	260.00		225.00

Back Design:
Large "3"
green.

REGULAR ISSUES

	A.B.P.	GOOD	V.FINE	UNC.
☐ With Light Portrait	13.00	19.00	33.00	170.00
☐ With Dark Portrait	14.00	20.00	40.00	310.00

FIVE-CENT NOTES

FIRST ISSUE	SPECIMEN	FACE	85.00	REVERSE	55.00
	PROOF	FACE	290.00	REVERSE	245.00

Face Design:
Portrait of
President
Jefferson,
brown.

Back Design:
"5" black.

REGULAR ISSUES

	A.B.P.	GOOD	V.FINE	UNC.
☐ Perforated edges, monogram ABNCO on back	8.00	12.00	30.00	325.00
☐ Perforated edges, without monogram on back	7.00	11.00	46.00	400.00
☐ Straight edges, monogram ABNCO on back	7.50	10.00	20.00	145.00
☐ Straight edges, without monogram on back	7.00	11.00	25.00	250.00

FIVE-CENT NOTES

SECOND ISSUE	SPECIMEN	FACE	90.00	REVERSE	60.00
	PROOF	FACE	195.00	REVERSE	170.00

Face Design:
Portrait of
President
Washington.

Back Design:
Shield and
brown, "5"s.

REGULAR ISSUES	A.B.P.	GOOD	V.FINE	UNC.
☐Value only in bronze on back	7.00	11.00	18.00	125.00
☐Surcharges 18-63 on back	7.00	10.00	18.00	125.00
☐Surcharges S-18-63 on back	8.00	12.00	19.50	140.00
☐Surcharges R-1-18-63 on back, fiber paper	10.00	16.00	52.00	500.00

FIVE-CENT NOTES

THIRD ISSUE	SPECIMEN	FACE	90.00	REVERSE	60.00
	PROOF	FACE	250.00	REVERSE	175.00

Face Design:
Portrait of
Spencer M.
Clark.

Back Design:
Green or
red.

REGULAR ISSUES	A.B.P.	GOOD	V.FINE	UNC.
☐Without letter "A" on face, red back	7.00	11.00	22.00	240.00
☐With letter "A" on face, red back	7.00	12.00	26.00	265.00
☐Without letter "A" on face, green back	6.00	10.00	18.00	150.00
☐With letter "A" on face, green back	6.00	10.00	19.00	150.00

This note was authorized to have the portraits of the explorers Lewis and Clark on the face. Mr. Spencer M. Clark, who was then head of the Bureau of Currency, flagrantly placed his own portrait on this note. This caused Congress to pass legislation forbidding the likeness of any living person on U.S. currency.

TEN-CENT NOTES

FIRST ISSUE	SPECIMEN	FACE	80.00	REVERSE	60.00
	PROOF	FACE	250.00	REVERSE	225.00

Face Design:
Portrait of
President
Washington.

Back Design:
"10,"
black.

REGULAR ISSUES	A.B.P.	GOOD	V.FINE	UNC.
☐ Perforated edges, monogram ABNCO on back	6.00	8.00	28.00	400.00
☐ Perforated edges, without monogram on back	6.00	8.00	30.00	425.00
☐ Plain edges, monogram ABNCO on back	6.00	10.00	16.00	185.00
☐ Plain edges, without monogram on back	7.00	12.00	38.00	275.00

TEN-CENT NOTES

SECOND ISSUE	SPECIMEN	FACE	90.00	REVERSE	60.00
	PROOF	FACE	225.00	REVERSE	185.00

Face Design:
Portrait of
President
Washington.

Back Design: "10," green.

REGULAR ISSUE	A.B.P.	GOOD	V.FINE	UNC.
☐ Value only surcharge on back	4.00	7.00	18.00	125.00
☐ Surcharge 18-63 on back	4.00	7.00	19.00	125.00
☐ Surcharge S-18-63 on back	5.00	8.00	20.00	130.00
☐ Surcharge I-18-63 on back	9.00	21.00	42.00	275.00
☐ Surcharge O-63 on back	150.00	410.00	1100.00	2200.00
☐ Surcharge T-1-18-63 on back, fiber paper	12.00	20.00	100.00	450.00

TEN-CENT NOTES

THIRD ISSUE	SPECIMEN	FACE	105.00	REVERSE	100.00
	PROOF	FACE	230.00	REVERSE	185.00

Face Design:
Portrait of
President
Washington.

Back Design: "10," green or red.

REGULAR ISSUES	A.B.P.	GOOD	V.FINE	UNC.
☐ Printed signatures Colby-Spinner, green back	6.00	10.00	18.00	130.00
☐ As above, figure "1" near left margin on face	6.00	11.00	18.00	135.00
☐ Printed signatures Colby-Spinner, red back	6.00	10.00	22.00	275.00
☐ As above, figure "1" near left margin, red back	7.00	13.00	31.00	300.00
☐ Autographed signatures Colby-Spinner, red back	10.00	17.00	27.00	275.00
☐ Autographed signatures Jeffries-Spinner, red back	10.00	17.00	51.00	300.00

TEN-CENT NOTES

FOURTH ISSUE	SPECIMEN	FACE	325.00	REVERSE	RARE
	PROOF	FACE	325.00	REVERSE	RARE

Face Design:
Bust of
Liberty.

Back Design:
Green with
TEN and
"10."

REGULAR ISSUES	A.B.P.	GOOD	V.FINE	UNC.
☐ Large red seal, watermarked paper	6.50	9.00	17.00	105.00
☐ Large red seal, pink fibers in paper	6.50	9.00	18.00	105.00
☐ Large seal, pink fibers in paper, right end blue	7.00	9.50	21.00	115.00
☐ Large brown seal	16.00	31.00	83.00	210.00
☐ Small red seal, pink fibers, right end blue	7.00	10.00	27.00	150.00

TEN-CENT NOTES

FIFTH ISSUE	PROOF	FACE	RARE	REVERSE	$400.00

Face Design:
William
Meredith.

Back Design:
Green.

REGULAR ISSUES

	A.B.P.	GOOD	V.FINE	UNC.
☐ Green seal, long narrow key	6.00	8.00	15.00	95.00
☐ Red seal, long narrow key	5.00	6.00	12.00	50.00
☐ Red seal, short stubby key	5.00	6.00	12.00	50.00

FIFTEEN-CENT NOTES
FACES AND BACKS PRINTED SEPARATELY
THIRD ISSUE ALL ARE SPECIMENS AND UNISSUED.

Face Design:
Sherman and
President
Grant.

Back Design:
Green
or red.

	SPECIMEN UNC.	PROOF UNC.
☐ With printed signatures Colby-Spinner	300.00	600.00
☐ With autographed signatures Colby-Spinner	2000.00	7500.00
☐ With autographed signatures Jeffries-Spinner	275.00	550.00
☐ With autographed signatures Allison-Spinner	300.00	500.00
☐ Green back	170.00	250.00
☐ Red back	165.00	250.00

FIFTEEN-CENT NOTES

FOURTH ISSUE   **PROOF**   **FACE**   **RARE**   **REVERSE** 475.00

Face Design:
Bust
of Columbia.

**Back
Design:**
Green
with "15"s.

REGULAR ISSUES	A.B.P.	GOOD	V.FINE	UNC.
☐ Large seal, watermarked paper	20.00	31.00	57.00	195.00
☐ Large seal, pink fibers in paper	20.00	32.00	62.00	210.00
☐ Large seal, pink fibers in paper, right end blue				
	20.00	32.00	57.00	205.00
☐ Large brown seal	26.00	46.00	170.00	RARE
☐ Smaller red seal, pink fibers, right end blue	20.00	31.00	60.00	210.00

TWENTY-FIVE-CENT NOTES

FIRST ISSUE	**SPECIMEN**	**FACE**	95.00	**REVERSE**	65.00
	PROOF	**FACE**	275.00	**REVERSE**	220.00

Face Design:
Five 5¢
Jefferson
Stamps.

**Back
Design:**
Black,
large "25."

REGULAR ISSUES	A.B.P.	GOOD	V.FINE	UNC.
☐ Perforated edges, monogram ABNCO on back	8.00	12.00	32.00	425.00
☐ Perforated edges, without monogram on back	8.00	13.00	57.00	535.00
☐ Straight edges, monogram ABNCO on back	8.00	10.00	19.00	185.00
☐ Straight edges, without monogram on back	9.00	15.00	67.00	585.00

TWENTY-FIVE-CENT NOTES

SECOND ISSUE	**SPECIMEN**	**FACE**	95.00	**REVERSE**	75.00
	PROOF	**FACE**	250.00	**REVERSE**	210.00

Time and climatic condition have changed the purple
color on the back of this note into many variations.

Face Design:
Portrait of
President
Washington.

**Back
Design:**
Purple with
"25."

REGULAR ISSUES	A.B.P.	GOOD	V.FINE	UNC.
☐Value only surcharge on back	7.00	11.00	21.00	225.00
☐Surcharge 18-63 on back	8.00	13.00	21.00	250.00
☐Surcharge A-18-63 on back	7.00	12.00	21.00	235.00
☐Surcharge 1-18-63 on back	19.00	37.00	200.00	595.00
☐Surcharge 2-18-63 on back	7.00	12.00	25.00	300.00
☐Surcharge S-18-63 on back	9.00	16.00	25.00	275.00
☐Surcharge T-1-18-63 on back, fiber paper	11.00	21.00	75.00	360.00
☐Surcharge T-2-18-63 on back, fiber paper	11.00	21.00	75.00	350.00

TWENTY-FIVE-CENT NOTES

THIRD ISSUE	SPECIMEN	FACE	140.00	REVERSE	82.00
	PROOF	FACE	250.00	REVERSE	170.00

All notes have printed signatures of Colby-Spinner.

Face Design:
Portrait of
Fessenden.

**Back
Design:**
Green or
red with "25"

	A.B.P.	GOOD	V.FINE	UNC.
☐Face—bust of Fessenden between solid bronze surcharges, fiber paper, back—green, surcharge M-2-6-5 in corners				
	120.00	190.00	750.00	3100.00
☐As above, with letter "A" in lower left corner of face				
	150.00	310.00	1050.00	4200.00
☐Face—Fessenden, open scroll bronze surcharges, fiber paper, back—green, surcharges M-2-6-5 in corners				
	12.00	21.00	82.00	425.00
☐As above with letter "A" in lower left corner of face				
	9.00	18.00	78.00	450.00
☐Face—Fessenden, open scroll surcharges, plain paper, back—green, value surcharges only				
	8.50	14.00	30.00	155.00
☐As before, letter "A" in lower left corner of face, back—green, plain paper	10.00	17.00	42.00	165.00
☐Face—Fessenden, red back, value surcharge only	12.00	19.00	45.00	240.00
☐As above, letter "A" in lower left corner of face				
	13.00	20.00	48.00	295.00

TWENTY-FIVE-CENT NOTES
FOURTH ISSUE SPECIMENS AND PROOFS RARE

Face Design:
Portrait of
President
Washington
and Treasury Seal.

**Back
Design:**
Green.

REGULAR ISSUES	A.B.P.	GOOD	V.FINE	UNC.
☐Large seal, plain watermarked paper	5.00	8.50	22.00	120.00
☐Large seal, pink silk fiber in paper	5.00	8.50	22.00	120.00
☐Large seal, pink fibers in paper, right end blue	5.00	8.50	23.00	120.00
☐Large brown seal, right end blue	35.00	70.00	282.00	1100.00
☐Smaller red seal, right end blue	5.00	9.00	22.00	120.00

TWENTY-FIVE-CENT NOTES
FIFTH ISSUE SPECIMENS AND PROOFS RARE

Face Design:
Portrait of
Walker and
red seal.

**Back
Design:**
Black.

REGULAR ISSUES	A.B.P.	GOOD	V.FINE	UNC.
☐With long narrow key in Treasury Seal.	6.00	8.00	16.00	53.50
☐With short stubby key in Treasury Seal	6.00	8.00	16.00	53.50

FIFTY-CENT NOTES

FIRST ISSUE	SPECIMEN	FACE	135.00	REVERSE	100.00
	PROOF	FACE	275.00	REVERSE	220.00

Face Design:
Five 10¢
Washington
stamps.

**Back
Design:**
Green.

REGULAR ISSUES	A.B.P.	GOOD	V.FINE	UNC.
☐Perforated edges, monogram ABNCO on back	10.00	14.00	81.00	675.00
☐Perforated edges, without monogram on back	13.00	20.00	75.00	700.00
☐Straight edges, monogram ABNCO on back	7.00	10.00	30.00	300.00
☐Straight edges, without monogram	14.00	20.00	85.00	400.00

FIFTY-CENT NOTES

FIRST ISSUE	SPECIMEN	FACE	135.00	REVERSE	105.00
	PROOF	FACE	330.00	REVERSE	260.00

Face Design:
Portrait of
President
Washington.

Back Design:
Red.

REGULAR ISSUES	A.B.P.	GOOD	V.FINE	UNC.
☐Surcharge 18-63 on back	7.00	11.00	35.00	500.00
☐Surcharge A-18-63 on back	6.00	11.00	26.00	325.00
☐Surcharge O-1-18-63, fiber paper	7.00	25.00	75.00	550.00
☐Surcharge R-2-18-63, fiber paper	10.00	17.00	46.00	455.00
☐Surcharge T-1-18-63, fiber paper	7.00	15.00	46.00	425.00

FIFTY-CENT NOTES

THIRD ISSUE	SPECIMENS	FACE	150.00	REVERSE	110.00
	PROOFS FACE		325.00	REVERSE	275.00

Face Design:
Justice with
sword,
shield,
scales.

Back Design:
Green
or red.

The following notes have printed signatures of Colby-Spinner and have *green backs*.

REGULAR ISSUES	A.B.P.	GOOD	V.FINE	UNC.
☐Value surcharge and S-2-6-4 on back, fiber paper				
			10,000.00	25,000.00
☐Value surcharge and A-2-6-5 on back, fiber paper				
	16.00	32.00	90.00	1150.00
☐As above with "1" and letter "A" on face, A-2-6-5 on back				
	55.00	85.00	700.00	3100.00
☐As above with "1" only on face, A-2-6-5 on back				
	16.00	32.00	75.00	625.00
☐As above with letter "A" only on face, A-2-6-5 on back				
	16.00	37.00	80.00	625.00
☐A-2-6-5 on back, *narrowly spaced,* plain paper				
	9.00	12.00	60.00	475.00

	A.B.P.	GOOD	V.FINE	UNC.
☐As above, numeral "1" and letter "A" on face				
	11.00	22.00	70.00	525.00
☐As above, numeral "1" only on face	6.00	12.00	65.00	475.00
☐As above, letter "A" only on face	11.00	18.00	71.00	525.00
☐A-2-6-5 on back, *widely spaced*, plain paper	10.00	18.00	71.00	535.00
☐As above, numeral "1" and letter "A" on face				
	20.00	40.00	300.00	1775.00
☐As above, numeral "1" only on face	7.00	13.00	70.00	650.00
☐As above, letter "A" only on face	6.00	12.00	70.00	650.00
☐Without position letters or back surcharges	6.00	12.00	60.00	475.00
☐As above with numeral "1" and letter "A" on face				
	15.00	26.00	150.00	1525.00
☐As above with numeral "1" only on face	5.00	11.00	60.00	485.00
☐As above with letter "A" only on face	6.00	12.00	66.00	475.00

The following notes have printed signatures of Colby-Spinner and *red backs*.

	A.B.P.	GOOD	V.FINE	UNC.
☐Value surcharge and S-2-6-4 on back, fiber				
	125.00	175.00	1400.00	31,000.00
☐As above, numeral "1" and letter "A"	150.00	350.00	2700.00	50,000.00
☐As above, numeral "1" only on face	125.00	200.00	750.00	30,000.00
☐As above, letter "A" only on face	135.00	225.00	850.00	30,000.00
☐Value surcharge and A-2-6-5 on back, plain				
	9.00	18.00	78.00	595.00
☐As above, numeral "1" and letter "A"	47.00	77.00	483.00	2130.00
☐As above, numeral "1" only on face	10.00	19.00	79.00	505.00
☐As above, letter "A" only on face	11.00	20.00	79.00	580.00
☐No surcharge on back, plain paper	11.00	20.00	85.00	680.00
☐As above, numeral "1" and letter "A" on face				
	25.00	48.00	258.00	2130.00
☐As above, numeral "1" only on face	12.00	24.00	145.00	930.00
☐As above, letter "A" only on face	12.00	27.00	103.00	655.00

The following notes have autographed signatures of Colby-Spinner and *red backs*.

	A.B.P.	GOOD	V.FINE	UNC.
☐Value surcharge and S-2-6-4 on back, fiber	37.00	80.00	200.00	1400.00
☐Value surcharge and A-2-6-5 on back, fiber	35.00	75.00	180.00	1100.00
☐Value surcharge only on back, plain paper	15.00	27.00	80.00	650.00

FIFTY-CENT NOTES

THIRD ISSUE	SPECIMEN	FACE	130.00	REVERSE	120.00
	PROOF	FACE	400.00	REVERSE	280.00

Face Design: Bust of Spinner with surcharges.
Back Design: Green or red.

The following notes have printed signatures of Colby-Spinner, and *green backs*.

REGULAR ISSUES	A.B.P.	GOOD	V.FINE	UNC.
☐Value surcharge and A-2-6-5 on back	10.00	27.00	95.00	335.00
☐As above, numeral "1" and letter "A" on face	22.00	41.00	225.00	710.00
☐As above, numeral "1" only on face	8.00	19.00	57.00	360.00
☐As above, letter "A" only on face	8.00	18.00	80.00	435.00
☐Value surcharge only on back	8.00	12.00	50.00	385.00
☐As above, numeral "1" and letter "A" on face	12.00	28.00	60.00	385.00
☐As above, numeral "1" only on face	8.00	14.00	50.00	385.00
☐As above, letter "A" only on face	8.00	14.00	50.00	435.00

TYPE II BACK DESIGN

	A.B.P.	GOOD	V.FINE	UNC.
☐No back surcharge	9.00	17.00	50.00	360.00
☐Numeral "1" and letter "A" on face	20.00	37.00	90.00	435.00
☐Numeral "1" only on face	10.00	17.00	57.00	375.00
☐Letter "A" only on face	10.00	20.00	75.00	435.00

The following notes have a portrait of Spinner, printed signatures of Colby-Spinner, *red backs*, and are Type I.

REGULAR ISSUES	A.B.P.	GOOD	V.FINE	UNC.
☐Value surcharge and A-2-6-5 on back	10.00	18.00	60.00	360.00
☐As above with numeral "1" and letter "A"	20.00	41.00	145.00	860.00
☐As above with numeral "1" only on face	12.00	17.00	60.00	410.00
☐As above with letter "A" only on face	12.00	24.00	73.00	510.00

The following notes have autographed signatures, *red backs,* and are Type I.

	A.B.P.	GOOD	V.FINE	UNC.
☐Autographed signatures COLBY-SPINNER, back surcharged value and A-2-6-5	11.00	28.00	75.00	485.00
☐Autographed signatures ALLISON-SPINNER, back surcharged value and A-2-6-5	11.00	28.00	90.00	560.00
☐Autographed signatures ALLISON-NEW, back surcharged value and A-2-6-5	400.00	650.00	1600.00	5200.00

FIFTY-CENT NOTES
FOURTH ISSUE SPECIMENS AND PROOFS RARE

Face Design:
Bust
of Lincoln.

**Back
Design:**
Green.

	A.B.P.	GOOD	V.FINE	UNC.
☐ Plain paper	17.00	23.00	65.00	525.00
☐ Paper with pink fibers	17.00	23.00	70.00	525.00

FIFTY-CENT NOTES
FOURTH ISSUE SPECIMENS AND PROOFS RARE

Face Design:
Bust
of Stanton.

**Back
Design:**
Green
with "50."

	A.B.P.	GOOD	V.FINE	UNC.
☐ Red seal and signatures ALLISON-SPINNER, paper with pink fibers, blue ends	10.00	15.00	42.00	265.00

FIFTY-CENT NOTES
FOURTH ISSUE SPECIMENS AND PROOFS RARE

Face Design:
Bust of
Samuel
Dexter.

**Back
Design:**
Green with
"50."

	A.B.P.	GOOD	V.FINE	UNC.
☐ Green seal, pink fibers, blue ends	7.00	11.00	23.00	180.00

FIFTY-CENT NOTES
FIFTH ISSUE SPECIMENS AND PROOFS RARE

Face Design:
Bust
of Crawford.

**Back
Design:**
Green with
"50."

	A.B.P.	GOOD	V.FINE	UNC.
☐ Signatures ALLISON-NEW, paper with pink fibers, blue ends	6.00	8.00	19.00	80.00

ERROR OR FREAK NOTES

Notes have been misprinted from time to time since the earliest days of currency. The frequency of misprintings and other abnormalities has increased in recent years due to heavier production and high-speed machinery. This has provided a major sub-hobby for note collectors. Freaks and errors have become very popular, their appeal and prices showing upward movement each year.

On the following pages we have pictured and described most of the more familiar and collectible Error Notes. Pricing is approximate only because many notes bearing the same general type of error differ in severity of error from one specimen to another. As a general rule, the less glaring or obvious errors carry a smaller premium value. Very valuable Error Notes include double denominations, or bills having the face of one denomination and reverse side of another.

Error and Freak Notes do turn up in everyday change. Specimens are located either in that fashion or from bank packs. As far as circulated specimens are concerned, some Error Notes have passed through so many hands before being noticed that the condition is not up to collector standards. This, of course, results in a very low premium valuation.

Values given below are for the specimens pictured and described. Different premiums may be attached to other specimens with similar errors, or notes showing the same errors but of different denominations.

MISMATCHED SERIAL NUMBERS

On ordinary notes, the serial number in the lower left of the obverse matches that in the upper right. When it fails to, even by the difference of a single digit, this is known as a "mismatched serial number." It occurs as the result of a cylinder or cylinders in the high-speed numbering machine becoming jammed. If more than one digit is mismatched, the value will be greater.

	V. FINE	UNC.
☐ $1 Federal Reserve Note, Series 1969, signatures Elston-Kennedy	115.00	258.00

	V. FINE	UNC.
☐ $1 Silver Certificate, Series 1957B, signatures Granahan-Dillon	110.00	220.00

	V. FINE	UNC.
☐ $1 Federal Reserve Note, Series 1977A, signatures Morton-Miller	115.00	205.00

INVERTED THIRD PRINT

The inverted third print is also known as "inverted overprint." The Treasury Seal, District Seal, Serial Numbers, and District Number are inverted on the obverse side of the note, or printed upside-down, caused by the sheet of notes (having already received the primary design on front and back) being fed upside-down into the press for this so-called "third print." (The back design is the "first print," the front is the "second print," and these various additions comprise the "third print." It is not possible to print these third print items at the same time as the obverse design, since they are not standard on every bill. At one time the signatures were included in the third print, but these are now engraved directly into the plate and are part of the second print.)

Though very spectacular, inverted third print errors are not particularly scarce and are especially plentiful in 1974 and 1976 series notes.

	V. FINE	UNC.
□ $5 Federal Reserve Note, Series 1974, signatures Neff-Simon	150.00	280.00

	V. FINE	UNC.
□ $2 Federal Reserve Note, Series 1976, signatures Neff-Simon	450.00	675.00

	V. FINE	UNC.
☐ $1 Federal Reserve Note, Series 1974, signatures Neff-Simon	160.00	350.00

	V. FINE	UNC.
☐ $50 Federal Reserve Note, Series 1977, signatures Morton-Blumenthal	420.00	675.00

	V. FINE	UNC.
☐ $20 Federal Reserve Note, Series 1974, signatures Neff-Simon	215.00	420.00

	V. FINE	UNC.
☐ $10 Federal Reserve Note, Series 1974, signatures Neff-Simon	200.00	380.00

COMPLETE OFFSET TRANSFER

Offset transfers are not, as is often believed, caused by still-wet printed sheets coming into contact under pressure. Though very slight offsetting can occur in that manner, it would not create notes as spectacular as those pictured here, in which the offset impression is almost as strong as the primary printing. These happen as a result of the printing press being started an instant or so before the paper is fed in. Instead of contacting the paper, the inked plate makes its impression upon the machine bed. When the paper is then fed through, it picks up this "ghost" impression from the bed, in addition to the primary impression it is supposed to receive. Each successive sheet going through the press will acquire the impression until all ink is totally removed from the machine bed. But, naturally, the first sheet will show the transfer strongest, and the others will be weaker and weaker. Obviously, the market value of such notes depends largely on the strength of the offset impression. The heavier and more noticeable it is, the more valuable the note will be—all other things being equal.

	V. FINE	UNC.
☐ $5 Federal Reserve Note, Series 1977, signatures Morton-Blumenthal, offset of reverse side of face		
Dark	125.00	300.00
Light	110.00	150.00

	V. FINE	UNC.
☐$1 Federal Reserve note, Series 1974, signatures Neff-Simon, offset of reverse side of face.		
Dark	100.00	290.00
Light	100.00	160.00

PARTIAL OFFSET TRANSFER

The most logical explanation for this error is that a sheet of paper fed into the press incorrectly became mangled or torn, and part of the inked plate contacted the printing press bed. Therefore, wet ink was left on those portions of the press bed not covered by paper. When the next sheet was fed through, it received the correct impression, plus it acquired a partial offset transfer by contacting this wet area of the press bed. Just as with offset transfers, the first sheet going through the press following an accident of this kind will receive the strongest transfer, and it will become gradually less noticeable on succeeding sheets.

	V. FINE	UNC.
☐$1 Federal Reserve Note, Series 1969D, signatures Banuelos-Schultz, offset of a portion of reverse side on face		
Dark	45.00	120.00
Light	40.00	100.00

PRINTED FOLD

Notes showing printed folds occur as the result of folds in the paper before printing, which probably happen most often when the sheet is being fed into the press. If the sheet is folded in such a manner that a portion of the reverse side is facing upward, as shown here, it will receive a part of the impression intended for its obverse. Naturally the positioning of these misplaced portions of printing is very random, depending on the nature and size of the fold.

	V. FINE	UNC.
☐ $20 Federal Reserve Note, Series 1977, signatures Morton-Blumenthal, Federal Reserve District seal and District number printed on reverse	140.00	320.00

THIRD PRINT ON REVERSE

The cause of this error is obvious, the sheet having been fed through the press on the wrong side (back instead of front) for the third impression or "third print." In the so-called third print, the note receives the Treasury and Federal Reserve District seals, district numbers, and serial numbers.

	V. FINE	UNC.
☐ $1 Federal Reserve Note, third print on reverse	150.00	300.00

BOARD BREAKS

The terminology of this error is misleading. It suggests that the fernlike unprinted areas were caused by a broken printing plate. Actually they must have resulted from something—probably linty matter—sticking to the printing ink. The assumption reached by the public, when it encounters such a note, is that the blank streaks were caused by the paper being folded in printing. This, however, is not possible, as that would yield an error of a much different kind (*see* Printed Fold).

It should be pointed out that board breaks are easily created by counterfeiters by erasing portions of the printed surface, and that the collector ought to examine such specimens closely.

	V. FINE	UNC.
☐ $20 Federal Reserve Note, board breaks on reverse	75.00	175.00

MISSING SECOND PRINT

The "second print" is the front face, or obverse of the note—the "first print" being the reverse or back. A note with a missing second print has not received the primary impression on its obverse, though the back is normal and the front carries the standard third print matter (Treasury Seal, serial numbers, etc.). These errors, while they probably occur frequently, are so easily spotted by B.E.P. checkers that such notes are very scarce on the market.

	V. FINE	UNC.
☐ $10 Federal Reserve Note, missing second print	250.00	525.00

PRINTED FOLD

This note was folded nearly in half before receiving the third print, which fell across the waste margin on the reverse side. Had the note not been folded, this waste margin would have been removed in the cutting process. This note, when unfolded, is grotesque in shape.

	V. FINE	UNC.
☐ $1 Federal Reserve Note, printed fold with Federal Reserve District seal, district numbers, and serial numbers on reverse. (Naturally, this note lacks the "third print" matter, such as the Treasury Seal, that was supposed to appear on the righthand side of the obverse.)	290.00	575.00

V. FINE   **UNC.**

☐ $5 Federal Reserve Note. Printed fold with entire Federal
Reserve District seal, portion of another Federal Reserve
District seal, and portion of two different serial numbers
on the reverse. It may be hard to imagine how a freak of
this nature occurs. This note was folded diagonally along a
line bisecting the Lincoln Memorial building slightly to the
right of center. The lefthand portion of the reverse side
was thereby drawn down across the lefthand side of the
obverse, extending well below the bottom of the note. It
reached far enough down to catch the district seal intended
for the note beneath it, as well as a bit of the serial number. This is why the two serial numbers are different; they
were supposed to go on two different notes. Obviously,
when something this dramatic happens in printing, not
only one error note is created but several—at least—at the
same time. Not all necessarily reach circulation, however.

         380.00   825.00

THIRD PRINT BLACK INK MISSING OR LIGHT

Though the machinery used is ultramodern, U.S. currency
notes are printed by the same basic technique used when
printing was first invented more than 500 years ago. Ink is
spread on the metal plates and these are pressed on the
sheets as they go through the press. Because the inking is
manually fed (as is the paper), an even flow is usually
achieved. When an under-inked note is found, it is generally
merely "light," giving a faded appearance. But sometimes
the plate will be very improperly inked, due to mechanical
misfunction or some other cause, resulting in whole
areas being unprinted or so lightly printed that they
cannot be seen without close inspection. These are not

especially valuable notes but counterfeit specimens are frequently made.

	V. FINE	UNC.

☐$1 Federal Reserve Note, Series 1977, signatures of Morton-Blumenthal. Federal Reserve District seal and District numbers missing from lefthand side, remainder of "third print" material light but distinct. If the lefthand serial number was strong, there might be suspicion of this being a counterfeit.   90.00   200.00

THIRD PRINT GREEN INK MISSING OR LIGHT

In this case, the green, rather than the black, ink was applied too lightly to the printing plate.

	V. FINE	UNC.

☐$5 Federal Reserve Note, Series 1977, signatures of Morton-Blumenthal   40.00   140.00

NOTE FOLDED DURING OVERPRINT

This note was folded as it was being overprinted and failed to receive the District seal and District numbers at the left side of its obverse. This kind of error, like all involving missing portions of printing, has been extensively counterfeited.

	V. FINE	UNC.
☐ $2 Federal Reserve Note, Series 1976, signatures of Neff-Simon	90.00	200.00

FAULTY ALIGNMENT

Notes of this kind were formerly called "miscut," and sometimes still are. "Faulty alignment" is a more inclusive term which encompasses not only bad cutting but accidents in printing. If the sheet shifts around in the press, it will not receive the printed impressions exactly where they should be. Even if the cutting is normal, the resulting note will be misaligned; the cutting machine cannot correct botched printing. It is very easy to determine where the fault lies. If one side of the note has its design higher than the opposite side, this is a printing error. If the misalignment occurs equally on both sides, the problem was in cutting. Since the two sides are not printed in the same operation, it would be a one-in-a-million chance for them to become equally misaligned.

The value of such notes depends upon the degree of misalignment. Collectors are especially fond of specimens showing a portion—even if very slight, as with the one pictured of an adjoining note.

	V. FINE	UNC.
☐ $5 Federal Reserve Note, bottom left of reverse shaved (or "bled"), corresponding portion of adjoining note just visible at top. This ranks as a "dramatic" specimen.		
Slight	60.00	125.00
Dramatic	50.00	240.00

INSUFFICIENT PRESSURE

Under-inking of the printing plate is not the only cause of weak or partially missing impressions. If the press is not operating correctly and the inked plate meets the sheet with insufficient pressure, the result is similar to under-inking. This probably happens as a result of a sheet going through just as the press is being turned off for the day, or at other intervals. Supposedly all action ceases at the instant of turnoff, but considering the rapidity of this operation, it is likely that a random sheet could pass through and be insufficiently impressed. The note pictured here received normal "third print," as is generally the case with notes whose first or second print is made with insufficient pressure.

	V. FINE	UNC.
☐ $20 Federal Reserve Note, Series 1977, signatures of Morton-Blumenthal	135.00	300.00

PRINTED FOLD

This note, along with a large portion of the adjoining note, became folded after the second print. When it passed through the press to receive the third print or overprints (seals, serial numbers, etc.), these naturally failed to appear on the folded area.

	V. FINE	UNC.
☐ $1 Federal Reserve Note, printed fold with overprints partially missing		
Small	75.00	200.00
Large	175.00	385.00

DOUBLE IMPRESSION

Double impressions have traditionally been traced to the sheet of notes passing through the press twice, which would be the logical explanation. However, in considering the method by which currency is printed, it would seem more likely that double impression notes have not made two trips through the press. They probably result from the automatic paper feed jamming. The sheet just printed fails to be ejected, and the printing plate falls upon it a second time instead of on a fresh sheet. This does not merely create a strong impression, but a twin, or a ghost, impression, since the sheet is not positioned exactly the same way for the second strike. Though the paper feed may not be operating properly, there will still be some slight movement—enough to prevent the second impression from falling directly atop the first.

	V. FINE	UNC.
☐ $1 Federal Reserve Note, Series 1977A, signatures of Morton-Miller, double "second print" impression		
Partial	175.00	375.00
Complete	410.00	850.00

DOUBLE IMPRESSION OF OVERPRINTS ("DOUBLE THIRD PRINT")

This note is normal as far as the primary obverse and reverse printings are concerned. It received twin impressions of the overprints or "third print." This was not caused by jamming of the paper feed as discussed above. Naturally, the serial numbers are different, as the automatic numbering machine turns with every rise and fall of the press.

	V. FINE	UNC.
☐ $20 Federal Reserve Note, Series 1950, signatures of Priest-Humphrey, double impression of overprints.		
Partial	240.00	465.00
Complete	450.00	750.00

THIRD PRINT (OR OVERPRINTS) SHIFTED

Whenever the overprints (serial number, seals, etc.) are out of position, vertically or horizontally, this is known as "third print shifted" or "overprints shifted." In the example pictured, shifting is extreme. This is a premium value specimen which would command the higher of the two sums quoted. Normally, the overprinting on a "shifted" note fails to touch the portrait, or touches it only slightly. The cause of this kind of error is a sheet feeding incorrectly into the press for the overprinting operation. As striking and desirable as these notes are to collectors, they often go unnoticed by the public.

	V. FINE	UNC.
☐ $100 Federal Reserve Note, Series 1969C, signatures of Banuelos-Schultz, third print shifted.		
Slight	175.00	375.00
Dramatic	210.00	390.00

INK SMEARS

Ink smearing is one of the more common abnormalities of currency notes. Generally it can be attributed to malfunction of the automatic inking device which inks the printing plate. When performing properly, ink is applied at a steady, controlled pace to the printing plate. A very minor disorder in the machine can dispense enough extra ink to yield very spectacular "smeared notes," such as the one illustrated. The value of ink smear notes depends upon the area and intensity of the smear. They are quite easily faked, so the buyer should be cautious.

	V. FINE	UNC.
☐ $1 Federal Reserve Note, ink smear		
Small	40.00	85.00
Large	60.00	135.00

PRINTING FOLD

This note was crumpled along the right side prior to the third printing or application of overprints. Hence the "third print" matter on the lefthand side is normal, but portions of the overprint on the right appear on the note's reverse side.

	V. FINE	UNC.
☐ $20 Federal Reserve Note, Series 1977, signatures Morton-Blumenthal.	130.00	250.00

BLANK CREASE

It occasionally happens that a note becomes creased prior to the reverse or obverse printing in such a way that a small fold is created. During the printing procedure this fold hides a portion of the note's surface, which fails to receive the impression. These notes are actually double errors—the cutting machine cuts them without knowledge of the fold, and when the fold is opened out the bill is then of larger than normal size. Since "crease errors" are difficult to spot in the Bureau of Engraving and Printing's checking, they find their way into circulation in rather sizable numbers. It is difficult to place standard values on them because the price depends on the exact nature of the specimen. The wider the crease, the more valuable the note will be. Premium values are attached to notes with multiple creases that cause the blank unprinted area to fall across the portrait.

	V. FINE	UNC.
☐ Blank crease note, any denomination. Value stated is collector premium over and above face value. (If note has additional value because of series, signatures, etc., this too must be added.)		
Single crease	35.00	75.00
Multiple crease	35.00	85.00

MIXED DENOMINATION

The two notes pictured are normal in themselves, and if they were not owned together as a set, no premium value would be attached to them. The error (which may be dubious to term as such) lies with their serial numbers. The $5 Note has a serial number one digit higher than the $1, suggesting that it was fed into the printing machine intended to print overprints (or "third prints") on $1 bills. Even when this does happen (probably infrequently), it is very difficult to obtain "matching" notes of the kind illustrated, in which the serial numbers are only a single digit apart. Even if you had a $5 Note and $1 Note (or other combination of denominations) from sheets that were fed one after the other, the odds on getting one-digit-apart serial numbers are extremely small.

The value is given for an Uncirculated set only, as there would be no possibility of finding such matched notes except in a bank pack. Once released into circulation, they may never again be mated.

	UNC.
☐ Mixed denomination pair from bank pack, $5 Federal Reserve Note within pack of $1 Federal Reserve Notes	3825.00

BLANK REVERSE

U.S. currency has its reverse printed before the obverse—in other words, back before front. The only logical explanation for blank reverse notes is that blank paper found its way into the batch of sheets on which reverses had already been printed. They were then fed—without detection—into the press for application of the obverse. They continued to escape notice during printing of the overprints, and miraculously got into circulation.

	V. FINE	UNC.
☐ $100 Federal Reserve Note, blank reverse	385.00	675.00

	V. FINE	UNC.

☐$20 Federal Reserve Note, Series 1977,
signatures of Morton-Blumenthal Blank reverse   160.00   345.00

	V. FINE	UNC.

☐$10 Federal Reserve Note, Series 1974,
signatures of Neff-Simon Blank reverse   160.00   310.00

	V. FINE	UNC.

☐$1 Federal Reserve Note, Series 1977,
signatures of Morton-Blumenthal Blank reverse   140.00   265.00

DOUBLE DENOMINATION COUNTERFEIT

This is a counterfeit or faked error. We include it to show the kind of work done by counterfeiters, and how such items can be made to resemble genuine errors. This happens to be a counterfeit of an error note that cannot exist in its genuine state. Thus, there can be no hesitancy in proclaiming it a fake. Anyone who is even slightly familiar with the way currency is printed should instantly recognize this item as a fraud.

Nevertheless, fakers succeed in selling (often at high prices) specimens of this kind, probably because some collectors want the impossible for their albums. Genuine double or twin denomination notes have the obverse of one denomination and the reverse of a different denomination. They do not consist of two obverses or two reverses, such as the one pictured. The note illustrated carries four serial numbers. For it to be genuine, it would have had to pass through the "third print" (overprinting) process twice. Obviously it was made by gluing a $1 and $5 Note together. Much more deceptive paste-ups are created with the notes correctly paired so that the obverse of one and reverse of the other shows. Beware!

INVERTED OBVERSE

U.S. currency is printed reverse first. Therefore, when the back and front do not face in the same vertical direction (as they should), the note is known as an "inverted obverse." The term "inverted reverse" is never used. This, of course, results from the sheet being fed through upside-down for the obverse or second print. Though these specimens are scarce in Uncirculated condition, they often pass through many hands in circulation before being spotted. The uninformed public is not even aware that a note with faces in opposite directions is an error and has premium value.

	V. FINE	UNC.
☐$2 Federal Reserve Note, Series 1976, signatures of Neff-Simon, inverted obverse	315.00	625.00

MISSING THIRD PRINT

This error is also known as "missing overprint." It consists of a note released into circulation without having gone through the "third print" operation.

	V. FINE	UNC.
☐$1 Federal Reserve Note, Series 1977, signatures Morton-Blumenthal, missing third print	170.00	325.00

FOREIGN MATTER ON OBVERSE

Sometimes foreign matter, usually paper scraps of one kind or another, gets between the printing plate and the sheet. This naturally results in the area covered being blank on the note. Because of the extreme pressure exerted in printing, the foreign matter is occasionally "glued" to the note and travels with it into circulation. If the appendage is paper, it will normally be found to be of the same stock from which the note is made—apparently a shred from one of the sheet margins that worked its way into a batch of sheets awaiting printing. The value of such notes varies greatly, depending on the size of the foreign matter and its placement. It's rare to find notes in which foreign matter became attached before the first or second print. Nearly always, they found their way to the note after the second print and before the third.

	V. FINE	UNC.
☐ $1 Federal Reserve Note, Series 1974, signatures Neff-Simon, foreign matter on obverse	135.00	235.00

	V. FINE	UNC.
☐ $1 Silver Certificate, Series 1935E, signatures of Priest-Humphrey. Foreign matter on obverse. More valuable than the preceding because of the note's age and the foreign matter being larger.	315.00	575.00

MISSING PORTION OF REVERSE DESIGN
(DUE TO ADHERENCE OF SCRAP PAPER)

In this instance, the foreign matter got in the way of the first print, or reverse printing. It prevented the covered area from being printed, but it later became dislodged and is no longer present. What appears on the illustration to be a strip of paper on the note is really the blank unprinted area once covered by the strip. Obviously a note that merely had a random strip of paper attached, over a normally printed design, would have no collector interest.

	V. FINE	UNC.
☐$1 Federal Reserve Note, missing portion of reverse design due to adherence of scrap paper	110.00	210.00

OVERPRINT PARTIALLY MISSING

The overprint or third print on this note is normal on the righthand side and missing entirely on the left. This was caused by the note being folded (more or less in half, vertically) immediately before overprinting. Had the lefthand side been folded over the face, this would have interfered with the overprints on the righthand side. Instead, this specimen was folded over the reverse side, or downward, with the result that the missing portion of overprint did not strike the note at all—it simply hit the printing press bed. The reverse side of this note is normal.

	V. FINE	UNC.
☐$1 Federal Reserve Note, Series 1963A, overprint partially missing	95.00	225.00

THIRD PRINT OFFSET ON REVERSE

This note is normal on the obverse but carries an "offset" of the third print or overprints on its reverse. It would appear that the overprints are showing through to the reverse, as if the note were printed on very thin paper. Actually, this "mirror image" is caused by a malfunction in the printing or paper-feeding machinery. The inked plate for printing the overprints contacted the machine bed without a sheet of paper being in place. Therefore, as the next sheet came through it received the normal overprint on its face and picked up the offset impression on its reverse from the machine bed. Each successive sheet going through the press also received an offset, but it naturally became fainter and fainter as the ink was absorbed. The value of a note of this kind depends on the intensity of the impression.

	V. FINE	UNC.
☐$5 Federal Reserve Note, offset impression of overprints on reverse	125.00	255.00

CONFEDERATE MONEY

The Civil War Centennial of 1961–65 has generally been credited with sparking an interest in the collecting and study of Confederate or C.S.A. Notes. This, however, is not totally borne out by facts, as C.S.A. currency had advanced steadily in value since the 1940s. It rides a crest of popularity today surpassing the early 1960s. This is due in part to the exhaustive research carried out since that time and numerous books and articles published. Even today, some C.S.A. Notes would still appear to be undervalued based on their availability vs. regular U.S. issues.

History. It became apparent upon the outbreak of the Civil War that both sides would experience extreme coinage shortages, and each took to the printing of notes that could be exchanged in lieu of bullion or "real money" (which always meant coined money until the 1860s). The South suffered more serious difficulties than the North, as it did not have as many skilled printers or engravers at its command. Also, with the war being fought on its territory rather than the North's, there was an ever-present danger of sabotage to plants printing money or engaging in related activities. The Confederacy tried by all available means to satisfy the currency demand and succeeded in distributing quite a large quantity of notes. Its shortage was taken up by notes issued by private banks, individual states, counties, railroads, and private merchants. Merchant tokens, to take the place of rapidly disappearing small change, poured forth in abundance during this period. All told, the Confederate Congress authorized the printing of about one and a half billion dollars' worth of paper currency. It is impossible to determine the total actually produced, but it would appear that this figure was far surpassed. At the war's conclusion, these notes were worthless, as the C.S.A. no longer existed and the federal government refused to redeem them. Many were discarded as scrap, but a surprising number were held faithfully by their owners who believed "the South will rise again." The South did indeed rise, industrially and economically, and those old C.S.A. Notes rose, too. They still aren't spendable, but many are worth sums in excess of face value as collectors' pieces. Until about 1900, however, practically no value was placed on Confederate currency—even by collectors.

Designs. Some surprising designs will be observed, including mythological gods and goddesses that seem to relate very little to the Southern artistic or cultural climate of the 1860s. Many scholarly efforts have been made to explain away the use of such motifs, but the simple fact is that they appeared not so much by choice as by necessity. Southern printers, not having the facilities of their Northern counterparts, were compelled to make do with whatever engravings or "stock cuts" were already on hand, as inappropriate as they might have proved. However, a number of original designs were created reflecting unmistakably regional themes and at times picturing heroes or leaders of the Confederacy. Slaves at labor, used as a symbol of the South's economic strength and its supposed advantage over the North, where labor was hired, was a frequent motif. Sailors were also depicted, as well as railroad trains and anything else that appeared symbolic of Southern industry. Probably the most notable single design, not intended to carry the satirical overtones it now possesses, is "General Francis Marion's Sweet Potato Breakfast" on the $10 1861 issue note.

In general, the C.S.A. Notes are not so badly designed a group as might be anticipated in light of conditions. The designing was, in fact, several leagues improved over the printing, which often left much to be desired. George Washington is depicted—not for being the first U.S. President but as a native son of Virginia. Jefferson Davis, President of the C.S.A., is among the more common portraits. He became even more disliked in the North than he otherwise might have been because of his picture turning up on currency. But after the war he took a moderate stand

and erased the old ill feelings; he even had words of praise for Lincoln. Other individuals whose portraits (not necessarily very faithful) will be encountered are:

- John C. Calhoun, U.S. Senator who led the battle for slavery and Southern Rights (later called "states rights")
- Alexander H. Stephen, Davis' Vice-President of the C.S.A.
- Judah P. Benjamin, holder of various official titles in the Southern government
- C.G. Memminger, Secretary of the Treasury and Secretary of War
- Lucy Pickens, wife of South Carolina's governor and the only woman (aside from mythological types) shown on C.S.A. currency
- John E. Ward
- R.M.T. Hunter

Printers. The study of printers of C.S.A. Notes is complex, made no less so by the fact that some contractors produced only plates, others did only printing (from plates procured elsewhere), and some did both. The principal Southern printer was the lithography firm of Hoyer & Ludwig of Richmond, Virginia. Also located in Richmond were Keatinge & Ball, which did commendable, if not exactly inspired, work, and B. Duncan, who also worked in Columbia, South Carolina. Another firm involved in quite a bit of note printing was J.T. Paterson of Columbia. The so-called "Southern Bank Note Company" was a fictitious name used to disguise the origin of notes prepared in the North. Some early notes were marked "National Bank Note Co., New York," but it was subsequently decided to remove correct identification from the notes of this printer, undoubtedly on the latter's request (fearing prosecution for aiding the enemy).

Cancellations. Two varieties of cancels are commonly found on C.S.A. Notes. First is the Cut Cancel (CC), in which a knife or similar instrument has been used to make piercings in a design or pattern. Unless roughly executed, such cuts do not materially reduce a specimen's value. In the case of some notes, examples without cancellation are almost impossible to find. The COC, or Cut-Out Cancel, is more objectionable because, instead of merely leaving slits, a portion of the paper was removed. The reduction of value for a Cut-Out Cancel averages around 25 percent. These are considered "space fillers" if the issue is fairly common, but a rare note with a COC may be very desirable. Pen Cancellations (PC) are far less frequently encountered. These show the word "Canceled" written out by hand across the note's face, in ink. Unless the ink is heavy or blotchy, a Pen Cancel will not have too much bearing on value. As the note is not physically injured, it would seem to be the least offensive of the three varieties. Whenever a note is being sold, presence of a cancel, of whatever type, should be plainly spelled out. Some collectors are not interested in canceled specimens. In time, as the scarce issues become even scarcer, they will probably have to be accepted as a fact of life.

Signatures. The first six notes issued, the four from Montgomery and T5 & 6 from Richmond, were hand-signed by the Register and Treasurer themselves. Thereafter, because the Treasury Secretary felt hand signatures helped prevent counterfeiting, and because of the quantities of notes spewing forth, clerks were hired to sign "for Register" and "for Treasurer." There were about 200 different people who signed for each Treasury official, making for thousands of signature combinations. Mostly the clerks were women, many the wives or daughters of soldiers who had been killed in action. Since the notes were signed in Richmond through April of 1864 (when all operations were removed to Columbia, South Carolina), most of the signers were from there. Some moved to Columbia, and others were hired there.

It is most interesting to many people to find that they had relatives who signed Confederate money, and many people search for such notes. A complete listing of all the names from the Confederate Records appears in Colonel Criswell's extensive book, *Confederate and Southern States Currency*.

Condition Grades. While condition standards are basically the same for Confederate currency as other notes of their age, some allowance must be made for paper quality and deficiencies in printing and cutting. These matters have nothing to do with the preservation or wear and can be observed just as frequently in Uncirculated specimens as in those in average condition. Without a source of good paper, printers were obliged to use whatever was most easily and quickly obtainable. Often the paper was thin, or stiff, or contained networks of minute wrinkles which interfered with printing. Cutting was generally not done by machine, as in the North, but by hand with a pair of scissors—workers actually took the sheets and cut apart notes individually. When paper-cutting devices were employed, they were apparently not of the best quality. In any case, regular edges on C.S.A. Notes are uncommon, and their absence does not constitute grounds for classifying an otherwise perfect specimen in a condition grade below Uncirculated. When the occasional gem is located—a well-printed, well-preserved note on good paper, decently cut—its value is sure to be higher than those listed. The collector is not advised to confine himself to such specimens, as his activities would become seriously limited.

Uncirculated—UNC. An Uncirculated note shows no evidence of handling and is as close to "new condition" as possible. An Uncirculated specimen may, however, have pinholes or a finger smudge, which should be mentioned in a sales offering. If these are readily noticeable, the note deserves to be classified as "Almost Uncirculated." Crispness is hardly a criterion of uncirculation as this quality is expected in notes graded as low as Very Fine.

Almost Uncirculated—A.U. Similar to the above grade, but not quite as good as an Uncirculated specimen. The note bears no indication of having actually circulated but has minor flaws resulting from accident or mishandling, such as individuals' counting crinkles.

Extremely Fine—X.F. An X.F. note is on the borderline between Uncirculated and Circulated. It has not been heavily handled but may reveal several imperfections: a pinhole, finger smudge, counting crinkles, or a light wallet fold. The fold is not so heavy as to be termed a crease.

Very Fine—V.F. Has been in circulation but is not worn or seriously creased. It must still be clean and crisp, without stains or tears. Fine to Very Fine condition is considered the equivalent of "Average Circulated" but not "Average" condition (which is another term for poor).

Fine—F. A note that has been in circulation and shows it, but has no physical injuries or just slight ones.

Very Good—V.G. A well-circulated note bearing evidence of numerous foldings. It may possibly have creased corners and wrinkles as well as light staining, smudging, or pinholes, but major defects (such as a missing corner) would place it into an even lower category.

Good—G. Good notes have been heavily circulated, worn, possibly stained or scribbled on edges, could be frayed or "dog-eared." There may be holes larger than pin punctures, but not on the central portion of design. This is the lowest grade of condition acceptable to a collector, and only when nothing better is available. Unless very rare, such specimens are considered space-fillers only.

Average Buying Prices—A.B.P. The Average Buying Prices given here are the approximate sums paid by retail dealers for specimens in Good condition. As selling prices vary, so do buying prices, and in fact they usually vary more. A dealer who is overstocked on a certain note is sure to offer less than one who has no specimens on hand. The dealer's location, size of operation, and other circumstances will also influence the buying price. We present these figures merely as approximate guides to what sellers should expect.

Type Numbers. Each Confederate Note pictured has a "Type" number as well as a "regular" Criswell catalog number. The Criswell numbers are listed in the beginning of each of the price listings, and the Type numbers appear immediately following in parentheses. These numbers are used for identification and are cross-referenced in Grover Criswell's publications.

FOR MORE INFORMATION

Considered to be the foremost authority on Confederate currency, Col. Grover Criswell has a variety of books available. His last release, *Confederate and Southern States Currency* ($75), covers all the currency issued by the

Confederate States Central Government, the Southern States, the Indian Territories, the Florida Republic and Territory, and the Republic and Independent Government of Texas. This edition also gives interesting discovery information that you are sure to enjoy. There are also current market values listed, as well as rarities. This is the best reference available for the serious collector, libraries, and the casual reader.

To order this book, or for a complete list of books that are available, write Criswell's Publications, Salt Springs, Florida 32134-6000, or call 352-685-2287.

CONFEDERATE STATES OF AMERICA—
1861 ISSUE, MONTGOMERY, ALABAMA
$1,000,000 authorized by "Act of March 9th."
Written dates "1861."
"NATIONAL BANK NOTE CO., NY"

TYPE 1

Face Design: Green and black, bears "Interest Ten Cents Per Day," 607 issued. John C. Calhoun left, Andrew Jackson right.

CRISWELL	NOTE	A.B.P.	GOOD	UNC.
☐1	$1000	5500.00	7500.00	50,000.00

"NATIONAL BANK NOTE CO., NY"

TYPE 2

Face Design: Green and black, bears "Interest Five Cents Per Day," 607 issued. Cattle crossing a brook.

CRISWELL	NOTE	A.B.P.	GOOD	UNC.
☐2	$500	5500.00	8500.00	51,000.00

CONFEDERATE STATES OF AMERICA—
1861 ISSUE
"NATIONAL BANK NOTE CO., NY"

TYPE 3

Face Design: Green and black, bears "Interest One Cent Per Day." Railway train, Minerva left.

CRISWELL	NOTE	A.B.P.	GOOD	UNC.
☐3	$100	2650.00	5500.00	28,000.00

"NATIONAL BANK NOTE CO., NY"

TYPE 4

Face Design: Green and black, bears "Interest Half A Cent Per Day." Negroes hoeing cotton.

CRISWELL	NOTE	A.B.P.	GOOD	UNC.
☐4	$50	2650.00	5000.00	26,000.00

CONFEDERATE STATES OF AMERICA—1861 ISSUE
"AMERICAN BANK NOTE CO., NY"
(Though ostensibly by the "SOUTHERN BANK NOTE CO.")

TYPE
5

Face Design: Green and black, red fibre paper, bears "Interest One Cent Per Day." Railway train, Justice left and Minerva right.

CRISWELL	NOTE	A.B.P.	GOOD	UNC.
☐5	$100	450.00	750.00	2750.00

TYPE
6

Face Design: Green and black, red fibre paper, bears "Interest Half A Cent Per Day." Pallas and Ceres seated on bale of cotton, Washington at right.

CRISWELL	NOTE	A.B.P.	GOOD	UNC.
☐6	$50	320.00	550.00	2450.00

CONFEDERATE STATES OF AMERICA—1861 ISSUE
$20,000,000 authorized by "Act of May 16th, 1861"
(All lithographic date "July 25th, 1861")
"HOYER & LUDWIG, RICHMOND, VA"

TYPE
7

Face Design: Ceres and Proserpina flying, Washington left.

CRISWELL	NOTE	A.B.P.	GOOD	UNC.
☐7-13	$100	375.00	600.00	2250.00

TYPE
8

Face Design: Washington, Tellus left.

CRISWELL	NOTE	A.B.P.	GOOD	UNC.
☐14-22	$50	75.00	90.00	385.00

CONFEDERATE STATES OF AMERICA—1861 ISSUE

TYPE
XXI

Face Design: Exists in a variety of colors.

CRISWELL	NOTE	A.B.P.	GOOD	UNC.
☐XXI	$20	60.00	100.00	250.00

The above type notes were bogus. For years it was thought they were a regular Confederate issue, and evidence exists that they were circulated as such. No collection of Confederate Notes is complete without one. There is no evidence as to who the printer was, but the authors have reason to believe he was located somewhere in Ohio. It is not a product of S.C. Upham, of Philadelphia, the well-known counterfeiter of Confederate Notes.

TYPE
9

Face Design: Large sailing vessel, "20" at left.

CRISWELL	NOTE	A.B.P.	GOOD	UNC.
☐23-33	$20	40.00	75.00	365.00

CONFEDERATE STATES OF AMERICA—1861 ISSUE

TYPE
10

Face Design: Liberty seated by eagle, with shield and flag.

There are at least forty-two minor varieties of this note, including a supposed ten or eleven stars on shield. Usually the stars are so indistinct that a note may show from six to fifteen stars. The other differences are minute changes in the size of the "10" in the upper corners. We list only the major type.

CRISWELL	NOTE	A.B.P.	GOOD	UNC.
☐34-41	$10	70.00	125.00	3100.00

TYPE
11

Face Design: Liberty seated by eagle, sailor left.

CRISWELL	NOTE	A.B.P.	GOOD	UNC.
☐42-45	$5	200.00	500.00	19,500.00

CONFEDERATE STATES OF AMERICA—1861 ISSUE
(Written date "July 25th, 1861")
"J. MANOUVRIER, NEW ORLEANS"

TYPE
12

Face Design: CONFEDERATE STATES OF AMERICA in blue on blue reverse.

CRISWELL	NOTE	A.B.P.	GOOD	UNC.
☐46-49	$5	440.00	1000.00	8750.00

$100,000,000 authorized by "Act of Aug. 19th, 1861."
$50,000,000 authorized by "Act of Dec. 24th, 1861."
"HOYER & LUDWIG, RICHMOND, VA"

TYPE
13

(Lithographic date "September 2nd, 2d, & s, 1861")
Face Design: Negroes loading cotton, sailor left.

CRISWELL	NOTE	A.B.P.	GOOD	UNC.
☐50-58	$100	50.00	80.00	275.00

CONFEDERATE STATES OF AMERICA—1861 ISSUE

TYPE
14

Face Design: Moneta seated by treasure chests, sailor left.

CRISWELL	NOTE	A.B.P.	GOOD	UNC.
☐59-78	$50	35.00	60.00	235.00

"SOUTHERN BANK NOTE CO., NEW ORLEANS"

TYPE
15

Face Design: Black and red on red fibre paper. Railway train, Justice right, Hope with anchor left.

CRISWELL	NOTE	A.B.P.	GOOD	UNC.
☐79	$50	900.00	1550.00	12,650.00

CONFEDERATE STATES OF AMERICA—1861 ISSUE
"KEATINGE & BALL, RICHMOND, VA"

TYPE
16

Face Design: Black and green, red fibre paper. Portrait of Jefferson Davis.

CRISWELL	NOTE		A.B.P.	GOOD	UNC.
☐80-98	$50		100.00	150.00	1250.00

"HOYER & LUDWIG, RICHMOND, VA"

TYPE
17

Face Design: Black with green ornamentation, plain paper. Ceres seated between Commerce and Navigation, Liberty left.

CRISWELL	NOTE		A.B.P.	GOOD	UNC.
☐99-100	$20		225.00	285.00	2450.00

CONFEDERATE STATES OF AMERICA—1861 ISSUE
"HOYER & LUDWIG, RICHMOND, VA"

TYPE
18

Face Design: Large sailing vessel, sailor at capstan left.

CRISWELL	NOTE	A.B.P.	GOOD	UNC.
☐101-136	$20	30.00	50.00	150.00

"SOUTHERN BANK NOTE CO., NEW ORLEANS"

TYPE
19

Face Design: Black and red on red fibre paper. Navigator seated by charts, Minerva left, blacksmith right.

CRISWELL	NOTE	A.B.P.	GOOD	UNC.
☐137	$20	700.00	1200.00	6200.00

CONFEDERATE STATES OF AMERICA—1861 ISSUE
"B. DUNCAN, COLUMBIA, SC"

TYPE
20

Face Design: Industry seated between cupid and beehive, bust of A. H. Stephens left.

CRISWELL	NOTE	A.B.P.	GOOD	UNC.
☐139-140	$20	40.00	55.00	195.00

"B. DUNCAN, RICHMOND, VA"

CRISWELL	NOTE	A.B.P.	GOOD	UNC.
☐141-143	$20	35.00	50.00	195.00

"KEATINGE & BALL, COLUMBIA, SC"

TYPE
21

Face Design: Portrait of Alexander H. Stephens.

YELLOW-GREEN ORNAMENTATION

CRISWELL	NOTE	A.B.P.	GOOD	UNC.
☐144	$20	150.00	250.00	2000.00

DARK-GREEN ORNAMENTATION

CRISWELL	NOTE	A.B.P.	GOOD	UNC.
☐145-149	$20	110.00	225.00	1750.00

CONFEDERATE STATES OF AMERICA—1861 ISSUE
"SOUTHERN BANK NOTE CO., NEW ORLEANS"

TYPE
22

Face Design: Black and red, red fibre paper. Group of Indians, Thetis left, maiden with "X" at right.

CRISWELL	NOTE	A.B.P.	GOOD	UNC.
☐150-152	$10	220.00	410.00	2450.00

"LEGGETT, KEATINGE & BALL, RICHMOND, VA"

TYPE
23

Face Design: Black and orange/red. Wagon load of cotton, harvesting sugar cane right. John E. Ward left.

CRISWELL	NOTE	A.B.P.	GOOD	UNC.
☐153-155	$10	335.00	520.00	3650.00

CONFEDERATE STATES OF AMERICA—1861 ISSUE
"LEGGETT, KEATINGE & BALL, RICHMOND, VA"

**TYPE
24**

Face Design: Black and orange/red. R.M.T. Hunter left, vignette of child
right.

CRISWELL	NOTE	A.B.P.	GOOD	UNC.
☐156-160	$10	85.00	185.00	1010.00

"KEATINGE & BALL, RICHMOND, VA"

CRISWELL	NOTE	A.B.P.	GOOD	UNC.
☐161-167	$10	60.00	135.00	910.00

"KEATINGE & BALL, RICHMOND, VA"

**TYPE
25**

Face Design: Hope with anchor, R.M.T. Hunter left, C. G. Memminger right.

CRISWELL	NOTE	A.B.P.	GOOD	UNC.
☐168-171	$10	55.00	125.00	615.00

CONFEDERATE STATES OF AMERICA—1861 ISSUE
"KEATINGE & BALL, RICHMOND, VA"

TYPE 26

Face Design: Hope with anchor, R.M.T. Hunter left, C.G. Memminger right.

Face Design: *Solid red "X" and "X" overprint.

CRISWELL	NOTE	A.B.P.	GOOD	UNC.
☐173-184	$10	60.00	125.00	695.00

*There are three types of red "X" and "X" overprints. That section of the note on which the overprints appear is illustrated in double size.

Face Design: *Coarse lace "X" and "X" red overprint.

CRISWELL	NOTE	A.B.P.	GOOD	UNC.
☐189-210	$10	60.00	115.00	675.00

CONFEDERATE STATES OF AMERICA—1861 ISSUE

Face Design: Fine lace "X" and "X" red overprint.*

CRISWELL	NOTE	A.B.P.	GOOD	UNC.
☐211–214	$10	55.00	115.00	675.00

TYPE
27

Face Design: Liberty seated by shield and eagle.

CRISWELL NOTE	A.B.P.	GOOD	UNC.
☐221-229, $10	1650.00	6150.00	44,500.00

CONFEDERATE STATES OF AMERICA—1861 ISSUE
"HOYER & LUDWIG, RICHMOND, VA"

TYPE
28

Face Design: Ceres and Commerce with an urn.

CRISWELL NOTE	A.B.P.	GOOD	UNC.
☐230-234 $10	35.00	60.00	545.00

"J. T. PATERSON, COLUMBIA, SC"

CRISWELL NOTE	A.B.P.	GOOD	UNC.
☐235-236 $10	40.00	80.00	575.00

"B. DUNCAN, RICHMOND, VA"

TYPE
29

Face Design: Negro picking cotton.

CRISWELL	NOTE		A.B.P.	GOOD	UNC.
☐237	$10		85.00	190.00	1550.00

CONFEDERATE STATES OF AMERICA—1861 ISSUE
"B. DUNCAN, COLUMBIA, SC"

TYPE
30

Face Design: Gen. Francis Marion's "Sweet Potato Dinner." R. M. T. Hunter left, Minerva right.

CRISWELL	NOTE		A.B.P.	GOOD	UNC.
☐238	$10		40.00	75.00	310.00

NO ENGRAVER'S NAME

CRISWELL	NOTE		A.B.P.	GOOD	UNC.
☐239-241	$10		40.00	50.00	320.00

"SOUTHERN BANK NOTE CO., NEW ORLEANS"

TYPE
31

Face Design: Black and red on red fibre paper. Minerva left; Agriculture, Commerce, Industry, Justice, and Liberty seated at center; statue of Washington right.

CRISWELL	NOTE	A.B.P.	GOOD	UNC.
☐243-245	$5	110.00	250.00	1550.00

CONFEDERATE STATES OF AMERICA—1861 ISSUE
"LEGGETT, KEATINGE & BALL, RICHMOND, VA"

TYPE
32

Face Design: Black and orange/red. Machinist with hammer, boy in oval left.

CRISWELL	NOTE	A.B.P.	GOOD	UNC.
☐246-249	$5	200.00	375.00	3680.00

"LEGGETT, KEATINGE & BALL, RICHMOND, VA"

TYPE 33

Face Design: Black and white note with blue-green ornamentation. C.G. Memminger, Minerva right.

CRISWELL	NOTE	A.B.P.	GOOD	UNC.
☐250-256	$5	60.00	120.00	1250.00

CONFEDERATE STATES OF AMERICA—1861 ISSUE
"KEATINGE & BALL, RICHMOND, VA"

TYPE 34

Face Design: C.G. Memminger, Minerva right.

CRISWELL	NOTE	A.B.P.	GOOD	UNC.
☐262-270	$5	45.00	100.00	750.00

"HOYER & LUDWIG, RICHMOND, VA"

TYPE 35

Face Design: Loading cotton left, Indian princess right.

CRISWELL	NOTE	A.B.P.	GOOD	UNC.
□271	$5	2200.00	6350.00	75,250.00

CONFEDERATE STATES OF AMERICA—1861 ISSUE
"HOYER & LUDWIG, RICHMOND, VA"

TYPE 36

Face Design: Ceres seated on bale of cotton, sailor left.

CRISWELL	NOTE	A.B.P.	GOOD	UNC.
□272	$5	30.00	50.00	335.00

"J. T. PATERSON & CO., COLUMBIA, SC"

CRISWELL	NOTE	A.B.P.	GOOD	UNC.
□274	$5	25.00	45.00	210.00
□276-282	$5	25.00	45.00	210.00

CONFEDERATE STATES OF AMERICA—1861 ISSUE
"B. DUNCAN, RICHMOND, VA"

TYPE
37

Face Design: Sailor seated beside bales of cotton, C.G. Memminger left,
Justice and Ceres right.

CRISWELL	NOTE	A.B.P.	GOOD	UNC.
☐284	$5	50.00	110.00	560.00

"B. DUNCAN, COLUMBIA, SC"

CRISWELL	NOTE	A.B.P.	GOOD	UNC.
☐285	$5	50.00	125.00	575.00

"B. DUNCAN, COLUMBIA, SC"

TYPE
38

Face Design: Personification of South striking down Union, J.P. Benjamin
left. Dated "September 2, 1861" through an error. No Confederate Note less
than $5 was authorized in 1861.

CRISWELL	NOTE	A.B.P.	GOOD	UNC.
☐286	$2	225.00	350.00	6850.00

CONFEDERATE STATES OF AMERICA—1862 ISSUE
$165,000,000 Authorized by "Act of April 17th."
"HOYER & LUDWIG, RICHMOND, VA."

TYPE
39

Face Design: Railway train, straight steam from locomotive, milkmaid left.
Bears "Interest at Two Cents Per Day."

CRISWELL	NOTE	A.B.P.	GOOD	UNC.
☐287-289	$100	45.00	75.00	175.00

Dated May 5 to May 9, 1862

J.T. PATERSON, COLUMBIA, S.C. (At Lower Left)

☐290-293	$100	35.00	55.00	125.00

VARIOUS WRITTEN DATES, MAY THROUGH OCTOBER, 1862

J.T. PATERSON, COLUMBIA, S.C. (At Lower Right)

☐294-296	$100	35.00	70.00	135.00

VARIOUS WRITTEN DATES, MAY THROUGH OCTOBER, 1862

TYPE
40

"J.T. PATERSON, COLUMBIA, S.C."

Face Design: Railway train, diffused steam from locomotive, milkmaid left
Bears "Interest at Two Cents Per Day."

CRISWELL	NOTE	A.B.P.	GOOD	UNC.
☐298-309	$100	40.00	55.00	135.00

VARIOUS WRITTEN DATES, MAY THROUGH OCTOBER, 1862

CONFEDERATE STATES OF AMERICA—1862 ISSUE
"KEATINGE & BALL, COLUMBIA, S.C."
On the following notes there are two types of ornamental
scrolls in the upper right corners.

**TYPE
41**

Face Design: "Hundred" overprint in orange/red. Bears "Interest at Two
Cents Per Day." Negroes hoeing cotton, J.C. Calhoun left, Columbia right.

CRISWELL	NOTE	A.B.P.	GOOD	UNC.
☐310-314	$100	55.00	90.00	225.00

Dated "August 26th, 1862" (Date all written, scroll No. 1.)

☐315-324	$100	45.00	85.00	165.00

Written dates, AUG. to DEC. "1862." ("186" of date is engraved.)

☐325-331	$100	45.00	85.00	185.00

Dated January 1 to January 8, 1863.

CONFEDERATE STATES OF AMERICA—1862 ISSUE

$5,000,000 authorized by "Act of April 18th, 1862"
$5,000,000 authorized by "Act of September 23rd, 1862"
"B. DUNCAN, COLUMBIA, S.C."

TYPE 42

Face Design: Personification of South striking down Union, J.P. Benjamin left.

CRISWELL	NOTE	A.B.P.	GOOD	UNC.
☐334-337	$2	30.00	45.00	310.00

TYPE 43

Face Design: "2" and "Two" in green overprint. Personification of South striking down Union, J.P. Benjamin left.

CRISWELL	NOTE	A.B.P.	GOOD	UNC.
☐338	$2	40.00	75.00	1800.00

CONFEDERATE STATES OF AMERICA—1862 ISSUE

TYPE 44

Face Design: Steamship at sea. Lucy Holcombe Pickens right. Liberty left.

CRISWELL	NOTE	A.B.P.	GOOD	UNC.
☐339-341	$1	40.00	65.00	250.00

TYPE 45

Face Design: "1" and "One" green overprint. Steamship at sea. Lucy Holcombe Pickens right. Liberty left.

CRISWELL	NOTE	A.B.P.	GOOD	UNC.
☐342-342A	$1	55.00	95.00	1550.00

CONFEDERATE STATES OF AMERICA—1862 ISSUE
"HOYER & LUDWIG, RICHMOND, VA."
This is a Sept. 2, 1861 note, dated through error
"September 2, 1862." No engravers' name, appears,
but it is a product of Hoyer & Ludwig, Richmond, VA.

TYPE
46

Face Design: Ceres reclining on cotton bales. R.M.T. Hunter at right.

CRISWELL	NOTE	A.B.P.	GOOD	UNC.
☐343-344	$10	35.00	60.00	475.00

(Essay Note, Printed Signatures.)
"KEATINGE & BALL, COLUMBUS, S.C."

TYPE
47

Face Design: Liberty seated on bale of cotton. R.M.T. Hunter right.

CRISWELL	NOTE	A.B.P.	GOOD	UNC.
☐345	$20		EXTREMELY RARE	

CONFEDERATE STATES OF AMERICA—1862 ISSUE
(Essay Note, Printed Signatures.)
"KEATINGE & BALL, COLUMBUS, S.C."

TYPE
48

Face Design: Ceres holding sheaf of wheat. R.M.T. Hunter right.

CRISWELL	NOTE	A.B.P.	GOOD	UNC.
☐346	$10		EXTREMELY RARE	

CONFEDERATE STATES OF AMERICA—1862 ISSUE
$90,000,000 authorized by "Act of Oct. 13th, 1862"
"KEATINGE & BALL, COLUMBIA S.C."

TYPE
49

Face Design: Fancy green reverse. Lucy Holcombe Pickens. George W.
Randolph right.

CRISWELL	NOTE	A.B.P.	GOOD	UNC.
☐347-349	$100	110.00	250.00	900.00

CONFEDERATE STATES OF AMERICA—1862 ISSUE
"KEATINGE & BALL, RICHMOND, VA." (THIRD SERIES)

TYPE
50

Face Design: Black and green. Ornate green reverse. Jefferson Davis.

CRISWELL	NOTE	A.B.P.	GOOD	UNC.
☐350-356	$50	110.00	235.00	1300.00

"KEATINGE & BALL, COLUMBIA, S.C." (THIRD SERIES)

CRISWELL	NOTE	A.B.P.	GOOD	UNC.
☐357-362	$50	70.00	175.00	710.00

CONFEDERATE STATES OF AMERICA—1862 ISSUE
"KEATINGE & BALL, COLUMBIA, S.C."

TYPE
51

Face Design: Fancy blue reverse. State Capitol at Nashville, Tennessee.
A.H. Stephens.

CRISWELL	NOTE	A.B.P.	GOOD	UNC.
☐363-368	$20	70.00	125.00	610.00

CONFEDERATE STATES OF AMERICA—1862 ISSUE

TYPE
52

Face Design: Fancy blue reverse. State Capitol at Columbia S.C., R.M.T.
Hunter. Printed on pink paper.

"B. DUNCAN."

CRISWELL	NOTE	A.B.P.	GOOD	UNC.
☐369-375IB	$10	30.00	50.00	145.00

"EVANS & COGSWELL"

CRISWELL	NOTE	A.B.P.	GOOD	UNC.
☐376-378	$10	30.00	50.00	145.00

Face Design: Fancy blue reverse. State Capitol at Richmond, VA., C.G. Memminger. Printed on pink paper.

There are many varieties of printers names on notes of this issue, though all have the same engraver's names. In general, the only valuable ones are those with two "Printers" names.

CRISWELL	NOTE	A.B.P.	GOOD	UNC.
☐379-390	$5	25.00	40.00	150.00

TYPE 54

Face Design: Judah P. Benjamin. Printed on pink paper.

CRISWELL	NOTE	A.B.P.	GOOD	UNC.
☐391-396	$2	35.00	65.00	250.00

TYPE 55

Face Design: Clement C. Clay. Printed on pink paper.

CRISWELL	NOTE	A.B.P.	GOOD	UNC.
☐397-401	$1	30.00	60.00	310.00

CONFEDERATE STATES OF AMERICA—1863
$50,000,000 authorized monthly, from April 1863 to January 1864, "By Act of March 23rd, 1863."

All notes of this year dated April 6th, 1863, but a red overprinted date appears on all the $5, $10, $20, $50, and $100 denominations showing the year and month of issue.

"KEATINGE & BALL, COLUMBIA, S.C."

TYPE 56

Face Design: Green reverse. Lucy H. Pickens. Two soldiers left. George W. Randolph right.

CRISWELL	NOTE	A.B.P.	GOOD	UNC.
☐402-404	$100	70.00	125.00	350.00

"KEATINGE & BALL, RICHMOND, VA."

**TYPE
57**

Face Design: Green and black, ornate green reverse, Jefferson Davis.

CRISWELL	NOTE	A.B.P.	GOOD	UNC.
□406-417	$50	50.00	95.00	275.00

CONFEDERATE STATES OF AMERICA—1863

**TYPE
58**

Face Design: Fancy blue reverse. State Capitol at Nashville, TN., A.H. Stephens.

CRISWELL	NOTE	A.B.P.	GOOD	UNC.
□418-428	$20	30.00	60.00	210.00

**TYPE
59**

Face Design: Blue back. State Capitol at Columbia, S.C., R.M.T. Hunter.

CRISWELL	NOTE		A.B.P.	GOOD	UNC.
☐429-447	$10		25.00	45.00	175.00

Engravers' names on lower margin.

**TYPE
60**

Face Design: Fancy blue reverse. State Capitol at Richmond, VA. C.G.
Memminger.

CRISWELL	NOTE		A.B.P.	GOOD	UNC.
☐448-469	$5		25.00	40.00	170.00

Pink Paper.

TYPE
61

Face Design: Judah P. Benjamin.

CRISWELL	NOTE	A.B.P.	GOOD	UNC.
☐470-473	$2	85.00	75.00	410.00

TYPE 62

Face Design: Clement C. Clay. Pink Paper.

CRISWELL	NOTE	A.B.P.	GOOD	UNC.
☐474-484	$1	25.00	50.00	210.00

"ARCHER & DALY. RICHMOND, VA."

TYPE 63

Face Design: Bust of Jefferson Davis. Pink Paper.

CRISWELL	NOTE	A.B.P.	GOOD	UNC.
☐485-488	50 Cents	20.00	40.00	65.00

CONFEDERATE STATES OF AMERICA—1864
$200,000,000 was authorized by "Act of February 17th, 1864."
All notes of this year are dated "Feb. 17th, 1864."

The actual amount issued was probably ten times the figure given above and the amount printed even greater. Thus there are many minor varieties of each type including color variations, flourishes, and more signature combinations than any other year. The authors list only the **important** types. The most common Confederate Notes appear in this year.

"KEATINGE & BALL, COLUMBIA, S.C."

TYPE
64

Face Design: Reddish horizontal line background. Equestrian statue of Washington and Confederate flag at left. Gen. T.J. "Stonewall" Jackson right.

CRISWELL NOTE	A.B.P.	GOOD	UNC.
☐489-489A $500	170.00	300.00	725.00

"A CONFEDERATE COUNTERFEIT."
Same as $100 Note illustrated on the next page, but
1/4 inch narrower, and 1/4 inch shorter.
This note only exists in Serial Letter "D."

CRISWELL	NOTE	A.B.P.	GOOD	UNC.
☐ 492	$100	60.00	75.00	190.00

Although a counterfeit, this note was listed in Bradbeer as a genuine, and evidence exists proving that it was accepted as such in the Confederacy. It is an excellent copy, in some ways better engraved than the genuine, but is easily distinguishable by its small size. The authors list it herein with the regular issues because few collectors desire to be without one. It is by far the most popular Confederate counterfeit.

TYPE 65

Face Design: Reddish network background. Intricate blue reverse with "Hundred" in large letters. Lucy Pickens. Two soldiers left. George W. Randolph right.

CRISWELL	NOTE	A.B.P.	GOOD	UNC.
☐490-494	$100	45.00	95.00	200.00

TYPE 66

Face Design: Reddish network background. Intricate blue reverse with "Fifty" in large letters. Jefferson Davis.

CRISWELL	NOTE	A.B.P.	GOOD	UNC.
☐495-503	$50	40.00	75.00	175.00

TYPE 67

Face Design: Reddish network background. Intricate blue reverse with "Twenty" in large letters. State Capitol at Nashville, TN. A.H. Stephens right.

CRISWELL	NOTE	A.B.P.	GOOD	UNC.
☐504-539	$20	25.00	35.00	65.00

"KEATINGE & BALL, COLUMBIA, S.C."
("PTD. BY EVANS & COGSWELL" On left end)

TYPE
68

Face Design: Reddish network background. Intricate blue reverse with "Ten" in large letters. Horses pulling cannon. R.M.T. Hunter at right.

CRISWELL	NOTE	A.B.P.	GOOD	UNC.
☐540-553	$10	20.00	30.00	55.00

"KEATINGE & BALL, COLUMBIA, S.C."

TYPE
69

Face Design: Reddish network background. Intricate blue reverse with "Five" in large letters. State Capitol at Richmond, VA. C.G. Memminger at right.

CRISWELL	NOTE	A.B.P.	GOOD	UNC.
☐558-565	$5	18.00	30.00	55.00

TYPE
70

Face Design: Reddish network background. Judah P. Benjamin.

CRISWELL	NOTE	A.B.P.	GOOD	UNC.
☐566-571	$2	35.00	60.00	145.00

TYPE 71

Face Design: Reddish network background. Clement C. Clay.

CRISWELL	NOTE	A.B.P.	GOOD	UNC.
☐572-577	$1	40.00	75.00	205.00

"ENGRAVED BY ARCHER & HALPIN, RICHMOND, VA."

TYPE 72

Face Design: Bust of Jefferson Davis. Pink Paper.

CRISWELL	NOTE	A.B.P.	GOOD	UNC.
☐578-579	50 Cents	18.00	32.00	62.50

The Blackbooks!

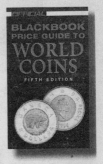

0-676-60173-1
$6.99 (Canada: $10.99)

0-676-60170-7
$8.99 (Canada: $12.99)

0-676-60176-6
$7.99 (Canada: $11.99)

The leading authorities on U.S. coins, U.S. postage stamps, and world coins!

All national bestsellers, these dynamic books are the *proven* annual guides for collectors in these fields!

- **Coins**—Every U.S. coin evaluated . . . features the American Numismatic Association Official Grading System
- **Postage Stamps**—Every U.S. stamp detailed . . . features a full-color, fast-find photo index arranged by the Scott numbering system
- **World Coins**—Features the most popular and collectible foreign coins from forty-eight countries around the world

BUY IT ● USE IT ● BECOME AN EXPERT™

Available from House of Collectibles in bookstores everywhere!

Collecting Coins Has Never Been More Fun!

There are fifty reasons to collect coins, and **The Official Guidebook to America's State Quarters** tells you why!

The new commemorative state quarters have become America's latest collecting craze, and this exciting book is packed with valuable information:

● How to identify mint errors and value your collection

● Learn the design process and how to be a part of it in future issues

● Find out when your state's coin will be released

Written by David L. Ganz, the driving force behind the fifty-state program, **The Official Guidebook to America's State Quarters** is a record of American history that will stand for all time.

0-609-80770-6 / $5.99 (Canada: $8.99)